The Influence of Women
on the Southern Landscape

1. An early photograph of the Welty garden in Jackson, Mississippi. Eudora Welty, well-known Southern writer, still lives in the family home, built by her parents in 1925. She and her mother, Chestina, developed the garden, which is currently under restoration by the Mississippi Department of Archives and History. This early spring view shows summer snowflakes, narcissus, spirea, and a flowering tree in bloom. Tender plants are covered with folded newspapers. Photograph courtesy of Eudora Welty collection—Mississippi Department of Archives and History.

The Influence of Women on the Southern Landscape

Proceedings of the
Tenth Conference on
Restoring Southern
Gardens and Landscapes

October 5–7, 1995
Old Salem,
Winston-Salem,
North Carolina

1995 Conference Planning Committee

Flora Ann Bynum, chairman, landscape restoration committee, Old Salem, Inc.

Kay Bergey, conference coordinator, Old Salem, Inc.

Gene Capps, vice-president and director of interpretation, Old Salem, Inc.

Sally Gant, director of education and special programs, Museum of Early Southern Decorative Arts, Old Salem, Inc.

Kenneth M. McFarland, site manager, Historic Stagville, Durham.

Darrell Spencer, director of horticulture, Old Salem, Inc.

Preston Stockton, superintendent, Reynolda Gardens of Wake Forest University, Winston-Salem.

Camilla Wilcox, curator of education, Reynolda Gardens of Wake Forest University.

Jo Ann Williford, assistant to the director, North Carolina Division of Archives and History, and administrator, Historic Stagville.

Proceedings chairman: *Flora Ann L. Bynum*
Proceedings editor: *Cornelia B. Wright*

Publication of these proceedings was supported by a generous grant from the Graham Foundation for Advanced Studies in the Fine Arts, Chicago, Illinois. Additional financial support was provided by the North Carolina Department of Cultural Resources, Raleigh.

©1997 Old Salem, Inc.
Drawer F, Salem Station
Winston-Salem, NC 27108

Design and typesetting of *The Influence of Women on the Southern Landscape* by Kachergis Book Design, Pittsboro, North Carolina.

LIBRARY OF CONGRESS CATALOGING-IN-PUBLICATION DATA
    The influence of women on the southern landscape : proceedings of the tenth conference, Restoring Southern Gardens and Landscapes, October 5–7, 1995, Old Salem, Winston- Salem, North Carolina.
        p.   cm.
    Includes bibliographical references.
    ISBN 1-879704-03-X
    1. Gardening—Southern States—History—Congresses. 2. Women gardeners—Southern States—History—Congresses. 3. Gardens—Southern States—History—Congresses.
I. Old Salem, Inc.
SB451.34.S68154   1997
635'.082—dc20   96-35958
                                                              CIP

Sponsoring Organizations of the Conferences on Restoring Southern Gardens and Landscapes

Old Salem, Inc., is a nonprofit educational corporation formed in 1950. It is responsible for the restoration of Old Salem, a Moravian congregation town founded in 1766, and its operation as a living history museum, and the operation of the Museum of Early Southern Decorative Arts, located in the historic district.

The Museum of Early Southern Decorative Arts (MESDA) is the only museum dedicated to exhibiting and researching the regional decorative arts of the early South. MESDA's collections, displayed in twenty-one period rooms and six galleries, include furniture, paintings, textiles, ceramics, silver, and other metalwares made and used in Maryland, Virginia, the Carolinas, Georgia, Kentucky, and Tennessee through 1820.

Reynolda Gardens of Wake Forest University, designed in 1916 by Thomas W. Sears of Philadelphia, was donated in 1958 to Wake Forest University by the Mary Reynolds Babcock Foundation. The gardens and greenhouses are located on the former estate of Richard J. Reynolds, founder of the R. J. Reynolds Tobacco Company.

Historic Stagville, located in Durham, North Carolina, is a state-owned historic site dedicated to education in the social and material history of the plantation South (with special emphasis on the diverse communities of the Bennehan-Cameron plantations) and historic preservation.

The Southern Garden History Society was founded in Winston-Salem in 1982 as an outgrowth of the conferences on Restoring Southern Gardens and Landscapes. Old Salem serves as headquarters for the society, which today has over six hundred members. The society functions in the District of Columbia and the fourteen Southern states.

Contents

vi

Introduction

The first conference on Restoring Southern Gardens and Landscapes was held in 1979, organized by Old Salem, Inc., Reynolda Gardens of Wake Forest University, and the Stagville Center (later Historic Stagville) of the North Carolina Department of Cultural Resources. In 1987, the Museum of Early Southern Decorative Arts was added as a sponsor. The Southern Garden History Society was formed at the third conference in 1982 and later became the fifth sponsor. All conferences have taken place in Winston-Salem, North Carolina, at Old Salem, a restored Moravian congregation town. Some lectures and activities have been held at Salem College, Reynolda Gardens, and at Historic Stagville in Durham, North Carolina.

The first three conferences occurred at eighteen-month intervals; from 1985, the conference has been held in October of every other year. Past themes have included "Many People, Many Cultures: The Shaping of the Southern Landscape," "The Southern Vernacular Landscape," and "Gardening for Pleasure in the South."

This volume represents the first time proceedings for the conference have been published. For each conference the committee has wanted to publish proceedings, but never managed to do so. However, the theme of the 1995 conference, "The Influence of Women on the Southern Landscape," was of such interest and had been so little explored that we felt an effort should be made to publish these papers.

In developing the conference theme, the planning committee quickly realized it would be impossible to recognize all women in the South who had contributed to and been a part of garden and landscape history. The committee therefore decided to emphasize themes and periods of history rather than individual women. The women discussed in these papers serve as examples, not as the only women who influenced the Southern landscape. Some well-known names have been left out. Those included represent the vast numbers of women who have influenced our Southern landscape.

Other questions confronted the conference committee. What did gardening mean to women, and what did women mean to gardening? How did it affect and influence their lives? How did the approach to gardening differ between men and women? Was the Southern woman's influence on the landscape different than women's influence in other areas of the country? Was the Southern woman herself different?

The committee realized that all questions could not be answered, all issues could not be addressed, all history could not be reported in one conference. But at the conference's conclusion, it was felt that stimulating, exciting progress had been made in addressing the role of women in shaping the Southern landscape.

The Restoring Southern Gardens and Landscapes conferences draw people from all over the South, plus other areas. Anyone interested in historical horticulture, garden history, and garden and landscape restoration has been welcomed. It is the only continuing conference on garden and landscape restoration in the country. To be informed about upcoming conferences, write: Landscape Conference Committee, Old Salem, Drawer F, Salem Station, Winston-Salem, NC 27108.

Flora Ann L. Bynum, conference chairman

E. Robert Friedrich
Phila.

2. A sketch of Salem Academy and College in the early twentieth century, with some buildings proposed. The college buildings facing Salem Square are (from left to right): Main Hall (1854), the Girls' Boarding School or South Hall (1805), and the Single Sisters' House (1786). The Single Sisters' garden, a series of garden squares, can be seen behind the Single Sisters' House in the upper right corner.

Salem Academy and College

The site of the 1995 conference, the campus of Salem Academy and College in Old Salem, Winston-Salem, was especially appropriate to the theme of "The Influence of Women on the Southern Landscape." The academy and college have led in the education of girls and young women in the South; begun in 1772 as a "school for little girls," the institution is one of the oldest in the country for women.

Botany was taught from the earliest days, and the girls were taken on botanical walks to study and gather native specimens. The Moravian minister Samuel Kramsch (1758–1824) compiled early floras of the Salem area and is recognized in the early botanical history of America. Kramsch was first principal of the Girls' Boarding School, established in 1802 when the Moravians decided to open their girls' school to those outside the Salem community. The herbarium of Christian Frederich Denke (1775–1838), Moravian minister, is in the botany department of Salem College; it is one of the earliest herbariums in the country.

Women were the first gardeners in the town of Salem, and the town's first garden was on what is today the Salem College campus. The Moravian records for April 27, 1771, note that "All the Single Sisters from Bethabara [the first Moravian settlement in North Carolina] went to Salem to plant their garden with beans, potatoes, corn and the like, returning in the evening." In February 1772, the Single Sisters moved from Bethabara to Salem, the records noting that "as soon as they were located they began to dig their garden, so that it might be ready for planting." For a hundred and fifty years, from 1771 until 1921, the land in back of Main Hall, South Hall, and the Sisters' House on the Salem campus had been gardened and farmed by the Single Sisters.

The Influence of Women
on the Southern Landscape

Valencia Libby

Women and Gardening

A Challenge in Writing History[1]

On 18 July 1995, less than three months ago, May Sarton died in the local hospital of a small community in southern Maine. For more than six-ty years, through her poetry, novels, and nonfic-tion, Sarton had revealed the depths of a creative woman's life. She had told her story with great honesty, turning the small occurrences of everyday life into timeless art. Sarton opened our eyes, and as we shared her life, we discovered that she, too, was a real dirt gardener:

Yesterday I did an hour's weeding, an attack on one small patch invaded by a monstrous weed, the roots of which seem to go everywhere, down and up and side-ways, which I tugged at and fought against until the small wheelbarrow was full of dead bodies and I was dripping wet. The result is that I am so stiff today I can't move. But I won a small victory.[2]

This conference is an opportunity to win a small victory, a victory that May Sarton the author and May Sarton the gardener would have rejoiced in. We are going to learn about women's contributions to the Southern landscape, share ideas and information, discuss what we learn, and explore new intellectual paths.

As an introduction, I would like to present some of the challenges that exist for those of us who want to write a women's history of the American landscape. They have become themes that my colleagues and I constantly face. Some relate to the past, some drive our work in the future.

The Anonymity of Women's Work

Historically speaking, women's work, whether in the home or outside it, was not considered important enough to record, describe, or quantify. Prior to the twentieth century, most working women received little or no recognition for their efforts, or when they worked, it may have been under the name of a male family member.[3] If a working woman went unnamed in the past, it is nearly impossible to recover her story. For example, we know that in the eighteenth century Martha Daniell Logan ran a nursery in Charleston, South Carolina, because she advertised in the local newspaper, but under her son's name.[4] Documents recording women's lives, whether public or private, are very difficult to find, and if they existed at all, they may well have been destroyed by now.

While this is frustrating, one can turn to other sources for historical information. For example, oral interviews have been a very important source for women's history. Documents generated by women like diaries and journals, domestic record books, and receipt files, as well as contemporary publications produced for a female audience such as manuals, guide books, how-to publications, and popular magazines, are valuable tools for piecing together a woman's life. Furthermore, there are artifacts themselves—plans, tools, the gardens and landscapes designed by women, and even plant cultivars named for women.

We need to work as the archaeologist does, reconstructing the past from physical evidence, and capitalize on the work of scholars in other disciplines. Material culture is a relatively new field of scholarship in which history is written from the study of both physical evidence and written documentation, rather than relying on the documents alone. Through research done in this field, valuable information has come to light which we can work with and interpret into landscape history. The Museum of Southern Decorative Arts in Winston-Salem fosters exactly this type of data collection and research. Let us collaborate on multidisciplinary teams to further our work.

Amateur or Professional?

Individual women working at home or out of their homes have often been labeled amateurs and their work dismissed. How do we define the difference between amateur and professional when it comes to women who work? By whether they were paid for their services? Received formal training? Or wrote a book about their work? Would the English garden designer Gertrude Jekyll have been considered a professional if she had worked alone for thirty years without her male colleague Edwin Lutyens? Probably not.

American culture has been inclined to diminish women's contributions to society under the labels of "amateur" or "volunteer." That is why the history of women's garden clubs, improvement societies, and volunteer organizations is so important to study, because there we can find very good records of how influential women changed the face of their communities as volunteers.

What about the history of women working in traditionally male-dominated professions such as horticulture, garden design, and landscape architecture? Their work was often not taken seriously by male colleagues and male critics, but, more tragically, they did not try to preserve their own work! Women, like Marian C. Coffin, who were among the first professional landscape architects at the turn of the century, discarded documents, as did the relatives who inherited their property, never dreaming that they would be important to posterity.

Contemporary Prejudice

There is also the need to combat contemporary prejudice against a subject whose work is known but has already been labeled, of which an opinion has been formed. A good example is Ellen Biddle Shipman, a garden designer working with Charles

Platt in the artists' community of Cornish, New Hampshire, after she was divorced. Her garden designs are well known in New England and the South, but regional foundations did not want to fund historical research and publications about her work for this very reason. However, a new book on Mrs. Shipman's career will appear shortly, published by the Library for American Landscape History and Sagapress.[5]

Women's Professional Education

Whether in horticulture, garden design, or landscape architecture, education for women has been poorly documented and even more briefly interpreted for the public. To date there has been only one book about American women's education in landscape architecture, *Women, Design and The Cambridge School,* published in 1980. That was fifteen years ago! Meanwhile, in England there has been an increasing demand for small works about the early twentieth-century women's gardening schools and the publication of volumes like Ursula Maddy's *Waterperry: A Dream Fulfilled.*[6] Several questions need to be answered: How accessible was formal training or professional education for women in these disciplines? Who could participate and what did they learn? Were they employable following graduation? Did education allow them to excel beyond their male peers?

Many young professionals today do not realize how difficult it was for women and minorities to obtain an education in the past. By studying the history of formal education we will learn how each field defined itself in a particular period and how it evolved. There are several schools, departments, and programs that need to produce their histories. I should know because I work for one of them: the Department of Landscape Architecture and Horticulture at Temple University was founded in 1910 as the Pennsylvania School of Horticulture for Women.

A Critical Template

We need to develop a critical template against which we can measure the professional accomplishments of women. It is not the historian's function simply to resurrect lives and document them, but rather to analyze a subject's work and place it within a greater context. Have you noticed that when work by a woman, such as an artistic piece or a garden design, is discussed, gender always comes up? This is not necessarily true when we discuss work by men because our society already assumes that a man's work *is* the standard. Can we overcome this bias and discuss the work of women without reference to gender? Women's work should be judged against both men's and women's work and weighed against time. It should be re-evaluated periodically as our knowledge of women's history expands.

Women's Biographies and Landscape History

As the scholar Carolyn Heilbrun has suggested in *Writing a Woman's Life,*[7] we need to change what we look for, conduct research on, write about, and relate to the public regarding the lives of important women. Our sub-themes and the way we pursue them can be the following:

1. Women Claiming Their Ambitions
   • Explore the subject's consciousness of her role as a worker, career person, or professional contributing to society.
   • Ask if the subject ever plotted a course for her life or simply let things happen (i.e., believed her life was shaped by fate, God, or destiny).
   • Was she consciously seeking a life's work? For example, Elizabeth Hall, one of the first graduates of the Pennsylvania School of Horticulture for Women, c. 1915, moved to New York City and taught science, then graduated from the Practical Gardeners' class at the New York Botanic Garden, the only woman in the class! She served as librarian for the Horticultural Society of New York and the New York Botanic Garden until her death in her nineties.

2. The Role of Marriage and Family
   • American women have for centuries believed that marriage and raising a family were the only important goals for them to achieve in life, the ideal role for women. Let us examine what marriage meant to our subjects.
   • Did they give up their work once married, or was their work necessary to produce income for their family?

• Did women select careers or work that could be bent around the demands of a family?

• What tensions existed between a woman's desires for a creative life and her personal life? For example, Celia Laighton Thaxter, an important writer in the late nineteenth century, hosted a salon of New England artists and writers in her home because she could not escape from the demands of her aging parents, husband, and children. She was fifty-eight when the artist Childe Hassam persuaded her to compose her gardening notes into a book which he illustrated. Called *An Island Garden,* it was published in 1894, the year that she died.[8]

3. Making Uncommon Choices

• One field of investigation that remains untapped in garden history is that of women serving in religious orders. The nuns of the Catholic orders that came to the New World, particularly New France (which includes Louisiana), brought with them herbs that they proceeded to cultivate in medicinal gardens associated with their schools and hospitals.

• Speaking of uncommon choices, women have often assumed careers and undertaken the bravest endeavors after the age of fifty. While men have traditionally found opportunities to pursue careers as young adults and continue to make major personal life changes throughout their years, women have been and are still, late bloomers. We need to carefully study and document the accomplishments of women after the age of fifty, in mid- to late life. One example is Silvia Saunders, the daughter of A. P. Saunders of Clinton, New York, a famous peony hybridizer. She was a professional photographer in New York City but returned home and gradually took over her father's business of the peony nursery after her father became incapacitated. She continued to distribute his rare cultivars well into her eighties.

4. Networks of Support

• Women have created circles of support, networks of relationships, around themselves in order to function and have some control over their lives in a strongly patriarchal culture. They have created spheres of influence by cultivating friends, allies, and comrades. It would be valuable to know how particular women have found, cultivated, and even perpetuated such circles historically. Focusing more of our efforts on understanding and documenting the support cast of each of our subjects can be fruitful because this is what distinguishes female from male social behavior in American culture. Behind every great woman there is a circle of allies.

As May Sarton said: "We can never stop learning, never cease to explore the mysteries of life, in which human relationships are the greatest mystery."[9]

Valencia Libby is associate professor of landscape architecture and horticulture at Temple University, Ambler, Pennsylvania.

NOTES

1. I would like to express my gratitude to Betsy Farrell, Catherine Howett, Robin Karson, Mary Beth Norton, Gayle Samuels, Neville Thompson, Gail Wagner, and many other women for sharing their thoughts and research on writing a women's history of landscape design.

2. May Sarton and Susan Sherman, *May Sarton: Among the Usual Days* (New York: W. W. Norton, 1993), 11.

3. Mary Beth Norton, *Liberty's Daughters: The Revolutionary Experience of American Women* (Boston: Little, Brown, 1980), 2.

4. Ann Leighton, *American Gardens in the Eighteenth Century* (Boston: Houghton Mifflin, 1976), 128–29, 211–15.

5. Judith B. Tankard, *The Gardens of Ellen Biddle Shipman* (Sagapanack, N.Y.: Sagapress, 1996).

6. Ursula Maddy, *Waterperry: A Dream Fulfilled* (Braunon, Devon, U.K.: Merlin Books Ltd., 1990).

7. Carolyn G. Heilbrun, *Writing a Woman's Life* (New York: Ballantine, 1988), 5.

8. Celia Thaxter, *An Island Garden* (Boston: Houghton Mifflin, 1894, reprint, 1988).

9. Martha Wheelock, "May Sarton: A Metaphor for My Life, My Work, and My Art," in *Between Women: Biographers, Novelists, Critics, Teachers, and Artists Write about Their Work on Women,* ed. Carol Ascher, Louise DeSalvo, and Sara Ruddick (New York: Routledge, 1993).

Gail E. Wagner

"Their Women and Children do Continually Keepe it with Weeding"

Late Prehistoric Women

and Horticulture in Eastern

North America

Despite a great deal of daily contact between Native Americans with their strong oral traditions and Europeans with their written language, we know few details about gardening or landscaping practices—and even less about women—in eastern North America at the time of European contact. Differences in language, a tendency to view the New World through European eyes, and the lack of written accounts from women have filtered the historic information we possess today. Archaeological evidence may be combined with historic accounts to re-create eastern North American Indian gardens and answer questions about what crops were grown, who did the gardening, where the gardens were located, and what the role of women was.

Two sources of information—archaeology and historic accounts—inform our understanding about the Southern landscape, Native American women, and Native American gardens before and after contact with Europeans; while valuable, both types of information have some drawbacks, which will be touched on here. While illustrating the prehistoric and early historic Indian societies in the Southeast, this article draws on historic information about Indians from as far west as the Great Lakes.

It is clear from the historic record that many of the southern Indians encountered by Europeans in the sixteenth and seventeenth centuries were agriculturalists who raised a number of domesticated plant crops. Today, we tell our children about the important role that the sacred triad of maize, beans, and squash played in the lives of eastern Indians. However, archaeology reveals that these crops were not important until relatively recently, that over 7,000 years passed before they came together in the garden, and for most of prehistory, other now unknown and lost crops were the staff of life for eastern Indians.

Archaeological Evidence

How can archaeologists make such a claim? Plant remains can be preserved in various forms at archaeological sites. The smallest of these, pollen and phytoliths, are microscopic in size and thus are called microbotanical remains. Phytoliths are made of the mineral silica, which is taken up by plants from the soil and water and deposited within the cells of the plant. There it may take on characteristic shapes peculiar to that type of plant. When the plant dies, the phytoliths retain their shapes and are deposited in the dirt, where they can be recovered and identified by archaeologists. Seeds, nuts, stems, wood, and other large plant parts may also be preserved (these larger remains are called macrobotanical remains). Because such organic remains are fated to rot away, only those that are desiccated, waterlogged, or charred are preserved for posterity. Archaeologists routinely recover charred plant remains that can be identified despite their crispy state.

Sequence of Domestication

The recovery of remains such as these allows us to construct a time line of domestication for eastern North America (Crites 1993; Fritz 1990). The first domesticated plant in the archaeological record is the bottle gourd *(Lagenaria siceraria),* found from 7000 B.C. in Florida. Soon thereafter we find squash *(Cucurbita pepo).* Unlike our squashes and pumpkins of today, this early squash had bitter flesh: only its seeds would have been edible. Both of these domesticates occur before the invention of ceramic pottery and would have been valued as containers.

By the Late Archaic period, or about 2500 B.C., we find domesticated marsh elder or sumpweed *(Iva annua),* which has an oily seed similar to sunflower; cultigen maygrass *(Phalaris caroliniana),* a grass with a starchy seed that matures in spring; and by 2200 B.C., domesticated sunflower *(Helianthus annuus),* another oily-seeded crop. All of these increased in importance over the next several thousand years. Domesticated goosefoot or lamb's-quarters *(Chenopodium berlandieri)* was added by about 1500 B.C., and by the Middle Woodland period, about 500 B.C. to A.D. 500, goosefoot and maygrass together generally constituted the most important plant foods in Indian diets, providing starch or carbohydrates.

The first evidence for maize is found as early as the Middle Woodland period, but this evidence is sparse. Maize at this time may have been part of the shaman or medicine man's bundle: it certainly was not yet part of the diet (Hastorf and Johannessen 1994; Scarry 1993b). It took over one thousand years for maize to rise to an important place in the diet, and not until about A.D. 800 does it show up with regularity and abundance at archaeological sites (Scarry 1993a). Also at that time its chemical isotopic signature becomes evident in the bones of the people who were eating it (Wagner 1987).

The earliest tobacco *(Nicotiana* sp.) thus far recovered dates to about 100 B.C., from the area around present-day St. Louis, Missouri. From there it spread out rapidly along the major river systems (Wagner *in prep.).*

Finally, about A.D. 700–800 the common bean *(Phaseolus vulgaris)* made its first appearance in eastern North America. At this same time, maize first surpassed goosefoot and maygrass in importance in the diet (Scarry 1993a). By this time the domesticated squashes had also long been grown for tasty flesh rather than as containers.

So, from 7000 B.C. until nearly A.D. 800, Indian gardens looked very different from what we popularly envision. By the time the Europeans arrived, eastern Indians had thousands of years' experience gardening crops never before seen by Europeans. Some of these crops had already faded into obscurity, and others soon followed suit. Those the Europeans adopted—maize, beans, squash, gourd, sunflower, and tobacco—continue to be grown today.

Indian Gardens

Archaeology can inform us about what plants the Indians gathered and grew and where they built their houses and towns. What archaeology rarely can identify is where they placed their gardens and how those gardens were arranged. During excavation of the late prehistoric A.D. 1100 Ocmulgee site in Georgia during the 1930s, archaeologists discovered that one of the mounds had been built on top of a set of fields separated by paths (Kelly 1938). The Indians mounded up the dirt into ridges and planted their crops on the tops of the ridges. At another prehistoric Indian ridged field in southwestern Wisconsin, dating to the fifteenth century, a profile cut through several ridges reveals that, like at Ocmulgee, ridges were constantly rebuilt as more dirt was deposited by flooding (Fowler 1969; Gallagher 1992; Gallagher and Sasso 1987).

Archaeologists who have recreated fields like these (Riley and Freimuth 1979) believe these ridges were used to improve tillage; that is, for weed control, aeration, improvement in soil structure, soil enrichment, erosion control, and control of insects (Gallagher 1992; Gallagher and Sasso 1987). In particular, ridges such as these would have served to raise the soil temperature, thereby allowing gardeners to grow crops in areas with marginal growing season lengths (Gallagher and Sasso 1987; Riley and Freimuth 1979; Riley, Moffat and Freimuth 1980). The valleys between the ridges funneled away the frost, while the raised, well-drained ridges would have warmed faster. Most eastern North American ridged agricultural fields have been found in Iowa, Wisconsin, and southern Michigan in areas where slight extensions of the growing season could have meant the difference between food and starvation.

Archaeologists point out that ridged fields in eastern North

America are a purely prehistoric phenomenon (Gallagher 1992; Riley 1987). The use of maize hills, however, is well recorded from the historic period. A combination of ridges and maize hills have been found at some prehistoric sites. Gallagher (1992) suggests that the eastern Indians did not begin to use maize hills until late, between A.D. 1500 and 1600. Indeed, maize hills last used in the mid-1600s were still visible in parts of Massachusetts in the early 1900s. The preserved hills averaged a little over four feet apart (Delabarre and Wilder 1920).

Only a few prehistoric fields have been identified in eastern North America. In one case, the archaeologist could tell it was a field not because of tilling patterns, but because the dirt contained large quantities of maize pollen and bits of wood charcoal (Cridlebaugh 1984; Delcourt et al. 1986). Maize pollen is so heavy it essentially falls to the ground immediately below the plants, and wood charcoal is one of the results of burning off vegetation to open up an area of woods. Incidentally, fragments of hoes and charcoal were recovered from ridged fields in Wisconsin (Gallagher and Sasso 1987) and Illinois (Fowler 1969), and piles of stones from field clearing were also recorded.

Instances such as these are rare, and still provide no details about what crops were grown where within a field. To flesh out our picture, we must turn to the historic record. I will ease into this subject by examining what the prehistoric record has to say about women and their role in gardening.

Prehistoric Women

Women, children, and agricultural motifs rarely are represented in the artifacts produced by the prehistoric Indians of eastern North America (Emerson 1989). One of the most common depictions of women occurs on effigy water bottles from the late prehistoric Southeast. These bottles show elderly female hunchbacks, perhaps representing "the life-giving blessings of water and fertility" (O'Connor 1995:38).

An Earth-Mother or Earth-Goddess, often identified as Old Woman or Grandmother, is a common theme in the mythology of eastern North American Indian groups. As pointed out by archaeologist Guy Prentice, she is "the mythological mother of all humans and vegetation. She is the womb from which life originates and to which all life returns with death. She is a symbol of the cycle of life" (Prentice 1986:249). Thus, she is symbolically connected to fertility, including agricultural fertility; water, rain, and lightning; serpents, death, and the Underworld; and the moon. Men, on the other hand, are associated with fire/sun; bird/falcon and through it thunder, lightning, rain, and fertility; warfare; and the Upperworld (Emerson 1989). The Iroquois myth on the origin of the human race exemplifies common concepts about women:

A beautiful woman was said to have fallen from the sky to an earth that was covered with water. A great turtle took this woman upon his back, and subsequently the turtle grew until he became an immense tract of land, which was the earth. The woman gave birth to twin sons—one good son who created maize, fruit, and tobacco, and a second evil son who created weeds and vermin (Smith 1883:76 in Prentice 1986:250).

Close analysis of symbolic motifs repeated on different female figurines leads archaeologists (Emerson 1982; Fortier 1992; Prentice 1986) to interpret a number of these as prehistoric representations of the Earth-Mother described in historic mythology. Premier among these are five remarkable bauxite figurines discovered at two late prehistoric sites in west-central Illinois near present-day St. Louis. These figures were ritually killed, or purposefully broken, and buried around A.D. 1100 next to religious structures (Fortier 1992; Prentice 1986). One of these, the Keller figurine, depicts a woman wearing a short skirt and calf-length moccasins kneeling on maize ears in front of a metate, or grinding stone base. Underneath the metate is a stand that may represent a cloud with falling rain (O'Connor 1995). A similar sandstone figurine was recovered from the Spiro site in Oklahoma. This figure, who kneels at a mortar, is probably a woman because, like other female figurines and unlike male figurines, she wears no earspools. In her left hand she holds an ear of maize, and in her right a mano or hand-held grinding stone. She is wearing a pack on her back (Emerson 1989).

Another bauxite figurine, the Birger figurine, depicts a kneeling woman wearing a short skirt and carrying a bundle fastened to her back with a tumpline (fig. 3). Her left hand rests on the

3. Birger figurine, bauxite, c. 20 cm tall, Stirling phase (A.D. 1050–1150). Recovered from the BBB Motor site (11MS595) in western Illinois. Note that the figurine was "killed," or intentionally broken, prior to burial. Reproduced with permission of the Illinois Transportation Archaeological Research Program, University of Illinois.

neck of a toothed, feline-headed serpent, while her right hand hoes the body of the serpent. The tail of the serpent splits and coils around and up the woman's back, where it produces at least six cucurbits (fig. 3a), most recently identified by their corky ridges as cushaw squash *(Cucurbita argyrosperma* ssp. *argyrosperma)* by Gayle Fritz (Fritz 1994).

Prentice (1986) can trace the following motifs to aspects of historic mythology about the Earth-Mother. The teeth exposed by the peeled-back lips signifies death or the supernatural (Emerson 1982). The serpent with the jaguar or puma head is also associated with death and the underworld. The pack carried on the back with a tumpline may represent the sacred bundles the Earth-Mother gave to humankind (Prentice 1986). The short skirt and tumpline are often associated with the Earth-Mother (Prentice 1986), and her well-defined breasts may be linked to milk, water, or fertility. Finally, the cucurbits may symbolize how Earth-Mother gave plants to humans (Prentice 1986). Please recall that gourds and cucurbits, not maize, are the earliest domesticated plants known in eastern North America.

Three other remarkable ritually killed bauxite figurines were

Prehistoric Women and Horticulture in Eastern North America

found at a nearby site (Fortier 1992). The Sponemann figurine fragments show the upper torso and head of a woman with well-developed breasts. She holds her bent arms out in front, palms up, and a stalk that sprouts out of each hand grows to her head. There, the stalks split into a coil of vines. On the left side of this coil is something that may be a sunflower seed head.

The Willoughby figurine is in two fragments, an upper torso and head, and a kneeling lower torso and basket. She has prominent breasts and wears a short skirt. She raises each hand up to her shoulders, where she holds square outward-facing plates. A vine curves up to her head from under the right plate, and on her head it branches into possible leaves or flowers. She is kneeling on top of an elaborate square basket, which is on top of a platform. The smooth lid of the basket may symbolize a cloud.

The West figurine is in many pieces, showing part of a head and upper torso, probably of a woman (she does not wear earspools). There is a coiled rattlesnake on her head and two other

3a. Detail of figure 3.

snakes and one rattle to the left of her face. She holds one of these down with her arm. She may be wearing a pack on her back.

Another bauxite figurine from farther north in Illinois, known as the Schild pipe, depicts a kneeling woman in a short skirt holding her left hand over her breast while her right hand ends in a round object (cucurbit or gourd? mano?). Something, possibly a short-handled hoe, is draped over her right shoulder. A serpent is coiled around the base of the bowl behind her (Emerson 1989).

This list should not mislead us into thinking there are many of these figurines depicting both women and agricultural themes or fertility; it includes practically every female figurine known to eastern North American archaeologists. Obviously, they do not depict everyday women as they are associated with gardens; rather, they illustrate mythological women loaded with symbolically significant motifs.

Only one other type of artifact and motif has been linked with late prehistoric Southern women: marine shell gorgets with stylized spider designs (Esarey 1990). This widespread but uncommon artifact has been found in the graves of women and children. The formal, repetitious styles, which vary by geographic region, nevertheless indicate that the style elements or motifs encoded special symbolic meanings. Ethnographically, spiders have been associated with women, earth, and fertility (Esarey 1990).

The Historic Record

None of the Indian groups in eastern North America kept written records before contact with Europeans; instead, they relied on oral traditions to pass their knowledge from one generation to another. For written records, we must depend on accounts from Europeans. Yet, despite a great deal of daily contact between Europeans and Indians during the exploration and colonial periods, we know relatively few details about the Indian way of life during those times. Captain John Smith wrote that in order to save the lives of the colonists during the lean year of 1608 at Jamestown, "Many [of the settlers] were billetted amongst the Salvages, whereby we knew all their passages, fields and habitation, how to gather and use their fruits as well as themselves" (Smith 1907:182). Despite such intimate knowledge, the colonists were not interested in writing about Indian life.

We do know that the agricultural Indian societies in the Southeast were organized into territories called chiefdoms. Chiefdoms were ruled by hereditary chiefs who also controlled religion. Chiefs were shown much respect by their followers. During state affairs they were carried on wooden litters, upon which they later were buried, and which are also represented in symbolic motifs. Chiefs often lived in houses elevated above the rest of the town on top of an artificial mound of earth, and their temples were also placed on the tops of these mounds. They could demand services, food, and goods from their followers (DePratter 1991; Hudson 1976:202–06; Swanton 1979), but they also were expected to distribute food or goods as needed. The chiefs in the Southeast were called *caciques* by the Spaniards, and *werowances* by the English.

We know that the majority of these societies were matrilineal, which means they figured kinship and inheritance through the female lineage. Children received their names from their mother's side of the family, not from their father's, and a man passed on his power and family obligations not to his children, but to the children of his sister. John Lawson (1966:51), in describing central South Carolina in 1700, put it as follows: "The Female Issue [carried] the Heritage, for fear of Imposters: the Savages well knowing, how much Frailty possesses the Indian Women, betwixt the Garters and the Girdle." Although in normal times men were the chiefs, more than one account from the mid-1500s describes a woman as chief. We can only wonder whether such an unusual succession resulted from population decimation caused by the spread of European diseases (DePratter 1991).

Language, Context, and Gender

We know frustratingly little about Indian women and gardening from the earliest historic records. The reasons we know so little can be put succinctly: language, context, and gender. At the earliest contact, no common language was shared between Europeans and Indians. Early explorers depended upon translators to talk with the people they met. These translators were often captured Indians who had been taught a European language, young European boys brought specifically to live with the Indians and learn their language, or shipwrecked Europeans who had been enslaved by the Indians. As explorers traveled from one area to another, they encountered so many different languages that they often had to depend on a chain of translators to bring the conversation around to a language they could understand.

Europeans faced a different sort of translation problem, as well: they could not help putting what they heard and observed into the context of their own culture. They saw the New World through the framework of the Old World they had left. This led to emphasis on some observations over others, and placed limits on the recognition of different ways of life and new plants and animals. Europeans did the best job they could of describing plants never before seen or named in Europe. Sometimes we can identify what they are drawing or talking about, and at other times we cannot. What fruit did Thomas Hariot compare in 1585 to the European medlar?

Medlars, a kind of very good fruit, so called by us chiefly for these respects: First in that they are not good until they be rotten, then in that they open at the head as our medlars, and are about the same bigness; otherwise in taste and colour they are far different; for they are as red as cherries and very sweet; but whereas the cherry is sharp sweet, they are luscious sweet (de Bry 1966:18).

We would recognize this as the persimmon. Even today, our reading of the historic record is colored first by the translation we depend upon, and second by our own cultural biases.

Finally, every single one of our earliest descriptions of Indian life in eastern North America was made by men. We have no written accounts from women, and none, as I have already said, from Indians of either gender. European men were most likely to observe all aspects of men's lives and tasks. We have many descriptions of bows and arrows, in part because the explorers were worried about how lethal these weapons could be. Men rarely had access to observing the full daily and seasonal round of Indian women, nor were they interested. This is unfortunate, since women seem to have played an important role in gardening. The following observations are based on historic sources from throughout eastern North America.

Who Gardened?

First, let us ask who did the gardening. Although the majority of descriptions mention women working in the fields, some also mention men and children. Accounts from the Caddo of Texas-Oklahoma, the Natchez of Louisiana, and other southern Indian groups describe communal planting of fields (DePratter 1991: 129–130; Van Doren 1955:400–401). A number of accounts mention that men helped to make a new field, but women were responsible for planting the crops and maintaining the fields after that. Given this intimate relationship between women and plants, we probably should credit women as the original domesticators of many of our food crops (Watson and Kennedy 1991). There is some indication that chiefs controlled when to commence planting and harvesting, and these occasions would have been marked by rituals (DePratter 1991:128).

In talking about his second voyage from 1535–36 to the area of Newfoundland, Jacques Cartier writes: "The women of that countrey doe labour much more then the men, as well in fishing (whereto they are greatly given) as in tilling and husbanding their grounds, and other things" (Burrage 1959:68). On December 28, 1539, while Hernando de Soto's men were near the coast in Apalache (northern Florida), "Eight men rode two leagues about the town in pursuit of Indians. . . . Two were discovered engaged in picking beans, and might have escaped, but a woman being present, the wife of one of them, they stood to fight" (Bourne 1904:49). Captain John Smith, who visited the Rapahanocks near Chesapeake Bay in 1608, found that "the people were most a hunting, save a few old men, women, and children, that were tending their corne" (Smith 1907:134). About maize and bean fields in Virginia, he says, "Their women and children do continually keepe it with weeding, and when it is growne middle high, they hill it about like a hop-yard" (Smith 1907:58–59). "When all their fruits be gathered, little els they plant, and this is done by their women and children" (Smith 1907:60). He goes on to say that while the men are "often idle," the women and children "make mats, baskets, pots, morters, pound their corne, make their bread, prepare their victuals, plant their corne, gather their corne, beare all kind of burdens, and such like" (Smith 1907:64). In all fairness, it should be pointed out that the European recorders usually observed Indian men at rest in the village, not at work out hunting, and so they were misled into thinking the men were idle (Rountree 1989:88–89).

Father Louis Hennepin, writing about Indian women of the Great Lakes and upper Mississippi Valley area, remarks, "While they are pregnant, they do not cease to be active, to carry very heavy loads, to plant Indian corn, and squashes, to go and come" (Shea 1880:283). He adds, "When these Indians go beaver hunting in the spring, they often leave their wives in the village to plant Indian corn, and squashes" (Shea 1880:294). André Penigault wrote about the Pascagoulas in the lower Mississippi Valley in 1699, "Next morning we took short walks into their countryside, where they sow their corn. The women were there to work with the men" (McWilliams 1981:20). He visited the Arcanssas in 1700 and wrote they "are very little devoted to the cultivation of the soil. It is the women who do the work here rather than the men" (McWilliams 1981:35).

Garden Care

Descriptions of how the Indians planted and tended their gardens detail the timing of plantings and harvests, the spacing within the fields, the mixture of crops, and the tools that were used. A few examples contain information concerning the timing and spacing of crops. Indians from Virginia to the lower Mississippi Valley were observed to plant more than one crop of maize. In his report to Sir Walter Raleigh of a voyage made to the Virginia coast in 1584, Captain Arthur Barlowe wrote that corn "groweth three times in five moneths: in May they sow, in July they reape, in June they sow, in August they reape: in July they sow, in September they reape" (Burrage 1959:234). Master Ralph Lane, a colonist in Virginia from 1585–86, mentions the planting of a second crop (Burrage 1959:264). Father Jacques Marquette, a French Jesuit missionary, observed the gardens of Indians in the vicinity of the Arkansas River in 1674–75: "It is true that they have an abundance of indian corn, which they sow at all seasons. We saw at the same time some that was ripe, some other that had only sprouted, and some again in the Milk, so that they sow it three times a year" (Thwaites 1673–1677:157).

Maize and beans were planted in clusters three to four feet apart. Samuel de Champlain noted that Indians in the St. Lawrence area in 1605 planted corn as follows: "Planting three or four kernels in one place they then heap up about it a quantity of earth. . . . Then three feet distant they plant as much more, and this in succession. With this corn they put in each hill three or four Brazilian beans" (quoted in Parker 1910:17). In his history of Virginia for the year 1608, Captain Smith (1907:58) says that to plant corn, the Indians "make a hole in the earth with a sticke, and into it they put foure greaines of wheate [corn] and two of beanes. These holes they make foure foote one from another."

Hariot, writing in 1585 about gardens in North Carolina, said:

For their corne, . . . they make a hole, wherein they put four graines . . . (about an inch asunder), and cover them with the mould againe, and so throughout the whole plot, . . . but with this regard, that they bee made in rankes, every ranke differing from [the] other halfe a fadome or a yarde. . . . By this meanes there is a yarde spare ground betwene every hole; where according to discretion here and there, they set as many Beanes and Peaze: in divers places also among the seeds of Macocqwer [squashes and pumpkins] Melden and Planta Solis [sunflower] (de Bry 1966:15).

Penigault observed gardening among the Pascagoulas of the lower Mississippi Valley in 1699: "They take a stick as big as one's arm and sharpened at one end and make a hole in the ground every three feet, into which they put seven or eight grains of corn per hole and cover it over with dirt. In this way they plant their corn and their beans" (McWilliams 1981:20). Much later, after hundreds of years of contact, Daniel Brodhead, who was detailed in September of 1779 by General Washington to destroy Seneca (New York) towns and fields, wrote: "I never saw finer corn altho' it was planted much thicker than is common with our Farmers" (quoted in Parker 1910:19–20).

Contrary to popular modern legend about Squanto and the use of fish, prior to European contact the Indians did not fertilize their fields. This was a practice followed by coastal Europeans who taught it to Squanto during his trip to England (Ceci 1975). Although Indians did use burning to help clear a field, there was no conscious effort on their part to use the ashes as fertilizer. During clearing, they often girdled the trees to kill them, then left the dead trees and stumps in the field and planted around them. They did practice field rotation, abandoning a field when production fell and either opening a new field, or returning to an older, partially overgrown field. Incidentally, ethnographic accounts plus archaeological plant remains indicate that these fallow fields in different stages of succession were rich sources of useful plants for prehistoric Indian societies. What to us today are weedy plants—such as maypops (Gremillion 1989), purslane, wild chenopod, blackberry, and sumac—although not planted, were encouraged in that the Indians did not weed them.

Where Were the Gardens Located?

Fields appear to have begun around the house or village, and extended along the trails for great distances. Captain Smith, writing of the inhabitants of Virginia in 1608, says, "Their houses are in the midst of their fields or gardens, which are small plots of ground. Some 20 acres, some 40. some 100. some 200. some more, some lesse" (Smith 1907:64). At Ocmulgee, Georgia, the late prehistoric ridged field was adjacent to the house discovered underneath the later platform mound.

The accounts of de Soto's travels through the Southeast in the early 1500s contain many descriptions of marches "through some great fields of corn, beans, squash and other vegetables which had been sown on both sides of the road and were spread out as far as the eye could see across two leagues of the plain. Among these fields there were sprinklings of settlements with houses set apart from each other and not arranged in the order of a town" (Varner and Varner 1988:182).

William Bartram, writing much later about southeastern Indians in 1777, says:

An Indian town is generally so situated, as to be convenient for procuring game, secure from sudden invasion, having a large district of excellent arable land adjoining, or in its vicinity, if possible on an isthmus betwixt two waters, or where the doubling of a river forms a peninsula. Such a situation . . . is taken in with a small expence and trouble of fencing, to secure the crops from the invasion of predatory animals. At other time however they choose such a convenient fertile spot at some distance from their town, when circumstances will not admit of having both together (Van Doren 1955:400).

Robert Gosnoll, in 1602, described a similar situation on Cedar Isle in Virginia: "Their cornefields being girded therein in a manner as Peninsulaes." (Smith 1907:47).

Gardens were on uplands and hills as well as bottomlands. In referring to the landscape in Virginia in 1606, Captain Smith says, "These hils many of them are planted, and yeeld no lesse plentie and varietie of fruit" (Smith 1907:49). In 1608, a young Indian who complained to Captain Smith about the intentions of the English colonists, threatened to leave them and their constant demands for food by saying, "Otherwise you will have the worse by our absence; for we can plant any where, though with more labour, and we know you cannot live if you want our harvest, and that reliefe we bring you" (Smith 1907:177).

Did the Indians Tend Trees?

Although the record concerning Indians planting and caring for trees is often ambiguous (this is an instance where the Europeans would not have always recognized the form of such care), it seems probable that they did. Archaeologist Pat Munson (1986) suggests that by the Middle Archaic, or by the sixth millennium B.C., eastern Indians were increasing the productivity of wild hickory trees by purposefully opening up and thinning the forest around them. This could easily have been done by girdling unwanted trees.

A number of times the de Soto accounts from the early 1500s describe groves of trees, often fruit trees, near or in villages. For example, on their way from Georgia to South Carolina in 1540, "At the end of three days, the army came to a halt in a very pretty place, cooled by great groves of mulberries and other trees heavy with fruit" (Varner and Varner 1988:296) [I must admit that this account does not relate the grove to a village]. Later, the approach to the village of Casquin was described: "Along the entire bank of that river and throughout the vicinity, there were numerous fields of corn and a great number of fruit trees, all of which proved the land to be fertile" (Varner and Varner 1988:430). At Casquin, de Soto made his camp in "an orchard which Casquin himself had pointed out when he perceived that his guests did not want the houses" (Varner and Varner 1988:431). Further south, at Mauvila, the de Soto chroniclers noted that a live tree formed part of the stockade around the village: "And this was not the only such tree in the fence, there being many others like it which had been preserved intentionally and which beautified it exceedingly" (Varner and Varner 1988:373).

Captain Smith noted in 1606 that in Virginia, "By the dwelling of the Salvages are some great Mulberry trees, and in some parts of the Countrey, they are found growing naturally in prettie groves" (Smith 1907:53). Much later, Alexander Nairne, the provincial Indian agent for South Carolina in 1708, visited the Chicasaw and observed that "Each house hath by it a grove of . . . plum trees, for it seems they bear best, when run up in thickets 4 or 5 foot asunder" (Moore 1988:59–60). He further noted ". . . their houses a Gunn or pistole shot asunder, with their improved ground peach and plum trees about them" (Moore 1988:58). The Iroquois are celebrated for their orchards of fruit trees that were burned in successive wars, beginning with the French in the early 1600s (Parker 1910). A General Sullivan reported in September, 1799:

[Colonel Butler] destroyed two hundred acres of excellent corn with a number of orchards one of which had in it 1500 fruit trees. . . . I flatter myself that the orders with which I was entrusted are fully executed, as we have not left a single settlement or a field of corn in the country of the Five Nations (Parker 1910:19).

Penigault, writing about the Natchez in the lower Mississippi Valley at the beginning of the 1700s, was impressed with their custom of planting fruit trees by their houses: "In front of their houses they have peach trees right in the open, which bear excellent peaches and make a pleasant shade for their houses" (McWilliams 1981:85). The peach, which is not native to North America, appears to have been an early and quite successful introduction from the sixteenth century Spanish (Sheldon 1978). Finally, Bartram, in his travels through the Southeast in the late 1700s, recognized a number of useful trees that occurred in old, abandoned Indian towns, including persimmon, honey locust, plum, mulberry, hickory, and black walnut. He said that he found Chickasaw plums "never . . . wild in the forests, but always in old deserted Indian plantations" (Harper 1958:25).

Plants Dispersed by the Indians

When plants are found in disjunct populations outside of their natural range, humans may have been the agents of dispersal. One such case known from the archaeological record is maygrass, an East Coast native found in abundance at prehistoric Midwestern sites (Cowan 1978). Three domesticated Old World crops—peaches, watermelons, and cowpeas—were adopted early by the Indians of eastern North America (Blake 1981; Gremillion 1993; Sheldon 1978). Peaches and watermelon spread especially far and quickly from their introduction to the Southeast by the Spanish in the sixteenth century (Blake 1981; Sheldon 1978). Archaeologists suggest that those new introductions most likely to be adopted are similar in aspect and care to traditional crops, with high yields and low risk (Blake 1981; Gremillion 1993).

We expect domesticated crops to be spread by humans. However, there is some evidence that Indians also dispersed wild plants (Black 1978). This occurred on a local level within the tended and successional fields of the Indians, when the gardeners did not selectively weed out useful weedy plants. One such that comes to mind is the maypop or passion flower, a perennial vine with a delicious fruit (Gremillion 1989). In describing the coastal Virginia Indians of the early seventeenth century, William Strachey wrote: "they plant also the Feild-apple, the Maracock a wilde fruict like a Pomgranet, which increaseth infinitely and ripens in August" (Wright and Freund 1953:79). Later he went on to say: "Here is a Fruict by the Naturells called a *Maracock;* this groweth generally lowe, and creepeth in a manner amongest the Corne . . . and in every feild where the Indians plant their Corne be Cart-loades of them" (Wright and Freund 1953:120–121). In the early eighteenth century, Robert Beverly wrote: "The Maracock, which is the Fruit of what we call the Passion Flower, our Natives did not take the Pains to plant, having enough of it growing every where; tho' they eat it with a great deal of Pleasure; this Fruit is about the Size of a Pullet's Egg" (Wright 1947:142 in Gremillion 1989:139).

Plant dispersal also occurred in a more active manner over greater distances. Sweet flag *(Acorus calamus),* which has an important medicinal root, had been spread northward by historic times (Black 1978). There are other examples, but I will mention only one more. I have heard that the late prehistoric archaeological site of Moundville in Alabama today is covered with the type of holly that was used by the southeastern Indians to make "black drink" or cassina, a drink much stronger in caffeine than the strongest coffee. The Indians drank large quantities of it out of elaborately carved whelk shell containers: the high intake of caffeine led to predictable results. This was an accepted way to purge oneself before undertaking important rituals. Traveling through northern Florida in 1771, a Sargent Wright observed, "Every Man and Man Child and Worships the New Corn and Cassina for four Days but Tastis No Salt in that time—the Woman Dos all the Work" (Calder 1935:242). This holly, aptly named *Ilex vomitoria,* normally grows only along the seacoast and would not occur naturally at places like Moundville. Today, interpreters at Town Creek Indian Mound in the Piedmont of North Carolina very appropriately grow it outside of the interpretive center.

Re-creating Indian Gardens

The archaeological and historical data about prehistoric and early historic Indian women and gardening have been brought alive at a number of re-created Indian gardens located at museums and parks throughout eastern North America. The majority of these showcase late prehistoric crops such as maize, beans, and squash; however, a few show gardens or crops of earlier times. I was involved with setting up a late prehistoric garden for a re-created Indian village in southwestern Ohio (Wagner 1990). Sun-Watch Village, which dates to about A.D. 1250, was built by Fort Ancient Indians who occupied the central Ohio River Valley from A.D. 950 to 1650. These agriculturalists lived in self-contained villages with several hundred inhabitants. A local museum planned to partially reconstruct the village, and wished to include an accurate garden in their reconstruction.

The problems and pleasures of this project were typical of any attempt to re-create a period garden. The types of crops I chose to grow and the types of weeds I chose to encourage were based on archaeological evidence gleaned from over fifty Fort Ancient sites. However, no historic records exist for garden design or gardening practices of this prehistoric society. I based the garden design—hills of maize and beans in blocks separated by aisles of squash and gourds, the entirety bordered by sunflowers—on general eastern historic accounts of Indian gardens (fig. 4). My focus was more on replicating the look of the crops themselves rather than the look of the entire garden.

Nevertheless, the look and feel of the garden was immediately

4. Re-created Fort Ancient (A.D. 1000–1650) garden at SunWatch Village, Dayton Museum of Natural History, Dayton, Ohio. Hills of maize and beans are separated by corridors of squash and gourds. The garden is bordered by sunflowers. The hills were made with river-shell hoes. G. Wagner photograph.

different and pleasing to the visitors to the site. The addition of other replicated tools and foods such as drying racks, underground storage pits, digging sticks, shell hoes, strings of dried squash, braided ears of corn, and dried squash blossoms stored in gourd containers added to the authenticity of the garden. Each of these provided starting points for questions from visitors and discussion by museum staff.

I should point out that replication was not complete: stone tools were not used to cut and shape the wooden digging stick; the ground was not cleared by girdling trees and using only digging sticks and shell hoes; and watchers did not sit on wooden

5. Re-created Catawba garden at Catawba Cultural Center, Rock Hill, South Carolina. The wooden stage in the background is for drying maize. The woods have been opened up by girdling trees (removing bark from the trunks). Useful weeds such as maypops *(Passiflora incarnata)* are allowed to grow among the maize, beans, squash, gourds, and sunflowers. G. Wagner photograph.

stages to throw stones at marauding birds and small boys. Behind the public scenes, we used modern tilling machines, modern tools, and artificial sources of water. Today we face different social constraints and schedules and simply do not have the time or resources to devote to total replication. Today we also have introduced pests and weeds that were not present 700 years ago, and these require modern methods of control.

I have since worked at or helped others re-create gardens in other areas and for other prehistoric periods (fig. 5), and I delight in growing a few of these unusual crops in my own garden at home. One of my favorites was a time-line garden that started with the earliest known domesticated crops at one end of a museum building and ended at the other with those crops encountered by the first Europeans. Anyone with a little space and the willingness to conduct a modicum of historical research can try their hand at re-creating an Indian garden.

Gail E. Wagner, Ph. D., is associate professor of anthropology and associate faculty member of the School of the Environment at the University of South Carolina at Columbia.

REFERENCES CITED

Black, M. Jean
1978 Plant Dispersal by Native North Americans in the Canadian Subarctic. In *The Nature and Status of Ethnobotany,* ed. Richard I. Ford, 255–62. Anthropological Papers No. 67. Museum of Anthropology, University of Michigan, Ann Arbor, Michigan.

Blake, Leonard W.
1981 Early Acceptance of Watermelon by Indians of the United States. *Journal of Ethnobiology* 1(2):193–99.

Bourne, Edward Gaylord [editor]
1904 *Narratives of the Career of Hernando De Soto.* 2 vol. New York: A. S. Barnes.

Burrage, Henry S. [editor]
1959 *Early English and French Voyages Chiefly from Hakluyt, 1534–1608.* New York: Barnes and Noble.

Calder, Isabel M. [editor]
1935 *Colonial Captivities, Marches and Journeys.* New York: Macmillan.

Ceci, Lynn
1975 Fish Fertilizer: A Native North American Practice? *Science* 188:26–30.

Cowan, C. Wesley
1978 The Prehistoric Use and Distribution of Maygrass in Eastern North America: Cultural and Phytogeographical Implications. In *The Nature and Status of Ethnobotany,* ed. Richard I. Ford, 263–88. Anthropological Papers No. 67. Ann Arbor: Museum of Anthropology, University of Michigan.

Cridlebaugh, Patricia
1984 American Indian and Euro-American Impact upon Holocene Vegetation in the Lower Little Tennessee River Valley, East Tennessee. Unpublished Ph.D. dissertation. Department of Anthropology, University of Tennessee, Knoxville.

Crites, Gary D.

1993 Domesticated Sunflower in Fifth Millennium B.P. Temporal Context: New Evidence from Middle Tennessee. *American Antiquity* 58(1):146–48.

de Bry, Theodore

1966 *Thomas Hariot's Virginia.* Readex Microprint.

Delabarre, Edmund B. and Harris H. Wilder

1920 Indian Corn-Hills in Massachusetts. *American Anthropologist* 22(3):203–25.

Delcourt, Paul A., Hazel R. Delcourt, Patricia A. Cridlebaugh, and Jefferson Chapman

1986 Holocene Ethnobotanical and Paleoecological Record of Human Impact on Vegetation in the Little Tennessee River Valley, Tennessee. *Quaternary Research* 25:330–49.

DePratter, Chester B.

1991 *Late Prehistoric and Early Historic Chiefdoms in the Southeastern United States.* New York: Garland.

Emerson, Thomas E.

1982 *Mississippian Stone Images in Illinois.* Circular 6, Illinois Archaeological Survey, Urbana.

1989 Water, Serpents, and the Underworld: An Exploration into Cahokian Symbolism. In *The Southeastern Ceremonial Complex: Artifacts and Analysis, The Cottonlandia Conference,* ed. Patricia Galloway, 45–92. Lincoln: University of Nebraska Press.

Esarey, Duane

1990 Style Geography and Symbolism of Mississippian Spiders. Paper presented at 48th Southeastern Archaeological Conference, Mobile, Ala.

Fortier, Andrew C.

1992 Stone Figurines. In *The Sponemann Site 2: The Mississippi and Oneota Occupations (11-Ms-517),* 277–303, ed. Douglas K. Jackson, Andrew C. Fortier, and Joyce A. Williams. American Bottom Archaeology FAI-270 Site Reports 24. Urbana: University of Illinois Press.

Fowler, Melvin L.

1969 Middle Mississippian Agricultural Fields. *American Antiquity* 34(4):365–75.

Fritz, Gayle

1990 Multiple Pathways to Farming in Precontact Eastern North America. *Journal of World Prehistory* 4(4):387–476.

1994 Precolumbian *Cucurbita argyrosperma* ssp. *argyrosperma* (Cucurbitaceae) in the Eastern Woodlands of North America. *Economic Botany* 48(3):280–92.

Gallagher, James P.

1992 Prehistoric Field Systems in the Upper Midwest. In *Late Prehistoric Agriculture: Observations from the Midwest,* ed. by William I. Woods. 95–135. Studies in Illinois Archaeology No. 8. Springfield: Illinois Historic Preservation Agency.

Gallagher, James P. and Robert F. Sasso

1987 Investigations into Oneota Ridged Field Agriculture on the Northern Margin of the Prairie Peninsula. *Plains Anthropologist* 32(116):141–51.

Gremillion, Kristen Johnson

1989 The Development of a Mutualistic Relationship Between Humans and Maypops *(Passiflora incarnata* L.) in the Southeastern United States. *Journal of Ethnobiology* 9(2):135–55.

1993 Adoption of Old World Crops and Processes of Cultural Change in the Historic Southeast. *Southeastern Archaeology* 12(1):15–20.

Harper, Francis [editor]

1958 *The Travels of William Bartram. Naturalist's Edition.* New Haven, Conn.: Yale University Press.

Hastorf, Christine A. and Sissel Johannessen

1994 Becoming Corn-Eaters in Prehistoric America. In *Corn and Culture in the Prehistoric New World,* ed. by Sissel Johannessen and Christine A. Hastorf, pp. 427–43. University of Minnesota Publications in Anthropology No. 5. Boulder, Colo.: Westview Press.

Hudson, Charles

1976 *The Southeastern Indians.* Knoxville: University of Tennessee Press.

Kelly, A. R.

1938 A Preliminary Report on Archaeological Explorations at Macon, Georgia. *Bureau of American Ethnology Bulletin* 119(1):1–68.

Lawson, John

1966 *A New Voyage to Carolina.* Readex Microprint.

McWilliams, Richebourg Gaillard [translator and editor]

1981 *Fleur de Lys and Calumet: Being the Penicaut Narrative of French Adventure in Louisiana.* Tuscaloosa: University of Alabama Press.

Moore, Alexander [editor]

1988 *Nairne's Muskhogean Journals: The 1708 Expedition to the Mississippi River.* Jackson: University Press of Mississippi.

Munson, Patrick J.

1986 Hickory Silviculture: A Subsistence Revolution in the Prehistory of Eastern North America. Paper presented at Emergent Horticultural Economies of the Eastern Woodlands Conference, Southern Illinois University, Carbondale, Ill.

O'Connor, Mallory McCane

1995 *Lost Cities of the Ancient Southeast.* Gainesville: University Press of Florida.

Parker, Arthur C.

1910 *Iroquois Uses of Maize and Other Food Plants.* Bulletin No. 482. Albany: New York State Museum.

Prentice, Guy

1986 An Analysis of the Symbolism Expressed by the Birger Figurine. *American Antiquity* 51(2):239–66.

Riley, Thomas J.

1987   Ridged-Field Agriculture and the Mississippian Economic Pattern. In *Emergent Horticultural Economies of the Eastern Woodlands,* ed. by Willian F. Keegan. 295–304. Occasional Paper No. 7. Center for Archaeological Investigations, Southern Illinois University, Carbondale, Ill.

Riley, Thomas J. and Glen Freimuth

1979   Field Systems and Frost Drainage in the Prehistoric Agriculture of the Upper Great Lakes. *American Antiquity* 44(2):271–85.

Riley, Thomas J., Charles R. Moffat and Glen Freimuth

1980   Prehistoric Raised Fields in the Upper Midwestern United States: An Innovation in Response to Marginal Growing Conditions. *North American Archaeologist* 2(2):101–15.

Rountree, Helen C.

1989   *The Powhatan Indians of Virginia: Their Traditional Culture.* The Civilization of the American Indian Series, Vol. 193. Norman: University of Oklahoma Press.

Scarry, C. Margaret [editor]

1993a   *Foraging and Farming in the Eastern Woodlands.* Gainesville: University Press of Florida.

Scarry, C. Margaret

1993b   Variability in Mississippian Crop Production Strategies. In *Foraging and Farming in the Eastern Woodlands,* ed. by C. Margaret Scarry, pp. 78–90. University Press of Florida, Gainesville.

Shea, John Gilmary [translator]

1880   *A Description of Louisiana, by Father Louis Hennepin, Recollect Missionary.* New York: John G. Shea. Readex Microprint.

Sheldon, Elisabeth

1978   Introduction of the Peach *(Prunus persica)* to the Southeastern United States. Paper presented at 19th Society for Economic Botany meeting, St. Louis, Mo.

Smith, John

1907   *The Generall Historie of Virginia, New England and The Summer Isles.* 2 vol. Glasgow, U.K.: James MacLehose and Sons.

Swanton, John R.

1979   *The Indians of the Southeastern United States.* Reprint of the 1946 Bureau of American Ethnology Bulletin 137. Washington, D.C.: Smithsonian Institution Press.

Thwaites, Reuben Gold [editor]

1673–1677   Voyages of Marquette. In *The Jesuit Relations, 59,* by Jacques Marquette. Vol. 59 Lower Canada, Illinois, Ottawas 1673–1677. Cleveland, Oh.: Burrows Brothers. Readex Microprint.

Van Doren, Mark [editor]

1955   *Travels of William Bartram.* New York: Dover.

Varner, John and Jeannette Varner [translators and editors]

1988   *The Florida of the Inca*. Austin: University of Texas Press.

Wagner, Gail E.

1987   Uses of Plants by the Fort Ancient Indians. Unpublished Ph.D. dissertation, Department of Anthropology, Washington University, St. Louis, Mo.

1990   Charcoal, Isotopes, and Shell Hoes: Reconstructing a 12th-Century Native American Garden. Expedition 32 (2):34–43.

in prep.   Tobacco in Prehistoric Eastern North America. In *Deer Person's Gift: Tobacco Use by Native North Americans,* edited and compiled by Joseph C. Winter. New Haven, Conn.: Yale University Press.

Watson, Patty Jo and Mary C. Kennedy

1991   The Development of Horticulture in the Eastern Woodlands of North America: Women's Role. In *Engendering Archaeology: Women and Prehistory,* ed. by Joan M. Gero and Margaret W. Conkey, pp. 255–75. Oxford: Basil Blackwell.

Wright, Louis B. and Virginia Freund [editors]

1953   *The Historie of Travell into Virginia Britania (1612) By William Strachey, gent.* London: The Hakluyt Society.

Kay Moss

"A Vertue of Necessity"

The Backcountry Housewife's

Reliance on Garden, Field, and Forest

The seventeenth-century herbalist John Parkinson offered sound advice toward the Ordering of the Kitchen Garden: "Who must like their habitations as they fall unto them, and cannot have time or meanes to alter them, they must make a vertue of necessity, and convert their places to their best advantage."[1]

Another famous English herbalist, listing the Indians' staple, corn, as turkey wheat, wrote, "We have as yet no certain proofe or experience concerning the vertues of this kinde of Corn; although the barbarous Indians, which know no better, are constrained to make a vertue of necessitie, and thinke it a good food; whereas we may easily judge, that it nourisheth but little, and is of hard and evill digestion, a more convenient food for swine than for men." Little did John Gerard suspect that in the following century corn was to become basic foodstuff for Europeans and Africans transplanted to America's Southern colonies. John

Lawson proclaimed Indian corn "the most useful Grain in the World; and had it not been for the Fruitfulness of this Species, it would have proved very difficult to have settled some of the Plantations in America." Necessity guided those early settlers to discover the virtues in unfamiliar subsistence crops, in wild fruits and herbs, and in adapting their kitchen gardening to new soil and climate conditions.[2]

Early adventurers published glowing descriptions of this land. At the dawn of the eighteenth century, John Lawson described the back parts of Carolina as "the most noble and sweetest Part of this Country. . . . Backwards, near the Mountains, you meet with the richest Soil, a sweet, thin Air, dry Roads, pleasant small murmuring Streams, and several beneficial Productions and Species, which are unknown in the European World." Lawson further embroidered his description of the backcountry as "adorn'd with pleasant Meadows, Rivers, Mountains, Valleys, Hills, and rich Pastures."[3]

As the Atlantic coastal areas became thickly populated, the more adventurous or the less prosperous immigrants moved into the backcountry to carve a life from the wilderness they found. Vast expanses of forest, prairie, and canebrake nurtured by fast-moving streams and mineral resources lured folks down the Great Wagon Road from Pennsylvania into the Valley of Virginia, the Carolinas, and Georgia. Another mid-eighteenth-century branch of settlement flowed from Charleston into the Carolina Upcountry. By the end of the eighteenth century, the tide of settlement overflowed the mountains into Kentucky following the Wilderness Road.

Imagine the Southern landscape that greeted early European pioneers—vast forests, open prairies, and extensive rivercane brakes, intersected by clear-flowing creeks and rivers. Before we focus on the manner in which settlers interacted with this landscape, let us reexamine a few myths and stereotypes.

First let us examine the common concept of the balance of nature. "Nature" is "balanced" only in a thoroughly dynamic sense. The natural balance is constantly readjusting to change. Human impact is only one of countless influences affecting its equilibrium. To the idea of the balance of nature one must add a tempering of chaos theory!

No ecosystem exists in a steady state. Each member of the system impacts every other. Each rock that ever weathered and crumbled, each mastodon that roamed the prehistoric Southeast, and in the eighteenth century each flock of passenger pigeons that roosted among giant oaks, each wolf pup born, each chestnut that fell to the forest floor impacted the early Southern backcountry environment.

Native Americans shaped the landscape. Agriculture accelerated change. Pressure from the eighteenth-century influx of newcomers out of Germany, Ulster, the Scottish Lowlands, England, Wales, France, Switzerland, and West Africa further quickened alterations to the landscape in the Southern backcountry.

Secondly, since there is no steady-state balance of nature, it is inaccurate to think of "living in harmony with nature." Humans, and all other animals, are components of the natural dynamic we call "balance." Neither Indians nor settlers lived *with* nature or *in* nature, but existed as *part of* nature. Early Piedmont folk may not have acknowledged this fact any more than we moderns generally recognize our dependence and impact on every other component of the natural world.

Apparent in our late twentieth-century society is a fresh welling of admiration for the "noble savage" with an accompanying aversion toward the greedy and destructive Euro-American—the Disney-Pocohontas story. Remember, however, that every human cultural group has used, often overused, and at times abused available resources. Agriculture and population density were high-impact forces throughout the eighteenth century. Late-century industrial development further shocked the environment and accelerated change. Each of these forces intensified with the coming of European settlers.

Let us consider here that segment of eighteenth-century Southern frontiersmen and women who delighted in this bountiful country—who cherished the native plants, who celebrated the abundance of game, who survived by the products of field and forest, and who added favored herbs and vegetables from their homelands to the scene—just as many Native Americans had done for centuries before. Both Indian and pioneer were focused on survival in this land.

Whatever conservation ethic they may have followed was based on budgeting of resources, warding off misfortune, or paying

6. The backcountry housewife tended a garden and took care of farm animals, as this view of a house at the Schiele Museum shows, and gathered plants from the wild, as well. Photograph courtesy of the Schiele Museum of Natural History, Gastonia, North Carolina.

homage to a benevolent Provider. This was not a Disney wilderness—there were enormous dangers and hardships to be braved, and carving a life from this landscape required intensive labor.

Here I wish to present evidence of early eighteenth-century Southerners who went beyond mere necessity in their everyday lives—hardworking, creative, optimistic individuals who made a "vertue of necessity." We will gently term the eighteenth-century Euro-American impact the "influence on the Southern landscape" and will note especially women's probable roles.

In the first days of frontier settlement, there was generally little differentiation between men's work and women's work among the commoner folk. Every family member pitched in to accom-

plish pressing tasks of each new day, foremost being the all-impor-
tant job of procuring food through farming, hunting, and gathering. Little evidence remains of the common gardens of the early
settlement period in the backcountry. When the basics of food
and shelter had been procured, the settlers began to seek comfort,
security, and a measure of refinement. The same spirit that led individuals to carve a fylfot on a blanket chest or press heart designs
onto gingerbread or embroider tulips upon a coverlet may have
inspired them to make a virtue of necessity in their gardens as
well.

The kitchen garden (figs. 6, 7) generally fell under a woman's
supervision. Here the backcountry housewife overstepped necessity, intermingling potherbs and "sallating" with medicinals and
dyestuffs, with resulting delectation of texture, color, and scent.

7. Squash and herbs grown together in an enclosure in a re-created early nineteenth-century garden. Photograph courtesy of the Schiele Museum of Natural
History, Gastonia, North Carolina.

The Virtues

Field, forest, and garden provided much more than food and pleasant flowers. The following eclectic assortment of plants was chosen to illustrate basic eighteenth-century theories, values, and lifeways. These examples are drawn from writings of eighteenth- and early nineteenth-century inhabitants and travelers and from published works documented as available in the southeastern frontier settlements. Some botanical virtues from two centuries ago are especially charming. Many of these plants enter less commonly into our twentieth-century lives, however you may discover several among them to deepen enjoyment of your garden—and of an abandoned field down the road!

Several Native Herbs of Interest

Native botanicals were gathered from the wild, and certain favorites were transplanted into the garden. John Lawson mentions that four sorts of snake roots "which are great Antidotes against that Serpent's Bite were easily rais'd in the Garden."[4]

The popular English *Gardeners Dictionary* by Philip Miller included detailed directions for cultivating the various snakeroots among numerous other native American plants.[5] English gardeners were more likely than Americans to have included pokeweed in their borders or to have encouraged specimen plantings of sumac. Inhabitants of the Southern backcountry settlements could easily collect such common wildings from the forest edge with no expenditure of gardening labor. Less invasive native species were given space in the American garden, however.

Trees and shrubs were counted among the herbs, following the broad eighteenth-century definition of that term. Early Southerners discovered many serviceable woody plants.

Tulip tree or *yellow poplar* wood is easily worked into boards, planks, bowls, dishes, spoons, all sorts of joiners' work, and canoes—"both the Indians and the Europeans often make their canoes from its trunk." A traveler reported seeing "a barn of considerable size whose walls and roof were made of a single [poplar] tree." Among huge poplar trees farther south one was of such "prodigious Bigness . . . wherein a lusty Man had his Bed and Household Furniture, and liv'd in it, till his Labour got him a more fashionable Mansion." In the spring the bark was peeled from the poplar and used to roof houses of Indian and pioneer. Medicinally, poplar leaves were applied to the forehead as a remedy for headache. The roots were said "to be as efficacious against the fever as the Jesuits' bark [quinine]."[6]

Persimmons were "commonly put upon the table amongst the sweetmeats and some people made a tolerably good wine of them." John Lawson warned that under-ripe persimmon fruit "draws your Mouth up like a Purse," further explaining, "The Fruit is rotten, when ripe." The practical Moravians noted of the persimmon, "It has a gum, and some years ago a premium was placed on this, to be paid to whoever gathered it."[7]

Domestic medical practitioners employed persimmon bark and roots internally against kidney and bowel complaints. Externally the bark found use in treatment of sores and cancers.

Of *sassafras*, the Moravian surveyor Christian Gottlieb Reuter wrote In 1764: "All has an odor, leaves, wood, and blossoms; and it is much used in medicine to purify the blood." While we generally think only of the sassafras root bark in medicine, the leaves and blossoms were also employed.[8]

Sassafras flowers were gathered and dried for tea "by the most curious." In his *Travels* of 1748–51, Peter Kalm wrote, "Some years ago it had been customary in London, to drink a kind of tea of the flowers of sassafras, because it was looked upon as very healthful, but upon recollecting that the same potion was much used against the venereal disease, it was soon left off, lest those who used it should be looked upon as infected with that disease."[9]

Among Southern manuscript sources sassafras root bark was used against cachexy, cancer, dropsy, consumption, pleurisy, rheumatism, and kidney problems. In addition, sassafras was included in a diet drink, a cancer salve, and a tea to drink along with Caesar's Cure (a plantain and horehound preparation for snake bite, dog bite, and other poisons).

Sassafras chips among woolen stuffs were said to expel moths. "Some people have their bedposts made of sassafras wood to expel bed bugs;" however, Peter Kalm noted that the scent of the wood remained only a few years. He was shown an older sassafras bed upon which he observed a multitude of the bugs! Another virtue of the sassafras wood was its durability, making it useful for

"Posts for houses and other Things that require standing in the Ground."[10]

A "fine lasting orange" dye was obtained by boiling the bark of the sassafras tree with urine in a brass pot. Interest in cultivating a convenient supply of this useful tree was indicated by Peter Kalm. He noted that as the shoots do not transplant well sassafras should be started from the berries, "which however is difficult, since the birds eat them before they are half ripe."[11]

The redbud tree was described "the best Sallad, of any Flower."[12] If you sprinkle redbud blossoms on your salad next spring, you will discover them to be pleasantly tart and lovely.

River cane greatly benefitted human inhabitants in their manufacture of tools, weapons, baskets, and mats; however, the native cane's greatest value may have been as cold weather food for grazing animals, both wild and domestic. Early writers noted the existence of extensive canebrakes in low ground along piedmont and mountain streams. Reuter catalogued cane as "Good winter forage for the cattle . . . In addition they furnish our pipe-stems."[13]

Pokeweed was celebrated as food and medicine. Philip Miller's popular gardening dictionary reported, "The Inhabitants of North America boil the young Shoots of this Plant, and eat it like Spinach," however period sources also warned of the poisonous nature of the mature plant. As a dye, pokeweed was disappointing. "The Juice of the Berries stain Paper and Linen of a beautiful purple Colour, but it will not last long. If there could be a Method of fixing the Dye, it might be very useful."[14]

The juice of the poke root furnished a familiar American purgative. The *Gardener's Dictionary* of 1759 warned against other medical usage. "Of late there have been some Quacks, who pretend to cure Cancers with this Herb [*Phytolacca,* pokeweed], but I have not met with one Instance of its having been serviceable in that Disorder." Nevertheless, that use persisted. Two manuscript commonplace books of the early nineteenth-century Carolina backcountry included pokeweed in cancer plasters.[15]

Sumac captured attention and was put to many uses. Several personal medical manuscripts which I have examined included sumac root bark used in applications to burns, sores, and cancers. Berries, leaves, and stems were employed in dyes for cloth and leather.[16]

Life Everlasting, Gnaphalium is the weedy native herb locally known as rabbit tobacco. Peter Kalm noted the use of this plant in his observations on mid-eighteenth-century domestic floral arranging. "The English ladies are accustomed to gather great quantities of this life everlasting. . . . For they put them into pots, with or without water, amongst other fine flowers which they gather in the gardens and in the fields, and place them as an ornament in the rooms. English ladies in general are much inclined to keep flowers all summer long about or upon the chimneys, upon a table or before the windows, either on account of their beauty or because of their sweet scent. . . . Gnaphalium was one of those which they kept in their rooms during the winter, because its flowers never altered."[17]

Traditional herbal usage for everlasting (cudweed) was followed. One backcountry Carolina manuscript of cures endorsed a poultice of everlasting for use against toothache. From the flowers and stalks a decoction was prepared "to bathe pained or bruised parts of the body, or they may be rubbed with the plant itself tied up in a thin cloth or bag."[18]

Yarrow was listed in both wild and cultivated plant inventories. The North Carolina Moravians reported yarrow "a good breast tea. Some eat it in the morning with bread and butter." Yarrow was widely recommended against wounds, hence its common name, woundwort.[19]

Another old name for yarrow, nosebleed, reflected a traditional treatment for migraine which involved stuffing the nostrils with yarrow leaves to create nosebleed. Whether this particular practice was common in the Southern colonies, it is certain that bloodletting was routinely performed for a multitude of ills and injuries.[20]

False Solomon's Seal "toward fall bears red berries, like currants, which taste good and are refreshing."[21] Another common name for this fruit was treacle berries, indicating their molasseslike flavor.

Selected Virtues from the Kitchen Garden

Roses were widely considered medicinal as well as a favored flavoring for foods. Red roses were included in the medical garden in the Wachovia settlements. A Guilford County, North Carolina, manuscript book of remedies suggested "for a gentle purge Take

Elder Roots peach Blossoms & Rose leaves [petals] Stew or Boyl them."[22]

Nicholas Culpeper summed up the rose's medical reputation as "very great Use and Effect." In five pages of recommendations, that herbalist included rose remedies similar to all encountered in Southern manuscripts. Petals of various *Rosa* species were considered effective both as a gentle purge and to stop a *lax* (diarrhea). Rose petals were common in gargles for sore throat, ointments to allay inflammations, and preparations to work on "melancholick Humours."[23]

Rose honey was considered mildly medicinal. You will also discover it to be absolutely delicious. Honey and fragrant petals are heated together, allowed to steep, and then the petals are strained out.[24]

In the kitchen, rose water or rose brandy entered into cakes and puddings as a major flavoring agent. Rose brandy is simply prepared by pouring brandy over rose petals and allowing to steep for a day or two. The brandy is then strained and poured over fresh petals. The process should be repeated until the scent and flavor is strong.[25]

Pinks, or Gillyflowers (Dianthus), were valued for flavor as well as for scent and ornament. Dianthus blossoms were infused in syrup or vinegar "to give it a pleasant taste and gallant color." In addition, these flowers were considered mildly medicinal, beneficial for "comforting the spirits."[26]

Nasturtium leaves and flowers were enjoyed in salads and as a garnish. Today's popular notion of adding edible flowers to the dinner plate is certainly not new! The seed pods of the nasturtium were commonly pickled for use as a substitute for capers. Eliza Smith's *The Compleate Housewife* included a receipt for pickling nasturtium "buds."[27]

Marigold petals added eye appeal to soups and color to cheese. Marigolds of the late eighteenth-century garden were likely to have been the pot marigold or calendula, although the French and African marigolds had been introduced by that time. To prevent the plague, the clergyman John Wesley recommended that one "eat marigold flowers, daily, as a salad, with oil and vinegar."[28]

Sage entered into both cookery and medicine; the backcountry housewife used the blossoms as well as the leaves. Sage tea was considered an especially salubrious beverage for the sick. For sunburn John Wesley suggested, "Wash the face with sage tea." Another eighteenth-century Methodist clergyman, Francis Asbury, gargled with sage tea "to scatter, if possible, the inflammation" of the throat. Sage tea might have been simply sage steeped in water; however, Hannah Glasse's famous cookbook directed steeping sage, baum (*Melissa*), and lemon in white wine and boiling water. Sage ointments were recommended for bruises and sores.[29]

Rosemary was esteemed in the backcountry garden, as elsewhere, for culinary and medicinal purposes and for its scent. John Wesley noted that he had tried washing his head every night with a decoction of rosemary to make hair grow. Hungary Water, a popular general restorative tonic, was manufactured by infusing brandy with rosemary.[30]

Chamomile (Roman) was commonly employed for an assortment of ills. John Wesley wrote of chamomile for "pain in the stomach . . . Take fasting, or in the fit, half a pint of camomile tea." Clystering (enema) solutions often contained chamomile. To alleviate pain of toothache or pleurisy a hot bag of boiled chamomile flowers was applied to "the part affected."[31]

A fancy for planting chamomile in walks and on banks to sit upon was suggested in early English herbals and gardening guides. We know this delightful idea traveled at least as far as the South Carolina lowcountry, for Eliza Lucas Pinckney's mid-eighteenth-century gardening plans included "seats of Camomile."

Parsley was widely cultivated as a culinary herb, then as now. The *Gardener's Dictionary* suggested parsley as a border in the kitchen garden. Parsley tops were employed in medicine as external application to bruises, swellings, and puncture wounds. The roots and tops were combined in a dose for dropsy.

Fennel and several relatives found special use against gastrointestinal complaints. The old herbals taught that fennel "consumes that phlegmatick Humour, which Fish most plentifully afford and annoy the Body" while *dill* "allayeth gripings and windinesse." *Caraway* seeds made with sugar into "Comfits are very good for the stomack."[32]

Gourds were important to Indians and settlers alike. Early North Carolina Moravians reported, "All sorts of vessels can be made from them; the hunters use them for powder flasks." Gourds were frequently called calabashes; however, true calabashes are fruits of a tropical tree rather than this relative of winter squash. Gourds were considered "particularly fit for keeping seeds of plants in, which are to be sent over sea, for they keep their power of vegetating much longer, if they be put in calabashes, than by any other means."[33]

Radishes of several sorts were planted in the kitchen garden every month of the year. Aside from a year-round fresh vegetable supply, the radish plant offered added virtues. Period receipts for pickling seed pods of the radish are intriguing. Preserved pods are certainly more appealing to my taste buds (and to my nose!) than the pickled radish roots, another eighteenth-century culinary offering.[34]

The radish entered into medicine. John Wesley recommended removing warts by rubbing daily with a radish root. To prevent the bite of a viper he directed, "Rub the hands with the juice of radishes."[35]

Cabbage, another kitchen remedy, provided a convenient poultice or a substitute for a cerecloth. Dr. Buchan recommended cabbage leaves applied warm to the side as relief for pleurisy. Other domestic receipts employed cabbage or collards in poultices for sore throat and for rheumatism.[36]

Poppy cultivation was encouraged. The North Carolina *Moravian Records* contain reference to the fact that (since 1761) a premium was being offered for production of opium from the poppies using the "best method of making Turkish Opium." It is interesting that the bounty for opium and for persimmon gum were the same, 2s. 6d. per pound. Similarly, a bounty was offered in the mid-eighteenth century for raising hemp.[37]

Tobacco, raised for home use or trade, also found varied usage in medicine. John Wesley recommended for an ear ache to "blow the smoke of tobacco strongly into it." Thomas Anburey, traveling through the interior of America during the Revolutionary War, advised, "Fumigate the parts affected with tobacco, which penetrating the pores, destroys the insects [seed ticks or chiggers]." John Tennent's domestic medical guide suggested a tobacco cure for "Worm-Fever" in children: "Soak a cur'd Leaf of Tobacco in Vinegar, and apply it warm to the Stomach, or Belly." He further noted, "It will make the Worms much sicker than it doth the Patient."[38]

Tobacco entered into preventative measures practiced by travelers passing through the North Carolina Moravian settlements during the smallpox outbreak of 1779. "It was customary . . . to have a leaf of tobacco which they smelled as a preventive, some stuck tobacco leaves in their nostrils."[39]

Mallows of "all kinds" were found growing around the Moravian settlements in 1764, especially the kind which could "be used in spring as salad." Hollyhock was listed among garden plantings, and marshmallow (*Althaea officinalis*) was listed in the medical garden at Bethabara.[40]

Close examination of mallow fruits yields the origin of two bits of lore. The common name "cheeses" (especially applied to the common mallow, *Malva neglecta*) was derived from the wheel-like shape of the fruit that reflected a customary shape for cheese. Individual seeds of many members of the mallow family are distinctly kidney-shaped. According to the doctrine of signatures, the use of mallows to allay kidney complaints was clearly indicated.

This random sampling of useful herbs illustrates the backcountry housewife's reliance on field, forest, and garden. Exploring and exploiting the landscape for materials was basic to survival. Indian, European, and African all impacted the environment of which they were part, tipping the "balance of nature," influencing the Southern landscape.

And, of course, today our reliance on field, forest, and garden is as strong as ever! Our impact on the landscape and the impact of the landscape on each of us is continuous with every step and every breath we take. Impact can be positive or negative—judging which may be simply a matter of attitude, a matter of making a virtue of necessity.

The dandelion was introduced to this landscape by those early European settlers. Today we can curse the dandelions in our gardens and further impact the landscape with herbicides, or we can dig up the offending plants and brew a gourmet beverage from roasted dandelion roots.

Your grandmother may have been one of many Southern women who ordered a fashionable new ornamental vine to shade, scent, and beautify her front porch. What early twentieth-century gardener would not have been tempted by a lovely climbing legume bearing large clusters of exceptionally fragrant violet-purple blooms in late summer? Well, few of her descendants appreciate kudzu today, yet with all its faults, even kudzu has virtues. If life gives you kudzu, you can weave a sturdy basket or concoct a delectable jelly!

Kay Moss is program specialist in eighteenth-century backcountry lifeways studies for the Schiele Museum of Natural History in Gastonia, North Carolina.

NOTES

1. John Parkinson, *Paradisi in Sole: Paradisus Terrestris,* (1629; reprint, New York: Dover, 1976), 461.

2. John Gerard, *The Herbal or General History of Plants* (New York: Dover, 1975), 83. John Lawson, *A New Voyage to Carolina*, ed. Hugh Talmage Lefler (Chapel Hill: University of North Carolina Press, 1967), 81.

3. Lawson, 89, 166.

4. Lawson, 84. The Moravian surveyor, Reuter, noted, "Practically all plants which the Indians are known to use as medicine are called 'Snakeroot.'" Adelaide L. Fries, ed., *Records of the Moravians in North Carolina*, II (Raleigh: State Department of Archives and History, 1968), 571. Medicinal snakeroots included *Polygala senega, Prenanthes serpentaria, Asarum canadense, Cimicifuga racemosa, Aristolochia serpentaria, Sanicula marilandica,* or *S. canadensis.*

5. Philip Miller, *The Gardeners Dictionary* (London, 1759).

6. Peter Kalm, *Travels in North America: The English Version of 1770,* Adolph B. Benson, ed. (New York: Dover, 1964), 108, 109; Lawson, 100.

7. Kalm, 69; Lawson, 109; *Records,* II, 561.

8. *Records,* II, 562.

9. Miller, 7U2; Kalm, 180.

10. Kalm, 180; Lawson, 101.

11. Kalm, 78.

12. Lawson, 106.

13. Lawson, 107; *Records,* II, 564.

14. Miller, 10M1; Kalm, 104.

15. Miller 10M1; Anne Cameron manuscript and William Lenoir manuscript, both in the Southern History Collection, Library of the University of North Carolina at Chapel Hill.

16. Kalm, 42; Miller, 11L4.

17. Kalm, 70.

18. Nicholas Culpeper, *The English Physician Enlarged with Three Hundred and Sixty-Nine Medicines made of English Herbs* (London, 1770), 100; John Quincey, *Pharmacopoeia Officinalis & Extemporanea. Or, A Complete English Dispensatory, in Four Parts* (London, 1736), 98; Lenoir manuscript; Kalm, 70–71.

19. *Records,* II, 571.

20. Gerard, 1072–73; Moravian records, among other sources, document bloodletting as a common practice.

21. *Records,* II, 570; John Josselyn, *New-Englands Rarities Discovered,* 45.

22. "Commonplace book of cures," John Allen papers, North Carolina Division of Archives and History, Raleigh.

23. Culpeper, 277–82.

24. Karen Hess, ed., *Martha Washington's Booke of Cookery* (New York: Columbia University, 1981), 274, 378.

25. Mary Randolph, *The Virginia Housewife* (Columbia: University of South Carolina Press, 1984), 172.

26. Gerard, 590, 597

27. E. [Eliza] Smith, *The Compleat Housewife: or Accomplishíd Gentlewoman's Companion,* 7th ed. (London, 1742), 81.

28. John Wesley, *Primitive Remedies* from 1791 (Santa Barbara, Calif.: Woodbridge Press, 1975), 96. Originally titled *Primitive Physick.*

29. Hannah Glasse, *The Art of Cookery Made Plain and Easy,* 1796 ed. (Hamden, Conn.: Archon Books, 1971), 270; Wesley, 116; *The Journal and Letters of Francis Asbury,* ed. Elmer T. Clark, (Nashville, Tenn.: Abingdon Press, 1958), 1:147.

30. Wesley, 77; *Records,* II, 575.

31. *Records,* II, 573; Wesley, 113; William Buchan, *Domestic Medicine: or, a Treatise on the Prevention and Cure of Diseases by Regimen and Simple Medicines,* 3d ed. (London, 1774), 178, 389, 701.

32. Culpeper, 132–33; Gerard, 1033, 1034.

33. *Records,* II, 573; Kalm, 183.

34. Robert Squibb, *The Gardener's Calendar for South Carolina, Georgia and North-Carolina,* 1787 ed. (Athens: University of Georgia Press, 1980); *Records,* II, 575; Smith, 85; Glasse, 93.

35. Wesley, 128, 124.

36. Buchan, 179.

37. *Records,* II, 575, 585.

38. Wesley, 59; Thomas Anburey, *Travels Through the Interior Parts of America* (New York: The New York Times and Arno Press, 1969), 396; John Tennent, *Every Man His Own Doctor: or The Poor Planter's Physician,* 3d ed., (1736; reprint, Williamsburg: 1984), 37.

39. *Records,* III, 1283.

40. Flora Ann Bynum, *Old Salem Garden Guide* (Winston-Salem, N.C.: Old Salem, Inc., 1979), 59

The Plantation Mistress

Lady Jean Skipwith of Prestwould

Catherine Edmondston and Her Garden

Martha Turnbull of Rosedown

Ann Pamela Cunningham of Rosemont

Kenneth M. McFarland

Introduction

In *The Golden Age of American Gardens,* authors Mac Griswold and Eleanor Weller have referred to the years just before the Civil War as the South's "Gilded Age."[1] Wealth created by the slave labor production of cotton, tobacco, and rice, to name but the main crops, became evident in various material ways, including, apropos of the subject at hand, gardens. This element of the plantation landscape can in turn be linked to the mistress of the plantation. Most often she was the wife (though sometimes the mother or sister) of a plantation "master" who bore the chief responsibility for plantation operations. However, at times she herself was the owner-operator of the whole plantation enterprise.

The four papers that follow help us learn something about four of these women and their gardens. As we consider their gardening lives, there is one point to be especially stressed: it is as easy to stereotype the plantation mistress as it is the plantation house. Her world is frequently depicted as an endless whirl of cotillions, crinolines, and camellias. And unarguably these were women born to, or married into, far greater material well-being than the vast majority of people of their era, black or white. It is therefore all too easy to forget the pain and suffering, and at times just plain hard work, that was often their lot in life.

At the 1989 Restoring Southern Gardens and Landscapes conference, landscape architect and garden historian Suzanne Turner, addressing the topic of "pleasure gardening," discussed the antebellum gardening activities of Louisiana's Rachel O'Connor. For the widowed Mrs. O'Connor, the pleasure of gardening meant far more than superficial enjoyment. Instead, the garden provided a critical psychological antidote—a "point of equilibrium," as Turner put it—in the face of multiple adversities.

In considering the women being discussed in the following papers, as an antidote to stereotype it might thus be useful to remember also such plantation mistresses as Sarah Gayle of Alabama, wife of one-time governor John Gayle, who died at the age of thirty-one. Having suffered all of her adult life with advanced tooth decay, she succumbed to tetanus contracted during her final excruciating visit to the dentist.[2] Or we can recall Charlestonian Mary McDowell Chaplin, wife of diarist Thomas B. Chaplin (owner of Tombee Plantation on St. Helena Island, South Carolina), who died a painful death at twenty-nine after having borne seven children and whose habit of taking snuff "by the mouthful" (perhaps laced with cognac to ease her pain), exacerbated already strained relations with her husband.[3]

Or, on a less serious level, we can remember Anne Ruffin Cameron, wife of North Carolina's richest citizen in 1860, Paul C. Cameron. In addition to being a prime mover behind creating the landscape gardens at Burnside in Hillsborough, every December she was also in charge of rendering lard from the nine hundred to one thousand hogs slaughtered at Fairntosh Plantation—a task described as a greasy job, indeed.[4]

For all such women, gardening could surely offer that "point of equilibrium" discussed by Suzanne Turner. They realized a "pleasure of gardening" that transcended simple definitions of the "pleasure" garden, just as their lives transcended simplistic images of the "plantation mistress." In each of the following instances our authors, Colonial Williamsburg's Laura Viancour, Jo Ann Williford of Historic Stagville, Texas garden historian Greg Grant, and South Carolina historic landscape consultant Christy Snipes, demonstrate how the women they studied also sought and found their own self-defined "pleasure of gardening" that in some instances made the difficulties even of civil war somehow easier to bear.

Moreover, these women have left a mark still apparent at sites like Virginia's Prestwould, Louisiana's Rosedown, and even Mount Vernon, as well as through the survival of garden-related diaries and correspondence. It is impossible to truly comprehend the influence of women on the Southern landscape without examining the impact of plantation mistresses such as Lady Jean Skipwith, Catherine Edmondston, Martha Turnbull, and Ann Pamela Cunningham.

Kenneth M. McFarland, a member of the board of the Southern Garden History Society and associate editor of its bulletin, Magnolia, is the site manager of Historic Stagville Plantation outside Durham, North Carolina.

NOTES

1. Mac Griswold and Eleanor Weller, *The Golden Age of American Gardens: Proud Owners, Private Estates, 1890–1940* (New York: Abrams, 1991), 222.

2. Elizabeth Fox-Genovese, *Within the Plantation Household: Black and White Women of the Old South* (Chapel Hill: University of North Carolina Press, 1988), 1–28.

3. Theodore Rosengarten and Susan W. Walker, eds., *Tombee: Portrait of a Cotton Planter,* with *The Journal of Thomas B. Chaplin* (New York: William Morrow, 1986), 171.

4. Jean Bradley Anderson, *Piedmont Plantation: The Bennehan-Cameron Family and Lands in North Carolina* (Durham, N.C.: Historic Preservation Society of Durham, 1984), 72.

Laura Viancour

Lady Jean Skipwith
of Prestwould[1]

The following description of Lady Jean Skip-with's garden was written by her daughter, Selina, in a letter to St. George Tucker, 1805: "A spacious, fine garden, to the cultivation of which she is totally devoted—if you are fond of gardening of flowers & shrubs, as well as fine vegetables, you would delight to see her garden, she will soon have a fine grove of the orange-tribe—as she has many thousands trees that will probably begin to bear at 3 or 4 years— her citrons already almost break off the slender branches, and she has had the bananas ripen last year."[2] Little did Selina know just how many people would take delight in her mother's garden, including myself two hundred years later.

Although it was not unusual for colonial women to enjoy plants and spend time in the garden, it *was* unusual for women to keep voluminous documents on plants, using their Latin names and recording various cultural requirements, as Lady Jean did. Many of her gardening notes survive today, full of information that tells about her gardening interests and, in a subtle way, tell us something about the personality of the woman who diligently wrote them. Fortunately for me, many of her gardening notes and numerous surviving family documents are kept at the College of William and Mary in Williamsburg. Not long into my research, I realized that Lady Jean was unique rather than typical of Virginia plantation women in the late eighteenth and early nineteenth centuries.

Jean Miller moved from her native Virginia to Scotland in 1760, when only twelve years old.[3] During Jean's formative years, she was exposed to the cities of Edinburgh and London, both of which had an excitement and energy not to be found in rural Virginia. While in England, Jean obtained as great an education as was then possible for a woman.[4] The age of enlightment was in full swing, fostering new ideas and providing fertile ground for Jean's independent mind to grow and develop.

In 1786, Jean decided to return to Virginia.[5] Back in Mecklenberg County, Jean settled in at Elm Hill, a plantation owned by her deceased sister Ann's husband, Sir Peyton Skipwith. At that time, Jean was thirty-eight years old and had never been married. This was the exception rather than the rule in an age when a young lady's destiny was to get married at a young age and have children.[6] Once married, a woman typically gave up all her property and rights[7]; from my research, I believe that not giving up her rights at such a young age was Jean's deliberate choice.

However, in 1788, two years after her return to Virginia, Jean Miller chose to marry Sir Peyton Skipwith. I believe that Jean saw in Sir Peyton a man who respected her intelligence and capabilities. Sir Peyton most likely saw in Jean a highly-educated, self-sufficient woman. Unlike most marriages in the eighteenth century where men held the "upper hand,"[8] the Skipwiths' marriage was one of mutual affection and respect.[9] In his will, Sir Peyton wrote about Lady Jean and his "well founded confidence I have in her prudent and careful management of my affairs."[10] Lady Jean had clearly not surrendered her independence.

Prestwould, built in 1794–95, is situated on the top of a knoll that slopes down to a point where the Dan and Staunton rivers merge to form the Roanoke River (fig. 8). During Lady Jean's reign as mistress, Prestwould consisted of 10,000 acres, extending ten miles down the river. An enormous plantation with extensive crop land, there were as many as seven hundred slaves and indentured servants at Prestwould. Lady Jean moved from Elm Hill, twenty miles away, to Prestwould in 1797.[11]

As the mistress of Prestwould, Lady Jean assumed many responsibilities typical of Virginia plantation women and some that were not. Besides entertaining guests, supervising house servants, and managing the daily chores, she found the time to build an extensive library[12] and pursue her interest in gardening. Gardening was obviously a passion for her; besides the kitchen garden and orchard, Lady Jean improved the grounds leading to the river and created a native plant garden on one island in the river and an orchard on another.[13] In October of 1800, Sir Peyton's friend, Wade Hampton wrote in a letter to Aaron Burr:

This edifice and its appendages stand on a very commanding height, half a mile from the Roanoke, which is formed opposite the door by a junction of the Dan and the Staunton. The ground to the river, is sloping, wavy, & highly improved, to a great extent up, & down, which affords a fine view of those rivers, & of an Island between the two latter, of upwards of 1,000 acre in which that of cultivation. Upon the whole, except about New York, or up the North River, I have never seen anything so handsome. I know not why I have been so minute, except that having the view before my window I can with difficulty keep my eyes off it.[14]

The island has long since disappeared. Although the view to the river is obscured by mature trees and other vegetation, the original stone wall separating the garden from the slope toward the island remains standing. Still visible in the wall today are the post holes left from the fencing system installed above to keep the deer out. The garden gate is a modern reproduction based on the original one that was still standing and photographed there in 1880.

Little is known about the garden Lady Jean cultivated on the island except for the "Island Map List" she wrote that identifies sixteen plants including claytonia, cyclamen, dog's tooth violet, and Solomon's seal.[15] Compelled to collect and classify plants, Lady Jean wrote several plant lists. Most of the lists contain ornamental plants and were perhaps for the garden next to the house. It is interesting that several plants on Lady Jean's "Island Map List" are also mentioned in her list titled "Wildflowers for the Garden."[16] Other lists written by Lady Jean include "Shrubs to be got when I

8. Prestwould Plantation, in a photograph taken by Francis Benjamin Johnston (1864–1952) for the Carnegie Architectural Survey of the South in the 1930s. Library of Congress.

can," "Bulbous roots to get when in my power," and "List of flowers for M. Boyd."[17]

In Wade Hampton's 1800 letter, the formal garden Lady Jean had created to the east of the house is not mentioned. The Skipwiths did not lay it out until the next year, 1801, one year after Lady Jean's daughters left Prestwould to receive an education in New York.[18] Without the responsibility of educating her daughters, Lady Jean would have had more free time to pursue her passion. In 1801, Samuel Dedman, a surveyor, was paid twenty-two dollars to build a garden at Prestwould.[19]

Unlike earlier plantation gardens in the colonial Chesapeake that were positioned between the house and river,[20] the garden at

Prestwould is situated along the east side of the house. Perhaps this location is an early indication of the shift in emphasis from the river side of the house to the land side. Or perhaps, by being visible from both sides and close to the house, it tells how important a priority the garden was for the plantation owners. It is not surprising to learn that Lady Jean's daughters, Helen and Selina, were influenced by their mother's garden and placed their own gardens on the east side of their homes. Like their mother, they laid their gardens out in squares bisected by paths and containing a variety of native plants, fruit trees, roses, and other fragrant shrubs.[21]

The garden you see today at Prestwould is an interpretive restoration made possible in 1980 by the Garden Club of Virginia and designed by Rudy Favretti. Mr. Favretti's garden plan was based on a 1930s interpretive drawing[22] which was copied from Lady Jean's original drawing, c. 1800, in her journal that is still in the possession of the Skipwith family.[23]

Surviving physical evidence supported the design shown in the drawing. Mr. Favretti told me that when he began his work at Prestwould, he could see undulations distinguishing the garden beds from the paths. These were in scale with the copy of the drawing. Surviving plant material, a garden house, and remains of the conservatory also still existed on the site.

The copy of the drawing shows that Lady Jean's garden consisted of six squares or parterres symmetrically arranged along an eighteen-foot-wide central drive. Four of the parterres were used for growing vegetables and herbs. The two other parterres were subdivided into smaller beds to be planted with flowers, bulbs, and "simples," with a small area of lawn next to the grape arbors. All of the borders around the six parterres were planted with an ornamental plant edging of some sort.

The outside perimeter of the garden, next to the main house, contained a path sandwiched between a border of accent plants or ornamentals and the horseshoe beds. Mr. Favretti told me that before the garden was restored, he could see the outline of the horseshoes because they were more pronounced than the other garden beds when the grass was greening in the early spring. This indicated a high amount of organic material present in the soil, suggesting that the horseshoe beds had been maintained well into the nineteenth century.

Unfortunately, we do not know specifically what plants Lady Jean had planted in the horseshoe beds. We know from surviving family letters that Lady Jean was always searching for certain plants, and that she exchanged plants with others.[24] One theory is that perhaps the horseshoe beds were used to grow these new plants and that the grass path gave her access to the beds for close observations.

Mr. Favretti believes several existing plants are survivors from Lady Jean's original garden. Corresponding with the drawing are figs near the bee house and a pecan tree near the grape arbor closest to the summer house. The figs are thought to be offshoots from the original plants, and age estimates of the pecan tree suggest that Lady Jean may have planted it. Several other pecans that ornament the garden are thought to be second- or third-generation plantings from seeds. The copy of the drawing also has several small dark circles indicating accent plants. Today these areas have large boxwood growing in them. Based on their present size, it is safe to assume that the accent plants shown on the drawing had actually been planted with these boxwood. (The boxwood were cut back by seventeen feet in 1988, and still stretch more than twelve feet high today! This emphasizes just how old these plants must be.)

In a corner of the garden nearest the house, the foundation of the conservatory was uncovered during the restoration. Measuring 12 by 28 feet, it provided a place for Lady Jean to grow the bananas referred to in the quotation mentioned earlier in her daughter's letter. The conservatory also housed the containers of orange and lemon trees Lady Jean wrote of in her list of house plants.[25] Surviving garden notes show that as well as tender fruit trees, Lady Jean was interested in hardier fruits[26] that she could plant in the orchard.[27]

The only surviving garden structure is the garden house, complete with a root cellar. The Garden Club of Virginia reconstructed the rose arbor under Lady Jean's bedroom window and the curved arbors in the two outside parterres. At the opposite end of the walk leading from the rose arbor is the family cemetery. Both Lady Jean and Sir Peyton are buried there.

Lady Jean Skipwith broke traditional molds in many ways. She was better educated than most Virginia women as evidenced by her large collection of books and garden notes.[28] In addition, Lady Jean studied Latin, a language she would use the rest of her life to classify her plants.

When Sir Peyton died in 1805, Lady Jean became the executrix of his property. Although she had the option to sell the plantation, she chose to take on the responsibility of managing Prestwould. Once again, Lady Jean was an independent single woman. As the mistress in charge, she was a prudent business woman and increased the landholdings and value of Prestwould.[29] When she died at the age of seventy-eight in 1826, she left behind no debts of her own, something that was uncommon for most people of that period.[30]

Described by her daughter as "totally devoted" to her garden, Lady Jean exhibited this devotion by keeping detailed records. Her surviving garden notes have provided valuable information for garden historians and gardeners. In a subtle way, her garden notes have revealed a remarkable woman whose passion for plants would be an inspiration to hundreds of people today. I find this ironic for a woman who in her will referred to "the same private manner in which I lived."[31]

Laura Viancour is coordinator of garden programs and training at the Colonial Williamsburg Foundation, Williamsburg, Virginia.

NOTES

1. I would like to express my appreciation to Kent Brinkley, Colonial Williamsburg Foundation landscape architect, for his time and expertise. Grateful thanks to those who shared their wisdom: Gordon Chappell and Patricia Gibbs, Colonial Williamsburg Foundation; Rudy Favretti, FASLA; and Julian Hudson and his staff at Prestwould. Thanks also to Willie Graham, Colonial Williamsburg Foundation, for use of his slide library.

2. Lisa A. Flick, "Stretching the Bounds, Lady Jean Skipwith, Mistress of Prestwould, 1748–1826," M.A. thesis, Department of History, the College of William and Mary, Williamsburg, Va., 1987, 50.

3. Sterling P. Anderson, Jr., "Prestwould and Its Builders: Address Given at Prestwould, 28 September, 1963" (pamphlet), 1.

4. Mildred K. Abraham, "The Library of Lady Jean Skipwith: A Book Collection from the Age of Jefferson," *The Virginia Magazine of History and Biography*, 91 (1983), 296–99.

5. *Ibid.*, 299.

6. Flick, 22.

7. Suzanne Lebsock, *The Free Women of Petersburg* (New York: W.W. Norton & Co., 1984), 23.

8. *Ibid.*, 18.

9. *Ibid.*, xviii.

10. Will of Sir Peyton Skipwith, August 1805 (typescript), Skipwith Papers, Earl Gregg Swem Library, College of William and Mary, Williamsburg, Va.

11. Ronald L. Hurst, "History in Houses: Prestwould near Clarksville, Virginia: Prestwould Furnishings," *The Magazine ANTIQUES,* January 1995, 162.

12. Abraham, 296.

13. Peter Martin, *The Pleasure Gardens of Virginia* (Princeton, New Jersey: Princeton University Press, 1991) 129.

14. Wade Hampton to Aaron Burr, 25 October 1800, Skipwith Papers, Valentine Museum, Richmond, Va.

15. Skipwith Papers, Earl Gregg Swem Library.

16. *Ibid.*

17. *Ibid.*

18. Wade Hampton to Aaron Burr, 25 October 1800, Skipwith Papers, Valentine Museum.

19. Samuel Dedman to Sir Peyton Skipwith, 24 April 1801, Skipwith Papers, Earl Gregg Swem Library.

20. Edward Chappell and Willie Graham, "Historic Houses: Prestwould near Clarksville, Virginia, *The Magazine ANTIQUES,* January 1995, 160.

21. Elizabeth Langhorne, *A Virginia Family and Its Plantation Houses* (Charlottesville: University Press of Virginia, 1987), 97–98.

22. Edith Tunis Sale, *Historic Gardens of Virginia* (Richmond: James River Garden Club, 1930), 268.

23. Telephone conversation with Rudy Favretti, FASLA, December 21, 1995. Mr. Favretti's efforts to secure a copy of the original drawing from the family were unsuccesful because the family did not want it published.

24. Samuel Goode to Lady Jean Skipwith, 4 Oct. 1789; J(oh)n H. Cocke to Lady Jean Skipwith, July 1808, Skipwith Papers, Earl Gregg Swem Library.

25. Skipwith Papers, Earl Gregg Swem Library.

26. *Ibid.*

27. Flick, 48.

28. Abraham, 296.

29. Flick, 59.

30. *Ibid.*, 64.

31. Will of Lady Skipwith, 5 May 1824 (typescript), Skipwith Papers, Earl Gregg Swem Library.

Jo Ann Williford

Catherine Edmondston
and Her Garden

Here I live quietly amid my groves & gardens, wandering from tree to tree to see how the apples ripen, the peaches blush, peep at the Figs, bring in baskets of choice Dahlias, red [sic], write, make Lavender baskets & Fly-brushes. . . .

Diary of Catherine Edmonston, July 30, 1862

"My garden is beautiful—how I love it!"(p. 7)[1] These words by Catherine Ann Devereux Edmondston come from one of the earliest entries in the diary she began in June 1860. For the next five and a half years, years filled with tumult and upheaval, she recorded events of her life and her hopes and her fears. Much of what she wrote concerned the news of war that surrounded her; still, it is impossible to thumb through many pages of her journal without finding a reference to gardening, a pursuit that for her was pleasurable and, with the advent of the war, increasingly practical.

Catherine Ann Devereux was born October 10, 1823, the daughter of a wealthy North Carolina planter. In 1846 she married Patrick Muir Edmondston of Charleston, South Carolina, at her father's plantation on the Roanoke River. As part of a $10,000 marriage settlement from Catherine's father, the young couple received two plantations in Halifax County in northeastern North Carolina—Looking Glass and Hascosea.[2] Ten thousand dollars seems like an exorbitant amount to pay for a marriage settlement in 1846, but then we don't know what settlement her five married sisters received. If the same amount was paid for all of them, it may explain why the seventh daughter never got married—her father probably couldn't afford it. Catherine may allude to another explanation when she writes, "What a gift beauty is! Perhaps I prize it too much as it has been denied me" (p. 7). But if physical beauty was not her gift, she did have others—a quick wit, a sharp intellect, and, obviously, a talent for growing things.

At the two plantations Catherine and Patrick, who had no children, lived the life of a typical planter family of that time. They split their time between the two plantations; Looking Glass became their winter home, Hascosea their summer residence. The 1860 census lists the Edmondstons as owning an estate of 1,894 acres.[3] Patrick was responsible for running the farming operations, while Catherine oversaw the activities of the household, including the kitchen and flower gardens, although gardening was a pursuit both of them enjoyed and which they often did together. On those occasions early in the war when Patrick was away from home, Catherine wrote that gardening did not seem to hold the same pleasure for her when he was not there (pp. 56, 62).

Although Patrick was instrumental in forming the Scotland Neck Mounted Riflemen, one of the first cavalry troops to volunteer its services to the governor at the start of the war, he resigned before the troop was ever called into active duty. During the training phase when he was a member, he was sometimes away from home for several days at a time, but never for an extended period. Therefore Catherine never faced the prospect of running the plantation on her own, as many plantation mistresses of that era did. She was free to pursue her gardening in much the same way she had done before the war, with some changes.

In 1860 the Edmondstons are listed as owning 88 slaves;[4] Catherine's attitude toward them was that of the stereotypical plantation mistress, at times maternalistic and always superior. She saw to it that slaves were trained to carry out many of the duties of the plantation, for as she stated herself in the journal, "I am fully of the old opinion that there is no use in having a dog & barking for one's self" (p. 300). When it came to gardening, however, the slaves worked with her, they did not simply do her bidding. Following an illness in 1862, Catherine wrote in her journal, "Despairing of being strong enough in time I sent Owen out to Hascosea to plant my Dahlia & Tube Rose roots, the first time it has ever been entrusted to other hands than my own!" (p. 171). At another point she describes getting her hyacinths in the ground. "Set out with my own hand 608 (six hundred & eight) splendid blossoming bulbs" (p. 634), she writes, although she does note that Owen dug the holes. On other occasions she describes how she and Patrick worked together, such as the time they planted fruit trees, with her holding them and Patrick throwing the dirt (p. 40).

Catherine's journal is full of references to many types of plants—vegetables, fruits, flowers, and spices—whose care she diligently guided. She mentions some varieties of different plants, but those few hardly scratch the surface of her holdings. (A list of the plants mentioned in her diary is provided in the appendix.) She obviously loved flowers: on one occasion at her parents' house, she told them she had spotted the first rose of the season, whereupon her stepmother kindly cut it for her (p. 145); on another occasion, she described her hyacinths as "truly exquisite" (p. 136). But it is not difficult to deduce from the journal that her favorite flowers were dahlias. Much time was devoted to planting and packing up her dahlia roots. "I thank God daily for the enjoyment I find in them," she wrote in October 1862, describing her dahlias. "They are perfect. 'Bethel'—my seedling named in honour of the battle—I shall divide with Mrs. D. H. Hill when I take it up. Her husband is the hero of Bethel & no one has a better right to it" (p. 276).

This was only one of many instances where Catherine wrote of sharing with friends, neighbors, and family. She was generous with her bulbs and her seeds as well as her flowers. Apparently her talents as a gardener were well known, for she describes a party for her husband's company, The Scotland Neck Mounted Riflemen, and states, "Mrs. Smith & I dressed the Pyramid of Flowers which were really beautiful! My Dahlias made a most magnificent show & won universal admiration" (p. 13). When a young neighbor died unexpectedly, she made a chaplet of delicate white lilacs, dahlias, evergreens, feverfew, and citarena to be laid on the coffin (p. 253). On a happier note, she could describe how a little girl ran out from the house of one of her neighbors to ask for flowers for their May party, which Mrs. Edmondston promised to send (p. 391).

I was struck by the attention to detail she paid to the growing seasons. She apparently kept a separate notebook where she recorded facts about not only plants, but birds as well. On February 21, 1861 she noted that the peach trees had begun to bloom; she then went on to write in her journal that in 1851 they first bloomed on February 25, in 1852 on March 6, and in 1856 they had a most backward spring for nothing had bloomed by April 1 (p. 39). We also know from her journal when the swallows arrived and on what day the dogwoods bloomed in various years of the decade of the 1850s (pp. 46, 47).

Her scientific approach to gardening is evident in her attention to the details of such things as how deep to plant and when to prune (pp. 343, 518, 524). Another indication of this can be seen in her never-ending battles with what she refers to as "that vile insect the apple tree borer" (p. 224) and the "sore pest" (p. 337) the peach tree borer. No soldiers mentioned in her diary put more effort in conquering the enemy than did Mrs. Edmondston in her pursuit of the borers. In her quest to defeat them, she studied their habits and spent hours eradicating them. For example, she wrote, "I have been since breakfast on my knees at the shrine of Pomona & it is now twelve o'clock. That is, I have been examining our young Peach Trees & cutting the borer out, & a tiresome job it is. I have had all of them scalded with boiling water at the collar & then well rubbed with sulphur & Lard, a process which I hope will destroy the eggs & make the tree so distasteful to the fly that she will deposit no more there" (p. 238). She would report with some disgust six months later that her efforts had little effect. "One thing is certain, that Sulphur does not revolt him, for I found him plentiful in the tree from whence I thought I had expelled him last summer, under bark which smells even now, after all the fall rains, like Pluto's dominions, he seemingly careless of his surroundings" (p. 337). She was particularly disgusted after she broke both of her knives trying to dig them out, since knives were extremely difficult to replace (p. 453). But despite her setbacks, she never gave up, reporting, "The price of Peaches will be similar to that of Liberty . . . Ceaseless vigilance" (p. 337).

The war meant that certain things had to be done differently. She remarked in March 1862 that her only horticulture purchase that year was two magnolias, one for each of the plantations. "When did that ever happen before?" (p. 131), she asks. In June of that same year she comments on how her quinces are loaded with fruit, and she writes, "Both themselves & the Strawberries seem to look at me saucily and defiantly as tho' they would say, '*Preserve me if you dare!*' for they must know that I have not sugar to spare for such luxuries" (p. 186). By 1864 she would note that she had a good stock of seeds given the times but that it seemed meager to what she once considered necessary for a good garden (p. 522). Her most obvious undertaking brought on by the war was the growing and drying of her own tea leaves. In 1864 tea was selling for $50 per pound in Petersburg and $25 per pound in Charleston, causing her to remark, "How I wish we had plants enough to supply us; we would laugh at Yankee Blockaders" (pp. 583, 624). She did raise and dry enough to take care of her own needs, giving a description of her drying method in her journal (p. 583). The Edmondstons were generous with other commodities as well, for she reported on one occasion that she had strawberries enough to feast a regiment: "My delight has been to gather & send them there" (p. 62). The war also affected the farming operations. Because they could not get roping and bagging necessary to store and ship cotton, in 1862 their cultivated acreage dropped to 40 acres from 300 the previous year (p. 140).

The journal reveals much about Catherine's character. She is obviously a woman of learning and of strong religious beliefs, and her journal is filled with literary and biblical quotes and references, many of them quite dramatic. Of the Yankees she writes at one point, "The sword of Damocles is suspended over us & at any moment these marauding thieves may be turned loose upon us to ravage & spoil us!" But a few sentences more she says, "However, in face of it all I planted my Hyacinth roots. I cannot tell who will enjoy their fragrance & beauty, but I plant in hope & with a strong faith in God's mercy" (p. 268).

She also had strong opinions about people and events, which she expressed without hesitation. Her conviction that slaves were totally incapable of knowing what was best for them was unwavering (pp. 709, 712–13). This maternalistic attitude also extended toward poor neighbors. An ongoing attempt to help one such neighbor is a recurring theme in the journal. Catherine found the woman a place to stay and also attempted to assist her with self-improvement. She wrote of "the girl Catherine Jackson," as she referred to her, "I tried to set forth, to her, her shortcomings & deficiencies in a firm yet kind light, particularly her utter want of veracity, her idleness, & her horrid unwomanly practice of chewing tobacco & her fancy for straying about the country alone" (p. 580). It is interesting to contemplate how one points out such things in a kind light, is it not? At any rate, this is a good indication of her straightforward manner.

As stated above, her comments on and observations of the war were the main focus of her journal. Unlike the majority of North Carolinians, who resisted secession until the firing on Fort Sumter, Catherine and Patrick were from early on staunch secessionists. Catherine lamented in February 1861, "O that North Carolina would join with her Southern sisters—sisters in blood, in soil, in climate & in institution" (p. 37). She was extremely knowledgeable about the events of the war, although like all people in her situation, she often fell victim to rumors. Her opinions of the war were usually stated with directness and assurance of accuracy. And her opinions of those who ran it were crystal-clear. Although she did criticize her own leaders at times, for the most part she considered those who shared her views to be "gentlemen" (pp. 330, 427, 439). On the other hand, she refers to Lincoln as "the underbred boor" (p. 51), to Sherman as the "Prince of Bummers" (p. 710), to Grant as "a monster" (p. 38), and to Stephen A. Douglas as a " vulgar whiskey drinker" (p. 16).

But even her philosophizing on the war often included allusions to her garden. At times her musings took a humorous turn, as when she contemplated the life of a vegetable. She mentions that the vegetation has "grown as tho there was no war to depress us. Who would not be a vegetable? she asks. No care. Ah! yes but we would have periodical enemies of our own—snails, worms, Guerrilla like Sparrows, & worse than all, 'Cooks.' War is to us an occasion evil, but 'Cooks' are to them a perpetual foe" (p. 150).

A diary entry in 1861 showed that she, like many Southerners, held an optimistic but unrealized view that the war would end quickly. She recalled digging up her dahlia roots which, she wrote, "blossomed splendidly all the Fall & had been a source of great pleasure to me; but I had not been called to 'strew them in the

Conqueror's path' nor to 'deck the Halls where the bright wine flows' in honour of Peace as I had fondly thought when I planted them" (pp. 97–98). If she were writing this in 1861, we can imagine how distressed she was when the war dragged on for four more long years.

By the end of the war, many of her observations took on a melancholy tone and her garden at times seemed to represent a stark contrast to the horrors of the outside world. In May 1864 she wrote," I walk in my garden where one hundred & twelve varieties of Rose all in splendid bloom salute me at once & think how many of my noble young countrymen have closed their eyes forever on all scenes of earthly beauty & enjoyment" (p. 567).

The last journal entry is dated January 4, 1866. Patrick and Catherine continued to live on their plantations following the war. Patrick died in 1871, Catherine in 1875 (pp. 732, 734), both of them only in their early fifties. Despite the vast changes the war brought to plantation life, I assume that to the very end of her days Catherine was still able to say as she had earlier, "Here I live quietly amid my groves & gardens, wandering from tree to tree to see how the apples ripen, the peaches blush" (p. 225).

Jo Ann Williford is assistant to the director, North Carolina Division of Archives and History, and administrator of Historic Stagville near Durham, North Carolina.

Appendix: Plants mentioned in Catherine Edmondston's Journal

Vegetables	leeks	rice
asparagus	lettuce of several kinds	salsify
beets	lima beans	snaps
cabbages	mustard	spinach
carrots	okra	squash
celery	onion	sweet potatoes
corn	parsley	tomatoes
cress	parsnips	turnips
cucumbers	peas	Vic cabbage
eggplant	pepper	watermelons
Irish potatoes	radish	

Fruits
apple
blackberry
cantaloupe
fig
grapes
muskmelon
orange melon
peach
pear
plum
quince
strawberry

Spices
sage
thyme

Flowering Plants,
Shrubs, and Trees
citarena
crab apple
dahlias
dogwood
feverfew
forsythia
hyacinths
Judas tree
lilac
magnolia

nasturtium
redbud
roses
syringa
tea
tuberoses

Varieties of Roses
Alex Backmetoff
Alpha
Beauty of Green-
mount
Bouisault
Fellenburg
Giant of Battles
Isabella Gray
Rivers
Sir Joseph Paxton
Thad Trotter
Woodland Margaret

Varieties of Dahlias
Bethel
Cheltenham Queen
Glory
Malakoff

Varieties of Peaches
Peach Stone Emilia
George the 4th

Miss Timmons
Old Mixon
President
Ravenel's Favorite
Grape Mignon
Newington
Early York
Honey

Varieties of Apples
Red Astrachan
Summer Rose
Summer Pearmain
Domine
Roman Stem
Mattamuskeet
Woolman's Harvest

Varieties of Peas
Tom Thumb
Ault's Extra Early

Varieties of Grapes
Concord
The Old North State
Scuppernong

Variety of
Strawberries
Albany

NOTES

1. All quotations are from *"Journal of a Secesh Lady": The Diary of Catherine Ann Devereaux Edmondston*, ed. Beth Golbert Crabtree and James W. Patton (Raleigh: North Carolina Division of Archives and History, 1979).

2. *Ibid.*, xi–xii.

3. Ibid., *xii.*

4. Ibid.

Greg Grant

Martha Turnbull
of Rosedown

The brochure information begins with the title, "Grandeur on the Mississippi." The description that follows is filled with with such words as "mansion," "millionaires," "opulence," "dynasty," and "treasures." Was Martha Turnbull's Rosedown just another example of excessive wealth for today's visitors to dream about? Does it really reveal "a portrait of the past," as the front of the brochure claims?

Rosedown Plantation (fig. 9) is located not far from the Mississippi River in West Feliciana Parish near the town of St. Francisville, Louisiana. It was originally owned by cotton planter Daniel Turnbull and his wife Martha Barrow Turnbull. Construction on the house began in 1834 and was completed in 1835. Work on the landscape appears to have begun in 1836, the same year that several shipments of plants arrived from William Prince and Sons[1] and Martha recorded her first entry in her garden diary.[2] The property was owned and inhabited by descendants of the Turnbulls until 1955. In 1956, the late Mrs. Catherine Fondren Under-

9. Rosedown Plantation. G. Grant photograph.

wood, with restoration landscape architect Ralph Ellis Gun, began
a massive restoration of the decayed home and its extensive gardens.

The tour guide passes along the information that the Turnbulls
visited Versailles and other formal gardens in Europe, which inspired their own landscape at Rosedown. It is its gardens that
make Rosedown special. Upon first visiting the plantation, one is
awestruck by the overwhelming scenic value of its landscape.
Close investigation, however, reveals that the gardens are not as
Mr. and Mrs. Turnbull planned them. Since the entire plantation
had fallen into near-ruin when Mrs. Underwood and Mr. Gun restored it to what they thought appropriate, most of the landscape
at Rosedown is not original, but a carefully planned imitation.

In photographs taken as the house restoration began in 1961
and 1962, the decay of the landscape was obvious. Many plants ap-

parently had died, many others had spread, and there were many trees that were obviously not original to the site. The gardens were selectively salvaged and amended to create the new Rosedown Plantation. While the landscape, scattered with original structures and plant material—including its majestic live oak (*Quercus virginiana*) alley—is grand and visually appealing, it is neither authentic nor a truly accurate representation.

This is a shame, because there is ample historical documentation available that describes Rosedown's gardens, the most significant being the diary Martha Turnbull kept for nearly sixty years, from 1836 to 1895. It contains a wealth of information concerning her landscape and plants. It also tells of a real working couple, an amazing horticulturist, terrible hardships, vegetables and animals galore, and financial ruin.

The original diary (with a number of pages missing or damaged), along with a 1958 transcription by C. A. Haines, is housed in the Lower Mississippi Valley Collection of the Hill Memorial Library on the Louisiana State University campus. Other valuable documents in the same collection are transcriptions by Lewis H. Flint of a number of papers and documents relating to Rosedown from the period 1765 to 1861. They include several nursery invoices. A collection of photographs taken by Louis "Red" Martel of the 1961 and 1962 restoration in progress is also housed here. They are very valuable in pointing out the dramatic changes that took place in the "cleanup." Still yet, the now out-of-print *Reflections of Rosedown* (1976), a bicentennial publication by Ola Mae Word, is kept here. Several other books that may prove very useful in ultimately deciphering the gardens at Rosedown are the *American Flower Garden Directory,* written in 1851 by Robert Buist (whom Martha referred to frequently), which details a whole assortment of gardening instructions and information; *The Rose Manual,* written in 1844 by Robert Buist; and *Prince's Manual of Roses,* written in 1846 by William Robert Prince, who supplied many of Martha's plants.[3]

Rosedown Plantation produced money-making crops, mainly cotton and sugar cane. Daniel Turnbull worked hard to grow his crops and get good prices for them. Rosedown produced its own food as well. For almost sixty years, the bulk of Martha's diary entries detail the growing and harvest of specific vegetables for the table. The fragile remains of the diary make little or no reference to the Civil War or to the death of her husband, which left Martha to manage the work of the plantation alone. She continued on as a truck and tenant farm manager as well as a deeply motivated, perfectionist landscape gardener. Only the once-mentioned words, "terrible times," give hint of the feast-to-famine scenario that was played out over the decades.

On 1 September 1895, Martha Turnbull penned her last entry in her diary. "My pension came—I had not one dime to pay Emma $2—this month, August or any debt what ever." She died penniless the following September at the age of 87.

Unfortunately, a trip to Rosedown today only suggests incredible wealth, fancy furnishings, and a brief mention of the ornamental gardens. Where are the ubiquitous field crops, vegetables, orchards, poultry, pigs, and turkeys mentioned in Martha's diary?

Martha loved the fresh vegetables she grew. Those mentioned in her diary included celery, peas, lettuce, cabbage, Irish potatoes, eggplant, radishes, asparagus, parsnips, carrots, onions, spinach, beets, salsify, mustard, turnips, English peas, cucumbers, cantaloupe, garlic, leeks, tomatoes, corn, watermelons, peppers, squash, cauliflower, artichokes, broccoli, okra, beans, and ground artichoke.

Her diary is filled with references to her avid preoccupation with vegetable gardening, of which only a few are offered here.

1836   Dec 7. Commenced hilling our celery. On the 29th had it to eat. Planted peas on the 10th they stood all the severe weather. Ate lettuce on the 22nd. This has been a very severe winter but our celery very fine—and cabbage tolerable—September is too late to sow cabbage seeds.

1837   Feb 8. Spring lettuce eggplants and radishes came up—Forked my asparagus bed—Planted parsnips, carrots, beets and salsify seed. 20th Salsify all dead others good—Mustard and turnips going to seed—peas planted 23.

March 12. Celery beginning to taste rancid, had asparagus to eat on the 16th and beets also that were planted in October—Planted all of my spring seed on the 16th and set out cabbage plants—wet spring.

May 19. Planted cucumbers, cantaloupe, and salsify seed—It begins to be hot-planted salsify the 4th time today, because none has come up before.

July 5. We had a cantaloupe and watermelon today and planted out celery 2 rows—made a scaffold over it to protect it from hot sun. 7th Egg plant to eat—Planted broom corn again. 9th Planted some cabbage plants—very heavy rains—Cabbage fine. 20th sowed some parsnips—Carrots and salsify useless.

1855   Sept 2. I have no tomatoes, snap beans, arbor beans, and c. [i.e., "etc."] to eat.

1864   April 15. Pea vines full of peas—Cold year and no seed will come up—Tomatoes and eggplant all out, but look badly—Irish potatoes came up very badly—Onions all running to seed.

May. I put out 2 beds of cabbage plants sowed in February—Beets are fine—Beets, carrots, spinach crop all seeding—eating peas for 10 days past, they are splendid—Lettuce splendid—Mrs. Matthews lettuce splendid heads.

June 2. Up to now we have had not one drop of rain since March—the March cabbage plants scarcely lived—no pepper out yet—I have all my English pea seed saved—the garden parching—I sewed [sic] some cabbage today.

1869   March 4. I suppose I cultivate in vegetables 5 acres.
April 9. Very little to eat in garden.

1871   Nov 25. It is useless to plant melons after June.

It is very apparent from reviewing the surviving documents that large quantities of fruit were produced at Rosedown for fresh eating, canning, and selling. A sample of references to the specific fruits and orchard trees mentioned in the diary include:

1837   Jan. On the 10th burnt off strawberry bed.

1855   October. We have 12 bought pear trees, 2 large figs, 2 green gage plums, plenty quince, plenty wild plums. But few of my peach buds took.
Nov. My pineapple are looking fine in the hotbed.
Nov. 20. My orange trees are full of oranges.

1856   April 20. Strawberries are very abundant. Picked off ⅓ of the bed enough for 30 people and still the bed red.

1864   June 6. 26 Apples planted, 12 figs, 6 Mrs. Smith's plums, 10 peach, 12 Aunt Sarah quinces, and 12 old kind. The above are living from the number set out in January. I now want in same orchard for fall—Aunt Isabelle's quince, peach, Aunt Sarah quince, Mrs. Butler's plums, and Mr. Smith's plums and figs. I will make a plum nursery.

1869   March 4. Truck patch orchard contains 8 acres.

1871   Nov. 25. For grafting—4 lbs. rosin, 14 ozs. tallow, 18 ozs. bees wax.

According to Martha Turnbull's records, she grew a tremendous number of annual flowering plants, roses, ornamental container plants, and even turf grasses. Many references to assorted plant materials were made in the diary. Among them were:

1837   On the 23rd [month unknown] planted out Peonies and Dahlias.
    May 6. Planted Olea cuttings—Myrtle and Hypericum under bell glass—and forked down some Pittosporum and Purple Fringe Tree.

1841   Feb 20. Sowed all kinds of flower seed.
    Nov 1. Set out shrubs and planted a variety of cuttings.

1842   Nov 8. Set out Pinks, Sweet Williams and other flowers in beds.

1855   Nov. Had 55 Olea—10 Metrosideros—100 Japonicas—10 Bird of Paradise—6 Azaleas—20 Heliotrope—20 Geraniums.
    Dec 20. We have set out 40 Lombardy Poplars up to gate.

1856   March 1. I am sowing all my flower and vegetable seed, putting out Chrysanthemums that were started out in Dec.—Hyacinths in bloom.
    March 11. Salvia splendens, Geraniums, Heliotrope must be cut down in Dept.

1869   *March 4. I suppose I cultivate . . . Flower garden 5 acres.*

1894   *Sept 19. The Chrysanthemums budding—Roses quite pretty.*

1894   *Nov 4. Harry's scythe broken and he put out Mamie's Violets and mowed Hydrangeas behind milk house.*

Many roses were grown at Rosedown. It doesn't take a horticultural genius to figure out that Martha Turnbull's favorite plants were the rose and the camellia. Camellias are still featured at Rosedown today, but roses are sorely neglected. Martha's first and two of her last entries in her diary were:

1836   *Nov 6. Planted rose cuttings, shrubs, and c—very dry.*

1893   *October. As it sprinkled so little, watered all my roses well and my japonicas only 11 left from the 25—many cisterns are dry from the drouth. No roses in bloom.*

1893   *Oct 18. Made a place for Marechal Neil and Reve d'Or*

Several references are made in the diary to a rockery. According to the diary, it was made in September 1858. The rockery is still intact at Rosedown today; however it is covered over with ivy and other volunteer plants and is not mentioned in any literature or descriptions of the landscape.

Martha Turnbull was a remarkable amateur horticulturist. She avidly experimented with new plants and was current in her horticultural practices. She commonly practiced the difficult task of budding roses, camellias, peaches, and other fruits. And she probably documented her garden better that any other American individual in the antebellum period, maybe ever. Martha did not just live in her garden, the garden lived in her. It seems that planting, enjoying, and documenting her garden allowed her to control the one pleasure in her life that could soothe all other problems. And like other fine gardeners through the ages, her garden diary allowed her to repeat past successes and avoid previous mistakes.

Although some reference is made during the house tour to

Martha's green thumb, the significance of her horticultural contributions and endeavors are sorely neglected. Several gardening groups that are interested in historic landscapes would like to be informed about the true gardens of Rosedown and the amazing woman who nurtured them. However, first the information must be deciphered and then spread to the rest of the interested horticultural and landscape world.

Times weren't always "rosy" at Rosedown. There were droughts, storms, marauding hogs, deaths, wars, financial burdens, stealing, and general hard times. Catherine Underwood is to be commended for rescuing Rosedown from total ruin. But, like many other plantation reclamations, the new Rosedown includes only the glossed-over fairy-tale images that appeal to today's sensation-minded public. The public needs to know that life during this period was tough, not necessarily a "garden of Eden."

To me, Rosedown is a combination school of history, public botanical garden, and shrine. It has the unique qualities of inherent scenic beauty and a wealth of surviving information that could eventually put it in the same category as Mount Vernon, Monticello, and the Hermitage. The amazing story of Martha Turnbull and Rosedown Plantation is too good to be hidden. But until its owners, operators, and admirers learn and appreciate its true story, Rosedown will always remain a hidden gem.

Greg Grant, a horticulturist and garden writer, was director of education and product development for Lone Star Growers in San Antonio, Texas at the time of the conference. In 1996, he became horticulturist for the Texas Agricultural Extension Service in Cherokee County.

NOTES

1. Rosedown Plantation Papers 1765–1861 (transcriptions by Lewis H. Flint), A-27, #2199, Louisiana and Lower Mississippi Valley Collections, Louisiana State University Libraries, Baton Rouge.

2. Martha Turnbull, Rosedown Plantation Diary, 1836–1895 (1958 transcription by C. A. Haines), Misc., Shelf #8, Folder #2357, Louisiana and Lower Mississippi Valley Collections, Louisiana State University Libraries, Baton Rouge.

3. Robert Buist, *The American Flower Garden Directory* (New York: C. M. Saxton, Barker, and Co., 1851); Robert Buist, *The Rose Manual* (1844; reprint, Crugers, N.Y., Earl M. Coleman, 1978), William Robert Prince, *Prince's Manual of Roses* (1846; reprint, Crugers, N.Y.: Earl M. Coleman, 1979).

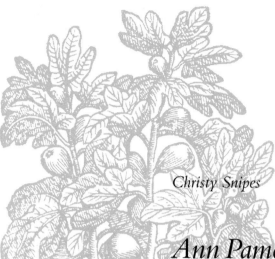

Christy Snipes

Ann Pamela Cunningham
of Rosemont

Rosemont Plantation (fig. 10), located in present-day Laurens County, is probably one of the
best-known of the upcountry South Carolina
plantations because of its association with the remarkable Ann Pamela Cunningham (1816–1875).
This visionary South Carolina lady founded the
Mount Vernon Ladies' Association of the Union,
which spearheaded the effort in the 1850s to purchase George Washington's home in Virginia and
to preserve it for generations to come. For her
efforts, Miss Cunningham has been called the
"First Lady of American historic preservation."[1]
Because Mount Vernon played such a great role in
this plantation mistress's life, it is discussed here
along with Miss Cunningham's home, Rosemont.
And there are actually two plantation mistresses to
examine: Ann Pamela and her mother, Mrs.
Robert Cunningham (1794–1873).

Ann Pamela Cunningham (fig. 11) was born in
1816 to Robert and Louisa Bird Cunningham of
Rosemont. Her mother was descended from a distinguished family, the Daltons of Alexandria, Virginia—frequent visitors to Mount Vernon during

10. Rosemont manor house, from an early twentieth-century photograph.

George Washington's lifetime. She also claimed the patriot Bird family of Pennsylvania in her ancestry.

The other side of Ann Pamela's family, her father's, presented a different picture but a no less heroic one. Ann Pamela's grandfather, Patrick Cunningham, came from Augusta County, Virginia, to the South Carolina upcountry in 1769. As a deputy surveyor general of the district, he prospered at his home on the Saluda River. During the Revolution, Patrick Cunningham supported the Loyalist cause but, because he was so well respected in the area, he enjoyed success even after the war.

Ann Pamela spent a cultured childhood at Rosemont Plantation and at fashionable boarding schools. A family painting, c. 1823, portrayed the mother Louisa at about 29 years of age with her children Ann Pamela at seven, John at five, and Ben Yancey at three. When Ann Pamela was about 17, she suffered an injury to her spine in a riding accident. This condition became chronic over time, and the infirmity kept her close to her parents and at Rosemont through her young adult years.

Rosemont was an active and lively plantation during this time, and the Cunningham family enjoyed great wealth. Census reports indicate the size and complexity of the working plantation. In 1860 it consisted of 3,700 acres of land, with the value of the "farm" set at $74,000. The personal holdings of the Cunningham family amounted to $120,000. A large number of livestock and the varied products of Rosemont were also listed, including wheat, corn, oats, wool, cotton, peas and beans, and butter.[2] There were 138 African-American slaves living and working on Rosemont.[3]

The family had the resources to enable Mrs. Cunningham to pursue her interest in landscape gardening. She was constantly "improving" the grounds with flowers and shrubbery. Letters to family members and acquaintances documented the fortunes of the crops at Rosemont, but they also noted the fruits and vegetables grown, their products (tomato catsup, fig preserves, and peach marmalade) the cooks made, the ornamentals that were blooming, and the changes accomplished in the design of her garden.[4] From these primary accounts, from our preliminary archaeological investigation sponsored by the Laurens County Historical Society, and from the remains of Rosemont's vegetation today, a conjectural layout of the grounds around the manor house was formulated. Also mentioned in correspondence are Mrs. Cunningham's gardeners, Sam and Austin; however, Sam is the only African-American cited specifically as a gardener in an inventory of the 1850s. Certainly Mrs. Cunningham, as lady of the plantation, was intimately involved with the workings of the "servants" in the house, the yard area (including the kitchen), and the gardens.[5]

Mrs. Cunningham's gardening expertise did not go unnoticed. She counted as friends some of the most noted horticulturists in the state: Joel Poinsett of Casa Bianca near Georgetown, and Mrs. William Seabrook, Jr., of Oak Island, Edisto Island. Both Mr. Poinsett and Mrs. Seabrook possessed renowned gardens in the low country. Louisa also generously shared plants and growing instructions with friends and relatives. She ordered plants from one of the premier nurseries in the South at that time: William Summer's Pomaria Nurseries of Pomaria, South Carolina, which carried the latest exotic imports and practical fruit-bearing plants.

Descriptions of the beauty of the gardens of Rosemont abounded over these years. Ann Pamela, the semi-invalid, often wrote in letters of "Rosemonte's gay outward attraction" to induce friends to visit her.[6]

By the 1850s Ann Pamela's condition had worsened. Her par-

11. Portrait of Ann Pamela Cunningham, the first Regent of the Mount Vernon Ladies' Association of the Union (1890, John Stolle, from a photograph). Private collection.

ents tried every possible means of treatment, including visits to a physician in Philadelphia. After leaving her daughter for treatment in the North in 1853, Louisa wrote to Ann Pamela of the pitiful, run-down condition of Mount Vernon.

This was the spark that lit the flame of Miss Cunningham's determination. Far from healthy at thirty-seven years of age, Ann Pamela proved strong in her determination to save Mount Vernon. The owner, John Augustine Washington, Jr., did not want to sell to a group of ladies, and he asked an exorbitant price for the property: $200,000. Miss Cunningham began her mission with the help of her mother and father in Laurens County. In future years, she would credit her mother with the original idea to save Washington's estate. Ann Pamela wrote countless letters across the nation soliciting funds for the cause. Amazingly, she reached her goal in a few short years, giving the Mount Vernon Ladies' Association of the Union control of the estate, a position it still holds to this day.

But the bounty of the early years soon ended. Ann Pamela became Regent of the Mount Vernon Ladies' Association in 1858; however, her father, Captain Robert Cunningham, died in 1859.

She ventured home to settle his estate and found herself stranded at Rosemont during the Civil War. Ann Pamela and her mother struggled to keep the plantation operating during the difficult war years and the great changes that occurred during Reconstruction. Their letters documenting the hardships at Rosemont during this time were sad and pitiful. Ann Pamela coped with an infirmed mother, an ineffective and debt-ridden brother, a plantation with workers to feed, and the vast social and economic changes of the period.

After six years away from Mount Vernon, Miss Cunningham returned to her position as Regent in 1866. After moving there in 1868, she tried to juggle the affairs of both Mount Vernon and Rosemont, shuttling between the two. Rosemont perhaps suffered more from Ann Pamela's absence, and Mrs. Cunningham now greatly resented her daughter's commitment to the Washington estate.

Rosemont's garden is mentioned infrequently during these difficult years, but there is a hint in correspondence that Louisa still worked in and treasured it. The landscape certainly lacked the maintenance it had received in the past. In a letter from 1871, Ann Pamela spoke of the garden:

If I live a thousand years I can never forget what I have endured this winter . . . trying to save my mother's remnant of property from being seized. . . . Our garden is alive with flowers! Poor mother! she is as much absorbed with interest in vines and flowers as if it could be her home while life lasts. I am afraid of the effect at her age when she realizes that it is given up forever![7]

It was a tragic period for Miss Cunningham. The responsibilities of two estates, coupled with illness and an increased dependence on the drug laudanum, began to take their toll. In 1872 the Council of Vice-Regents strongly encouraged Miss Cunningham to give up her residence at Mount Vernon, but it was not until 1873 that she resigned. Louisa Cunningham died that year at Rosemont. Elswyth Thane wrote poignantly in her history, *Mount Vernon Is Ours,* "She [Miss Cunningham] returned to an empty, run-down house, on a poverty-stricken plantation, deserted by all the best of its once loyal servants. But, it was her home, the only one she had, and her life in the North had failed her, and she did not know where else to go."[8] Ann Pamela Cunningham died at

Rosemont in May 1875. She was buried as she had requested at First Presbyterian Church in Columbia.

Under Miss Cunningham's leadership, the restoration of the mansion and grounds at Mount Vernon had progressed. She had left the Association solvent with a balance exceeding $1,000. The greenhouse was making a profit from the production and sale of plants and bouquets, and the grapery (which had been her idea) was holding its own. Certainly, Ann Pamela had used her love of the garden and plants at Rosemont to advantage at Mount Vernon. A visit to the property today reveals the importance of this South Carolina lady's first efforts for Mount Vernon. The house, estate grounds, and gardens are meticulously restored to their state in Washington's time.

Before her death, Miss Cunningham made arrangements with her brother to save Rosemont Plantation for the family. The land remained in the family well into the twentieth century. The manor house burned in 1930, but parts of the land were farmed by Cunningham descendants and tenant farmers—some descendants of the African-American slaves from Rosemont—until it was sold in the 1940s. Today, the property shows remnants of its cultivation by Mrs. Cunningham, for old magnolias tower in the forest, huge boxwoods and crapemyrtles reside in lines and patterns in the woods, and a Japanese cryptomeria hangs on for dear life. Rosemont still has much to offer to the fledgling study of up-country South Carolina plantation life, including the aspect of landscape gardening. Rosemont Plantation is a valuable archaeological resource; it remains a noteworthy existing historic landscape; and it survives as a lasting tribute to the visionary Ann Pamela Cunningham.[9]

Christy Snipes heads the consulting firm, Historic Landscape and Garden Design, in Columbia, South Carolina.

NOTES

1. Charles B. Hosmer, Jr., *Presence of the Past: A History of the Preservation Movement in the United States before Williamsburg* (New York: G. P. Putnam's Sons, 1965), 47–51.

2. Eighth Census of the United States: 1860, State of South Carolina, Laurens District, 237, South Carolina Department of Archives and History (SCDAH), Columbia, S. C.

3. Slave Schedule, Eighth Census of the United States: 1860, State of South Carolina, Laurens District, 183–84, SCDAH.

4. Letters in various collections: Benjamin Yancey Papers, Southern Historical Collection, the Library of the University of North Carolina at Chapel Hill; and Benjamin F. Perry Papers, Alabama Department of Archives and History (ADAH, Montgomery, Ala.

5. Ann Pamela Cunningham, Journal, June 1, 1836, to July 12, 1836, and January 1, 1837, Cunningham family records, private collection.

6. Ann Pamela Cunningham, letter to Mrs. Benjamin Perry, February 20, 1847, Perry Papers, ADAH.

7. Ann Pamela Cunningham, letter to Mrs. Nathaniel Halsted, March 20, 1871, Mount Vernon Archives, Mount Vernon, Virginia.

8. Elswyth Thane, *Mount Vernon Is Ours: The Story of the Preservation and Restoration of Washington's Home* (New York: Duell, Sloan, and Pearce, 1966), 441.

9. Christy Snipes, *Rosemont Plantation, Laurens County, South Carolina: A History of the Cunningham Family and Its Life on the Land* (Laurens, S.C.: Laurens County Historical Society, 1992), 243.

Susan E. Schnare

Women Garden Writers

"Gardening, Reading about Gardening,
and Writing about Gardening are all One"

There was a saying, probably Victorian, that a re-
spectable woman had her name in print three
times—at her birth, at her marriage, and at her
death. Perhaps because of this attitude, although certain individuals stand out, the contributions of wom-
en to the gardening world are less noticeable, and
therefore seen to have been less important, than
those of men.

In *The Story of Gardening*, Martin Hoyle speculates
that women are invisible in garden history partly because of their exclusion from gardening pursuits and
partly because what they did was not recorded.[1] As
an example, *The Oxford Companion to Gardens* assumes that the earliest role of women in gardens was
as weeders, because there are few garden records relating to women besides those of payments to
women weeders.[2]

The lack of records makes the work of women
writers even more significant. Unwritten events may
be forgotten, but the work of even the least popular
writer will still be found on some library shelf to
shed light on the lives of women and their concerns.[3]

Gardening requires a small amount of land, fertilizer, seeds, and a few basic implements. To write about gardening implies expert knowledge gained from experience, enough education to write with skill, and time. Most women garden writers have been wealthy, intelligent, and educated, with ample time in which to garden, observe, and write. They usually wrote for women, perhaps because they felt men would not listen to them. Often they directed their work toward women of all classes, but many of their recommendations excluded all but their wealthier readers.

Gardening was consistently seen as good for women because it was healthy and made them more useful to their families. The first chapter, entitled "The Florist," of *The Young Ladies Book: A Manual of Elegant Recreations, Exercises, and Pursuits,* published in Boston in 1830, defined the level of gardening expected of women:

It is not recommended to a young lady to dig up the earth, study the modes of manuring it, or prepare compost; it will suffice for every purpose of health and pleasure, that she can sow the seeds in their fit season; transplant the seedlings . . . , trim them and train them give them sun or shade; water or keep them dry, as their different habits may require. A garden offers many light and graceful occupations to a young lady.[4]

During Victorian times, particularly, the garden provided a sense of freedom from social, economic, and political restrictions.[5]

The earliest gardening books for women were instructive works by men. Thomas Tusser's *Five Hundredth Points of Good Husbandry* in 1573, to which he added *As Many of Good Housewiferie, First Devised and Now Lately Augmented with Divers Approved Lessons Concerning Hopps and Gardening &c* to the second edition in 1610.[6] In verse, gothic script, and archaic English, it now proves difficult reading. A few years later, Thomas Lawson wrote his well-known *Countrie Housewifes' Garden* (1617).

Painting was considered an eminently suitable pastime for women, and flowers were popular subjects.[7] From flower painting, determined women sometimes made the step to serious botanical illustration, which required knowledge of botany and access to specimens. Several eighteenth- and many nineteenth-century women made this transition successfully.[8]

The first important botanical work by a woman was published to get her husband out of debtor's prison. The five hundred illus-

12. Engraving from *A Curious Herbal* by Elizabeth Blackwell, published in 1737 and 1739.

trations that Elizabeth Blackwell drew, engraved, and painted for *A Curious Herbal, Containing Five Hundred Cuts, of the Most Useful Plants, Which Are Now Used in the Practice of Physick* were accompanied by descriptions copied from Philip Miller's *Gardener's Dictionary* and published in two volumes in 1737 and 1739 (fig. 12).[9] From jail, her husband Alexander (1709–1747) contributed the plant names in other languages. Elizabeth Blackwell's work was supported and praised by the most distinguished botanists of her day, including Sir Hans Sloan and James Sherard.

The Blackwells were second cousins who married secretly while he was in university in Aberdeen, Scotland. Alexander, a distinguished classics scholar, and Elizabeth, the daughter of an Aberdeen stocking merchant, moved to London, where Alexander worked for a printer and in 1730 opened his own shop. This was not a time of free enterprise, and Alexander stumbled into a hornet's nest. He was soon charged and convicted with practicing a trade without going through an apprenticeship. He got into debt and was sent to prison for nearly two years.[10]

Little is known about Elizabeth's education, but her massive undertaking demanded intelligence, artistic ability and training, and a thorough knowledge of engraving. Was this learned in her husband's print shop, or did Alexander go into printing because of her skill?

Elizabeth's successful venture apparently resulted in her husband's employment as Director of Improvements for the Duke of Chandos, who was laying out the grounds for his new mansion, Cannons. However, Alexander must have committed some blunder in his new career, since it was said that the "occasion of it kept him from other employment."[11] The next year, he anonymously published a pamphlet, entitled *A New Method of Improving Cold, Wet, and Barren Lands* (1741), and in 1742, went to Sweden as an agricultural expert. He had some success in agriculture, but became involved in a conspiracy concerning the Swedish line of succession, was arrested, convicted and executed in 1747.[12]

A Curious Herbal was translated into German and continued to sell well into the nineteenth century. Apparently it supported Elizabeth, who had remained in England, until she died in 1759.[13]

By the late eighteenth and early nineteenth centuries, botany had become an accepted part of a lady's education, and gardening, botanizing, and plant collecting were considered admirable pursuits. This was in part attributable to relaxed social customs and in part because of the popularity of the Romantic picturesque.

A fictional Spaniard in the novelist Southey's *Letters from England* (1807) described how the search for the picturesque, outdoor activities, and the collection of natural-science specimens had become popular pastimes:

A course of summer travelling is now looked upon as essential. . . . While one of the flocks of fashion migrates to the sea-coast, another flies off to the mountains of Wales, to the lakes . . . or to Scotland; some to mineralize, some to botanize, some to take views of the country,—all to study the picturesque.[14]

Evidence for this appreciation exists in the garden Thomas

Johnes had built in 1794 for Mariamne, his eleven-year-old daughter, and her collections of plants at Hafod, Wales, that merged her botanical studies with his appreciation of the picturesque.[15] Also in the late eighteenth century, Caroline Powys commented in her diary on Lady Jersey's hobby: "As her Ladyship is, according to the present taste, a botanist she has a pretty flower-garden going out of the library."[16]

The popularity of natural-science studies in England in the late eighteenth and early nineteenth centuries had its counterpart in the American South. The Charleston Botanic Society and Garden were founded in 1805, and about that time a Mr. Whitlow gave a series of lectures on botany that "upwards of fifty young ladies" attended "for the purpose of acquiring a regular knowledge of this delightful science, many of whom were making the most flattering progress."[17]

Despite increased education and freedom for women, writing was not considered "womanly." Women writers often published at least the first edition of their work anonymously, possibly to spare their families humiliation, or to test their audience. The usual pseudonym was "A Lady." Perhaps this was a reply to Jean Jacques Rousseau's popular *Letters on the Elements of Botany Addressed to a Lady.*

In 1799, Lady Charlotte Murray (1754–1808) published *The British Garden: A Descriptive Catalogue of Hardy Plants Indigenous or Cultivated in the Climate of Great Britain*. It contained 767 pages of plant names and information in two volumes. The first edition was published under the pseudonym "A Lady," but "the Rt. Hon. Lady Charlotte Murray" appeared on the title page of the second printing, also in 1799, and the third in 1808.[18] *The British Garden* was popular during the early nineteenth century, and referred to by one critic as a "useful, convenient, and well compiled repertory; forming an instructive companion to young botanists, and to the numerous dilettante, while on a visit to botanic gardens."[19]

Dr. James Smith reported in *English Botany* (1797) that Charlotte Murray had found a double cranesbill geranium, a variety of *Geranium pratense*, near Attol in 1793,[20] which suggests she did her own field work. Charlotte, who never married, moved to Bath, perhaps for her health, and died there in 1808 at the age of fifty-four.

Charlotte's brother, "Planter John," the fourth duke of Athol, was famous for his forestry projects at their family home at Athol, Scotland, but there is little information on Charlotte's life. In the archives of her family home, a castle of some size and antiquity, there was some initial confusion over which Charlotte Murray she was.[21]

Like Charlotte Murray, Maria Jacson published most of her work as "A Lady." She first wrote three botanical text books for children, but is best known for *The Florist's Manual; or, Hints for the Construction of a Gay Flower Garden* (1816). While the first edition bore only her initials, the second included her name and home in Shropshire on the last page.

Maria and her sister were well educated, especially after they had spent several years reading to their blind father, a vicar. At his death, they turned to writing as a source of income. Her sister wrote five novels, and Maria wrote on botany and gardening.[22]

Maria Jacson's *Florist's Manual* was perhaps the first book on gardening by a woman to become widely known and used. John Claudius Loudon gave it some good publicity by quoting from it extensively in *The Floricultural Cabinet and Florist Magazine* (1837).[23]

A 1917 review of the Biographical Index of British and Irish Botanists in the Journal of Botany complained that anyone who had written a book, "however trivial and even useless," was included. As an example the reviewer pointed to Henrietta Maria Moriarty's *Viridium*, first published by the author in 1805, and in 1807 reprinted as *Fifty Plates of Greenhouse Plants*. Her work was intended to have two purposes: to teach young ladies the art of flower drawing, and provide to instructors with a textbook free of smut:

Those who have the instruction . . . and even the fashioning of young minds most at heart, often find it difficult to obtain representations . . . sufficiently accurate, and . . . entirely free from those ingenious speculations and allusions, which, however suited to the physiologist, are dangerous to the young and ignorant . . . I have taken as little notice as possible to the system of the immortal Linneus, and . . . nay I have not once named the fanciful Doctor Darwin.[24]

The *Journal of Botany* review speculated, from the list of contributors, that Mrs. Moriarty had been a governess in families of position; noted that she copied her paintings with only slight alterations from *Curtis's Botanical Magazine;* and pointed out that her spelling showed that she was unfamiliar with the plants she had painted.[25] The paintings themselves are clumsy and the colors are muddy.

In contrast, Elizabeth Kent's *Flora Domestica: or the Portable Flower Garden with Directions for the Treatment of Plants in Pots and Illustrations from the Works of the Poets,* was published in 1823 and reprinted in 1831. In it she described nearly two hundred plants, mixing mythology, poetry, anecdotes, and folklore with botanical and cultural information.[26]

Elizabeth Kent gave lessons in botany and wrote learned articles, including the scholarly "Linnean System of Plants," published in *Magazine of Natural History* (1829). According to a glowing review of *Flora Domestica* in Loudon's *Gardener's Magazine* (1830), she was a competent horticulturalist, and in the heart of London kept a "thriving garden of pots on top of the house; not of sickly geraniums, but of pretty little natives."[27]

Jane Webb Loudon (1807–1858) is said to have led the way for women to play an increasingly important role in the garden.[28] She wrote some twenty books, including *The Young Lady's Book of Botany* (1838), *The Ladies' Country Companion* (1845), and *The Ladies' Florist Garden of Ornamental Annuals* (1840). She founded *The Ladies Magazine of Gardening* in 1842, which she edited for many years, and, after her husband John Claudius Loudon's death in 1843, edited his considerable body of work.

Gardening for Ladies (1840) and *Ladies' Companion to the Flower Garden* (1842) were bound together, edited by Andrew Jackson Downing, and published in America in 1843 (fig. 13). Downing hoped Mrs. Loudon's book would encourage American women to garden:

Mrs. Loudon's works are intended especially for the benefit of Lady gardeners,—a class of amateurs, which in England, numbers many and zealous devotees, even among the highest ranks. It is to be hoped, that the dissemination in this country of works like the present volume, may increase among our own fair country women, the taste for these delightful occupations in the open air, which are so conducive to their own health, and to the beauty and interest of our homes.[29]

Despite her impressive publication record, Jane is known primarily as the formidable wife of John Claudius Loudon. She raised their daughter, ran a household, cared for some 4,500 pot-

13. Title page of Jane Loudon's *Gardening for Ladies,* first published in Britain in 1840 and in the United States in 1843.

ted plants, maintained their quarter-acre garden, and took dictation from her husband many nights until 2 A.M.[30]

Compared to Mrs. Loudon's works, Louisa Johnson's two books were not radical but perhaps slightly subversive. *Every Lady Her Own Flower Gardener* (1840), a tiny book of three by four inches, which went through many editions, was, according to its author, written in response to a real need by women:

"We require," they say, "a work small in compass, which will enable us to become our own gardener: we wish to know how to set about everything 'ourselves,' without expense, without being deluged with Latin words and technical terms, and without being obliged to pick our way through multiplied publications, redolent of descriptions, and not always particularly

lucid. . . . We require to know the hardiest flowers, and to comprehend the general business of the garden, undisturbed by fear of failure, and at the same time at the most economical scale of expense."[31]

While she stressed economy, Mrs. Johnson did see the lady gardener as requiring "the services of an old man, a woman, or a stout boy."[32]

In her introduction, she explained the importance of gardening for women:

Nothing humanizes and adorns the female mind more surely than a taste for ornamental gardening. It compels the reason to act, and the judgement to observe; it is favorable to meditations of the most serious kind; it exercises the fancy in harmless and elegant occupation, and braces the system by its healthful tendency. A flower garden to the young and single of my sex, acts upon the heart and affections as a nursery acts upon the matronly feelings. It attaches them to their home; it throws a powerful charm over the spot dedicated to such deeply-interesting employment; and it lures them from dwelling too deeply upon the unavoidable disappointments and trials of life, which sooner or later disturb and disquiet the heart. . . . Floriculture ranges itself under the head of female accomplishments in these our days; and we turn with pity from the spirit which will not find in her 'garden of roses' the simplest and purest of pleasures.[33]

In *Every Lady's Guide to Her Own Greenhouse* (1851), Mrs. Johnson recognized that a semblance of the power lacking in women's lives could be gained from a greenhouse:

Those who attend to plants themselves know the pleasure of being the mistress of their own greenhouse . . . you do as you please, your will is not disputed; there is nobody to question your judgement nor condemn your acts. . . . I do not insist on a lady doing all the drudgery of a greenhouse; she may have a man-servant or a maid-servant to assist her—but they will be servants. A professional gardener would be a lady's master: she must not cut this nor give away that, or remove the other. As to watering, pruning, or taking a flower, it is high treason against the monarch of the garden, and is perhaps punished with a threat of abdication. I declare I know ladies who submit to black looks, impertinent remarks, rude sneers, and other uncouth behavior in a manner that I would not submit to even from my husband—that is, if I could help it.[34]

There were many earlier botanical and horticultural books written for children, but Julia Horata Ewing's *Mary's Meadow* (1883) is unusually enjoyable. It tells the fictional story of two brothers and a sister who study the classical garden literature, mainly John Parkinson's, adopt a meadow, and create a wild garden there, despite threats from the mean old owner. In the end the owner, who was under the impression the children were vandalizing the meadow, realizes the depth of Mary's love for the place and gives it to her, thereby rewarding her goodness and the love of nature with land ownership—a rare state for a woman, let alone a pre-adolescent girl.

Women writers often looked inward and examined their own lives and gardens, since that was what they knew best. Toward the end of the nineteenth century, a style emerged that came to characterize the garden literature of the early twentieth century. The weaving of garden information with personal details of the author's home life occurred in most of the garden literature from the 1880s to the end of World War II. Although a number of men, including Alfred Austin, Dean Hole, and Beverly Nichols, used this personal approach, women wrote in this style extensively, and for a time nearly exclusively.

Eleanor Vere Boyle and "Elizabeth" were two of the earliest to write in this style. In fact, Mrs. Boyle (1825–1916) may have created this style in 1884 with her popular *Days and Hours in A Garden*, which blended folklore, poetry, plant histories, and archaeology with events in her life and garden. It began in October 1882 with "Nuns and White Owls; Yews, Thrushes and Nutcrackers," and continued in diary form through September of the following year. *Days and Hours*, illustrated with her line drawings, was reprinted at least seven times. *A Garden of Pleasure,* also in diary form, covered 1894 complete with weather reports. Mrs. Boyle's personable style of sharing her gardening life may have been noted and approved by Elizabeth.[35]

Elizabeth, as she became known after the publication of her first book *Elizabeth and her German Garden*, was Countess Mary Annette von Arnim (1866–1941), the young alienated English wife of a German nobleman.[36] Her first book, which also began with nuns and owls, concerned her life in rural Pomerania and how she found in gardening an antidote to the dullness and the stuffiness of pre-World War I German culture. *Elizabeth and her German*

Garden first appeared in 1898 and was an instant bestseller, going through eleven reprints in the first year. It was followed the next year by a sequel, *Solitary Summer*, in which the young wife, fed up with the constant stream of German visitors, begs her husband (the Man of Wrath) for one summer with no house guests. She declares to her husband,

I want to be alone for the whole summer, and get to the very dregs of life. I want to be as idle as I can, so that my soul may have time to grow. Nobody shall be invited to stay with me, and if any one calls they shall be told I am out, or away, or sick. I shall spend the months in the garden, and on the plain, and in the forests. . . . I shall be perpetually happy, because there will be no one to worry me. Out there on the plain there is silence, and where there is silence I have discovered there is peace. "Mind you do not get your feet damp," said the Man of Wrath, removing his cigar.[37]

Elizabeth's two garden books, which bordered on fiction, told of her gardening mistakes, deep love of nature, and general distrust of anything German. The rest of her twenty-two books were fiction, although always semi-autobiographical, and often involved gardens. One of the most popular, *Enchanted April*, was recently made into a movie.

After the death of her first husband, Elizabeth moved to Switzerland and then, for the duration of World War I, to England, where she mistakenly married Francis, Earl Russell, brother of Bertram Russell. He was an abusive husband, whom she soon left and on whom she took revenge in her book *Vera*. World War II forced her to flee from her villa in the south of France to the United States, where she died in Summerville, South Carolina, in 1941.[38]

Dawn MacLeod excluded Elizabeth and Marian Cran from her study of gardening women, *Down to Earth Women* (1982), because of grave doubts that either of them did much actual gardening.[39] Marian Cran chronicled her education as a gardener in an entertaining, personal style: *The Garden of Ignorance* (1913), was followed by *The Gardens of Good Hope* and then *The Garden of Experience* (1921).

The Story of My Ruin (1924) told of the rescue of Cran's fourteenth-century house, Coggers, in rural Kent. While the description of her garden may have been mainly dreams and plans of how it might have been,[40] her love of Coggers was real. Late in her life Marian Cran lost her house to the bank and was evicted, but broke back in and lived there illegally for some years until she could make payments.[41] As well as publishing several books, Marian Cran wrote a regular gardening column, and during World War II was the first woman to broadcast a radio garden show.

Gertrude Jekyll (1843–1932) may well be the most influential garden writer, male or female, ever. Her writing style was more authoritarian than chummy, but her standards were high and her taste was superb. Munstead Wood, her home and garden in Surrey, figured prominently in her writings, which ranged from the very personal *Home and Garden* (1900) and *Children and Gardens* (1908) to the more instructional *Wood and Garden* (1899) and *Colour in the Flower Garden* (1908).

Gertrude Jekyll's books and ideas on gardening soon became extremely popular in North America, and American travelers plagued her with pilgrimages to Munstead Wood and requests to meet her. As she wrote in a letter to a friend, "You can have no idea what I have suffered from Americans, Germans, and journalists."[42]

Early in the twentieth century, many American authors adapted her gardening and writing styles to their own gardens and distinctive personalities, but paid homage to Miss Jekyll as the source of their inspiration. Three of the most popular of these were Helena Rutherford Ely, Louise Beebe Wilder, and Mrs. Francis King.

Helena Rutherford Ely was one of the first American women garden writers to write in this style. *A Woman's Hardy Garden* was published in January 1903 and reprinted eleven times in the next five years. In the introduction she humbly explained,

Many friends have asked me to tell them when to plant or transplant, when to sow this or that seed, and how to prepare beds and borders; in fact, this has occurred so often that it has long been in my mind to write down what I know of hardy gardening, that other women might be helped to avoid the experiments and mistakes, which only serve to cause delay.[43]

Ely warned against trends, particularly the contemporary one for Italian gardens, saying, "what is beautiful in one place becomes incongruous and ridiculous in another."[44] She preferred "the simple formal gardens of a hundred years ago, with Box-edged paths, borders and regular Box-edged beds, [that] are always beautiful, never become tiresome, and have the additional merit of being appropriate either to the fine country-place or the simple cottage."[45]

She recognized the garden as a sanctuary for women and suggested the old-fashioned sunbonnet as a way to maintain it:

Retired behind its friendly shelter, you are somewhat deaf to the world; and at the distant house, people may shout to you and bells may be rung at you, and if your occupations be engrossing, the excuse "no one can hear through a sun-bonnet," must be accepted."[46]

Ely wrote several other books, including *The Practical Flower Garden* (1911), which were based on her experiences in her New York garden.

Louise Beebe Wilder (1879–1939), who also wrote and gardened in New York, produced over a hundred articles for *House and Garden* and ten books.[47] *My Garden* (1916) was much like Helena Ely's *Woman's Hardy Garden* in its lists of flowers and cultural recommendations, but Mrs. Wilder's later books referred to gardens from Maine to Florida, and quoted from works as diverse as *Mary's Meadow* and John Gerard's 1597 *Herbal*.

A true disciple, Mrs. Wilder mentioned Gertrude Jekyll fifteen times in *Fragrant Path* (1932) alone. She told of a visit to Munstead Wood where she saw large bushes of "Rosemary trained against the walls where the sun draws out its sharp sweetness to greet you as you pass."[48]

Mrs. Francis King, or Louisa Yeomans King (1863–1948), was a prolific and skilled writer. From her first book, *The Well-Considered Garden* (1915), she dealt with many of the same subjects in much the same way as Miss Jekyll, whom she referred to as "my own adored preceptress."[49] Mrs. King wrote, "If we take up such a book as Miss Jekyll's *Garden Ornament* and turn to the marvelous illustrations under the heading 'Steps and Balustrades' we need not make any serious mistakes."[50]

Mrs. King, who lived and gardened in Michigan, was a national officer in the Garden Club of America for many years.[51] Among her many honors was the George Robert White medal awarded to her by the Massachusetts Horticultural Society in 1921 "in recognition of her service to horticulture by increasing the love of plants and gardens among the women of the United States."[52]

In *A Woman's Hardy Garden*, Helena Rutherford Ely admitted

that, while the most attractive books on gardening were English, "beyond the suggestions given for planting, and the designs given in the illustrations," the cultural directions could not be used in northeastern United States.[53] The same could probably be said by Southern gardeners about Northern garden books. Southern gardeners were probably more strongly influenced by English garden literature than by that from the North.

Elizabeth Lawrence often quoted the English authors, particularly Mrs. Loudon. In "The Loudons," an article that appeared in the *Charlotte Observer*, Miss Lawrence wrote: "Since Bayswater, a suburb of London, has winters very like ours, Mrs. Loudon's books have a particular interest for gardeners in these parts."[54]

Elizabeth Lawrence surely needs no introduction here, as North Carolina was her home for most of her life. She was the first woman to receive a degree in landscape architecture from the North Carolina State University School of Design, and was awarded the Herbert Medal of the American Horticultural Society. Her gardens, first in Raleigh and later in Charlotte, provided the setting and subjects for her books, including *A Southern Garden* (1942), *The Little Bulbs* (1956), and *Gardens In Winter* (1961).

None of this explains the depth of knowledge exhibited in her writings on such a wide range of subjects, or the perception and charm that glows through her books and articles. Miss Lawrence counted among her many friends and correspondents personalities like Eudora Welty, Carl Krippendorf, and Vita Sackville-West.[55] She admired Gertrude Jekyll's work and edited selections of Miss Jekyll's writings into a book, *On Gardening* (1964). In the introduction, Miss Lawrence reflected on Elizabeth, the Countess von Arnim's, visit to Munstead Wood: "I can think of no two gardeners less likely to be charmed with one another than Elizabeth and Miss Jekyll. I should like to know what each one of them wrote in her journal that night."[56]

The experience and skill of the hundreds of competent and often fascinating women writers of two hundred and fifty years perhaps culminated in the work of Elizabeth Lawrence. Well aware of the legacy of garden writing, she wrote, "Gardens are so perishable; they live on only in books and letters; but what has gone on before is not lost; the future is the past entered by another door." She concluded, "Gardening, reading about gardening, and writing about gardening are all one; no one can garden alone."[57]

Susan E. Schnare, Ph. D., is a landscape historian and consultant on landscape preservation and garden design. She lives in Andover, New Hampshire.

NOTES

1. Hoyles, Martin, *The Story of Gardening* (London and Concord, MA: Journeyman Press, 1991), 187–88.

2. *Oxford Companion to Gardens*, ed. Sir Geoffrey Jellicoe, Susan Jellicoe, Patrick Goode, and Michael Lancaster (Oxford and New York: Oxford University Press, 1986).

3. As an example, no information is available on the life of Dora Maw, author of "The Romance of a Garden," a history of the Montpellier Botanical Garden, France, (London: Royal Horticultural Society, 1940). Professor William Sterne, Librarian at the Lindley Library during World War II, remembers her as the daughter of George Maw, the famous plant hunter and crocus breeder, but Dora does not appear on the family tree.

4. Anonymous, *The Young Ladies Book: A Manual of Elegant Recreations, Exercises and Pursuits* (Boston: A. Bowen, 1830), 36–37. This was rewritten for American girls from an earlier English edition.

5. Dianne Harris, "Cultivating Power: the Language of Feminism in Women's Garden Literature, 1870–1920," *Landscape Journal* 13:2 (Fall 1994):113.

6. Thomas Tusser, *Five Hundredth Points of Good Husbandry, and as Many of Good Housewiferie, First Devised and Now Lately Augmented with Divers Approved Lessons Concerning Hopps and Gardening,* 2d. ed. (London, 1610).

7. See Henrey, Blanche, "Botanical Drawing Books," *British Botanical and Horticultural Literature before 1800,* vol. 1 (London: British Museum, 1975), 585–87.

8. The Dutch botanical artist and naturalist Maria Sibylla Merian (1647–1717) of Amsterdam was known and respected by the botanists of her day, according to Henrey (p. 426). Ray Desmond lists many women botanical artists who exhibited flower paintings in *The Bibliography of British and Irish Botanists and Horticulturalists* (London: Taylor and Francis, 1977). Two women who published their work were Margaret Meen, *Exotic Plants from the Gardens at Kew* (1790) and Mary Lawrence, *Collection of Roses* (1799).

9. Miller was Director of the Chelsea Physic Garden from 1722 to 1770. Mrs. Blackwell lived across the street from the Chelsea Physic Garden from 1734 to 1739, while working on *A Curious Herbal,* to have access to the specimens she needed.

10. Henrey, "Botanical Drawing Books," 128–36.

11. Henrey, "Botanical Drawing Books," 236, quoting *Gentlemen's Magazine* 17 (1747), 425.

12. *Ibid.*

13. *Ibid.*

14. H. Sprague Allen, *Tides in English Taste*, vol. 2 (New York: Rowman and Little-field, 1969), 211, quoting Robert Southey, *Letters From England* (1807).

15. For an account of Hafod and the Johnes family, see Elizabeth Inglis-Jones, *Peacocks in Paradise* (London: Golden Grove, 1988).

16. Caroline Powys, *Passages from the Diaries of Mrs. Philip Lybbe Powys of Hardwick House, Oxon, A.D. 1756 to 1808*, ed. Emily J. Climenson (New York, London, and Bombay: Longmans, Green, and Co., 1899), 197–98.

17. Loutrel Briggs, *Charleston Gardens* (Columbia: University of South Carolina Press, 1951), 16.

18. Rt. Hon. Lady Charlotte Murray, *The British Garden: A Descriptive Catalogue of Hardy Plants Indigenous, or Cultivated in the Climate of Great-Britain*, 2 vols., 2d. ed. (Bath: S. Hazard, 1799).

19. Henrey, "Botanical Drawing Books," 584, quoting *The Monthly Review* 31 (1800):202.

20. J. Sowerby and James Smith, *English Botany*, vol. 6 (1797), 404.

21. Letter to the author from Christopher Dingwall, Ardler, Perthshire, 25 October 1991. Mr. Dingwall and Mrs. Jane Anderson, archivist at Attol, provided this information, for which I am most appreciative.

22. Joan Percy, "Maria Jacson," *Garden History* 20, 1 (Spring 1992):45–56.

23. Review of *The Flower Garden* in *The Floricultural Cabinet and Florist Magazine* 5 (1 July 1837):176–77.

24. Henrietta Maria Moriarty, *Fifty Plates of Greenhouse Plants,* 2d.ed. (London, 1803), vi. The Darwin referred to here is Dr. Erasamus, author of *Plan for the Conduct of Female Education, in Boarding Schools* (1797).

25. *Journal of Botany* (1917):52–54.

26. [Elizabeth Kent], *Flora Domestica: or the Portable Flower Garden with Directions for the Treatment of Plants in Pots and Illustrations from the Works of the Poets* (London, 1823).

27. *Gardener's Magazine* (1830):487.

28. Hayden, Peter, *Biddulph Grange, Staffordshire: A Victorian Garden Rediscovered* (London: George Philip and the National Trust, 1989), 19.

29. Andrew Jackson Downing in the introduction to *Gardening for Ladies and Ladies' Companion to the Flower Garden* by Jane Loudon (New York: Wiley and Put-nam, 1843).

30. For an account of Jane Loudon's life see Bea Howe, *Lady with Green Fingers: the Life of Jane Loudon* (London: Country Life Ltd., 1961).

31. Louisa Johnson, *Every Lady her own Flower Gardener*, 5th ed. (London, 1843), foreword.

32. *Ibid.*

33. *Ibid., 4–5.*

34. [Louisa Johnson], *Every Ladies' Guide to her own Greenhouse* (London, 1851), 7.

35. Elizabeth is known to have read Alfred Austin's *The Garden that I Love* (1894)

just prior to writing *Elizabeth and Her German Garden*. Leslie de Charms, *Elizabeth of the German Garden* (New York: Doubleday & Co. Inc., 1959).

36. For more information on Elizabeth, see Karen Usborne, *'Elizabeth': The Author of Elizabeth and Her German Garden* (London: Bodley Head, 1986).

37. Elizabeth [Mary Annette von Arnim], *Solitary Summer* (New York: Macmillan, 1899), 3–4.

38. Obituary, *The New York Times,* 10 February 1941.

39. Dawn MacLeod, *Down to Earth Women* (Edinburgh: Wm. Blackwood, 1982), 174.

40. *Ibid.*

41. Personal communication from Coggers' current owner.

42. Gertrude Jekyll, *On Gardening*, with an introduction by Elizabeth Lawrence (New York: 1964), 17.

43. Helena Rutherford Ely, *A Woman's Hardy Garden* (New York: Grosset & Dunlap, 1903), 5–6.

44. *Ibid.,* 22.

45. *Ibid.,* 23.

46. *Ibid.,* 199.

47. Obituary, *Florists Exchange and Horticultural Trade World*, 30 April 1938.

48. Louise Beebe Wilder, *The Fragrant Path* (New York: Macmillan, 1932), 169.

49. Mrs. Francis King, *Chronicles of the Garden* (New York: Charles Scribner's Sons, 1925), 39.

50. *Ibid.,* 98–99.

51. Obituary, *Bulletin of the Garden Club of America*, March 1948.

52. A. P. Saunders in the introduction to *From a New Garden* by Mrs. Francis King (New York: Alfred A. Knopf, 1930).

53. Ely, *Hardy Garden*, 19–20.

54. Elizabeth Lawrence, *Through the Garden Gate*, edited and with an introduction by Bill Neal (Chapel Hill: University of North Carolina Press, 1990), 4–5. See also "Scattering Seed," 160–61.

55. Elizabeth Lawrence, *Gardening For Love: The Market Bulletins*, edited and with an introduction by Allen Lacy (Durham: Duke University Press, 1987). Her friends are frequently mentioned in *Gardening for Love* and *Through the Garden Gate.*

56. Elizabeth Lawrence in the introduction to *The Gardener's Essential Gertrude Jekyll* (1991); reprinted from *On Gardening* (1964).

57. Elizabeth Lawrence, *Through the Garden Gate*, ix.

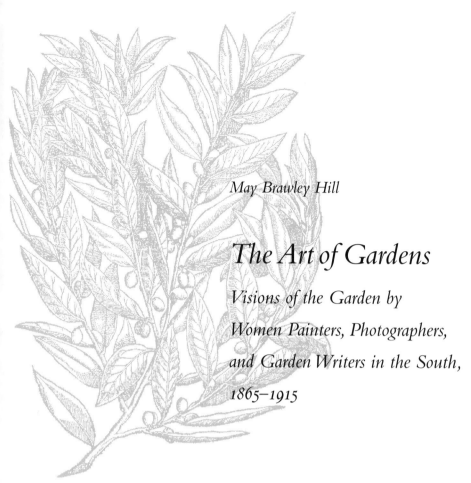

May Brawley Hill

The Art of Gardens

Visions of the Garden by
Women Painters, Photographers,
and Garden Writers in the South,
1865–1915

Pleasure gardens have been painted and written about as long as there have been gardeners making them. When the gardener is also an artist or writer, the results are usually noteworthy and often influential far beyond their locale and time. American painter Anna Lea Merritt, who married an English artist in the 1880s and went to live in Hampshire, wrote *An Artist's Garden,* illustrated with her own paintings of her flowers, in 1908. Like the women I will consider, Mrs. Merritt felt that a garden "should be considered as a living picture and designed as carefully as a painting." She continued, "There must be composition both as to form and color. The value of flat spaces, empty places must be observed. . . . Masses of shadows are required as a foil for the colors painted by the gayest flowers."[1]

The idea of the garden as a living picture is a fairly recent one. In the seventeenth century, the pleasure garden was conceived architecturally, with broad avenues, geometric parterres, and water features—structure rather than plants—having priority. In the mid-eighteenth century, Humphrey Repton and his English contemporaries began to visualize the garden as landscape painting. The ordered Arcadian world painted by Nicholas Poussin or Claude Lorrain was translated into spacious parkland, punctuated by groups of trees allowing vistas of placid lakes and classical temples. By the nineteenth century, the English landscape garden had been domesticated into the "gardenesque," with curving paths, artfully placed trees, and ornamental flower beds. At mid-century these flower beds resembled geometric Berlin-work embroidery, rendered in brilliantly colored annuals.

Since the 1860s, the flower garden was a favored motif with painters in Europe and America, many of them also avid gardeners. These artists tended to avoid geometric beds of annuals for more free-form arrangements that reflected new movements in painting. French impressionist Claude Monet's garden is perhaps the best-known artist's garden today. From its inception in the 1880s it has had a marked influence on gardens far from Giverny, both through Monet's own paintings and in those of other artists. The first American painters arrived in Giverny in 1887, among them John Leslie Breck, who sent back to Boston several views of the garden. By the 1890s, Monet's garden was not only an attraction to the scores of American Impressionist painters who studied in France but also a tourist destination.

In this country, the garden that poet and painter Celia Thaxter created on the Isle of Shoals off the coast of Maine in the 1870s played an equally influential role. Appledore House, the hotel on the island run by her family, attracted educated and cultivated vacationers who gathered in her parlor for informal concerts and picture viewing. Her garden's generosity of planting and painterly sense of color, texture, and mass was, for Mrs. Thaxter's aesthetically sophisticated friends, a welcome contrast to the garish carpet beds and ribbon borders that were so popular. The color effects she achieved charmed impressionist Childe Hassam and inspired some of his loveliest paintings. Some of these were used as illustrations in Thaxter's widely read book, *An Island Garden* (1894), a poetic evocation of one season among her flowers.

Celia Thaxter's old-fashioned garden of hardy perennials with its symmetrical rectangular bordered beds and its use of old-fashioned flowers and native plants, looked back to imagined colonial prototypes. Old-fashioned perennial gardens, snubbed for a generation, had begun to appear in books and magazines around the time of the 1876 Centennial celebrations. This old-style garden was embraced by those who saw in the values, virtues, and gardens of colonial times a refuge from the social and economic upheavals of industrialization, labor unrest and massive immigration. It also appealed to artists, as much taken with the aesthetic possibilities of an exuberant and informally planted garden that could be maintained by one person as by its links to America's past.

Perhaps the most endearing book about making such a garden was novelist Anna Bartlett Warner's *Gardening by Myself* (1872), which recorded her experiences making a flower garden with neither money nor gardeners. Miss Warner's book was but one in a succession of American gardening books for ladies but the first to advocate a woman doing all the work herself. By the 1870s, however, the radical idea that women were not by nature weak or delicate and ought to enjoy the physical health and abundant exercise expected of men began to gain acceptance. The home and garden were culturally sanctioned places for a woman to begin a physically active life.

For Anna Warner, old-fashioned flowers were rich in associations and as she put it, offered both "the scent of present fragrance and the perfume of olden times." Their "rich, soft, mingled bloom and tender tints" reflected as well the taste for muted colors and informal arrangements that were beginning to appear in interiors as well as gardens in the wake of the Aesthetic movement.[2] This change in taste, combined with a fascination with all things colonial generated by the centennial celebrations, created a new appreciation for native forms in both decoration and gardens.

Mariana Griswold Van Rensselaer, best known as an art critic, also wrote *Art Out-of-Doors: Hints on Good Taste in Gardening* (1893). Here she argued that gardening shared principles of composition, color, light, and shadow with landscape painting. The harmonious association of the plants was important, but she gave equal weight to the garden's accord with its site and the natural landscape. Mrs. Van Rensselaer's insistence on national character— as she put it, "We want American gardens, American landscapes,

American parks and pleasure grounds, not the features of those of a dozen different countries huddled together"—led her to champion native plants. Not surprisingly, she advised those with limited space to give up a lawn and "arrange in front of the house an old-fashioned garden with as many beds and walks and box hedges as the space will allow."[3]

Journalist Helen Ash Hays, who contributed "Garden Letters" to the *New York Evening Post,* wrote in *A Little Maryland Garden* (1909) of her own old-fashioned garden years after it was begun. Here she relied on American natives to contribute bloom from March to November; she used as her guide Bernard McMahon's *American Gardener's Calendar,* first published in 1806. As she put it, "I had never heard of William Robinson. . . . It was, therefore, instinct that led me to keep my flowers back in borders rather than cut up the lawn with circles and ovals. And it was necessity that guided me in the choice of hardy plants to fill the borders."[4]

Designer Candace Wheeler was a notable influence on American decorative arts in the 1880s and 1890s through her New York firm Associated Artists, which employed women designers exclusively. After her husband's death in 1907, she moved from her family's Long Island home and began spending winters at a new home in Thomasville, Georgia. Here at the age of eighty she began a garden relying on dogwoods and other natives, as well as spring bulbs that lined a path to a friend's house next door.

Mrs. Wheeler had begun her first garden in 1854 in Roslyn, New York. Her second garden and the subject of her book *Content in a Garden* (1901) was made in Onteora, in the Catskill Mountains, where the Wheelers had a summer home. Mrs. Wheeler's half-acre garden there, bounded by a rough stone wall wide enough to plant on, was filled with native American plants and proven old-fashioned flowers. She sought to suggest the lavishness of nature's plantings on a small scale through color modulations, gradual intensification of color by a number of tints leading up to a mass of one hue. When Mrs. Wheeler moved to Georgia she found that this garden was already well known through her book. As she wrote in her autobiography, "the influence of the Onteora garden followed me for one and another of my new southern neighbors alluded to it as an old acquaintance."[5]

The old-fashioned garden was given a tremendous boost

through the writings of popular historian Alice Morse Earle. Her article on "Old Time Flower Gardens" appeared in 1896 and was reprinted as the last chapter of her best-selling *Home Life in Colonial Days* (1898). Her comprehensive *Old-Time Gardens* (1901) was illustrated with nearly sixty surviving early gardens and an equal number of old-fashioned flowers that were, as she put it, "true representatives of old families.[6]

Among the Southern gardens included were Tudor Place in Georgetown, D.C.; Greenwood in Thomasville, Georgia; and the Hampton-Preston garden in Columbia, South Carolina, all featuring box borders. Boxwood for Mrs. Earle and many others at the time implied not only a garden's antiquity but that of the gardener's family as well. As an 1908 article on old-fashioned gardens put it, "Box implies . . . human life on a certain scale, leisurely, decorous, well-considered. It implies faith in an established order and an assured future."[7]

For young women coming to maturity in the South after the devastation of the Civil War, there was neither an established order nor an assured future, but there was plenty of century-old box. Unlike Long Island, where early gardens were being ransacked of enormous boxwoods for new country estates,[8] Southern gardens were left in peace and decay at least until the full-blown colonial revival of the 1920s.

Some Southern gardens dating to early in the century were inherited by young women who lovingly kept them up, as did artist Myra Thompson of Spring Hill near Nashville. Miss Thompson had studied at the National Academy of Design in New York and at the Pennsylvania Academy; she had a studio in Nashville, where she taught a large drawing class. After her father's death in the 1890s, she spent her later years at Spring Hill engaged in the upkeep of the well-known garden begun by her great-grandfather. Here roses, iris, lilies, and other old-fashioned flowers shared box-bordered beds with flowering shrubs.[9]

Kate Helms, a Kentucky artist and writer, lived at Helm Place in Fayette County, where the old garden on one side of the house had grass walks bordering beds of old-fashioned perennials and shrubs. Such gardens could be very informal. Another Kentucky garden of the time, made by the writer's great-aunt, was once described as "just an old-fashioned garden in which lilacs and lettuce lived amicably side by side and the cabbage and cosmos were near neighbors."[10]

America's historic preservation movement, begun in mid-century with the Mount Vernon Ladies' Association, had been given a boost by the centennial celebrations. The enthusiastic amateurs—many of them women—who restored, documented and maintained their own early houses and gardens, were in the forefront of the movement. The Association for the Preservation of Virginia Antiquities, for example, was founded in 1889 by Cynthia Coleman and Mary Jeffery Galt, the niece of sculptor Alexander Galt and herself a trained artist. Among the first of the buildings saved from destruction was the home of Mary Ball Washington in Fredericksburg, its garden notable for the double row of ancient box flanking the walk. The same year the Ladies' Hermitage Association was organized, and restoration of Andrew and Rachel Jackson's garden begun.

The nascent historic preservation movement in Charleston, South Carolina, was given a boost by the work of resident painter Alice Ravenel Huger Smith. Like so many other young women in the South after the war, she faced the necessity of earning her own living and never married. She had studied drawing at the Carolina Art Association but was essentially self-taught as a watercolorist. The growing attraction of Charleston for tourists created a market for Miss Smith's charming low-country landscapes and vignettes of the town. Her Charleston views not only documented the appearance of the many ancient houses and gardens that were rapidly disappearing, but through her two books carried a preservation message far afield. With her father she published in 1914 *Twenty Drawings of the Pringle House on King Street* (now known as the Miles Brewton House) and in 1917 *The Dwelling Houses of Charleston.*[11]

Although old Charleston gardens were seen to have their origins in the ordered geometry of the eighteenth century, their appearance in the years around 1900 owed more to a taste for the old-fashioned garden than to accurate preservation efforts. The garden at 58 South Battery, for example, restored in 1984 to elaborate patterned beds of four ovals surrounding a central diamond, in the early years of this century looked quite different.

Novelist Alice French, after taking tea with the Misses Ravenels (where she noted "a delightful wildsome garden"), visited 58 South Battery; there she found "Mrs. Brawley's house and iron gate and sunken garden and comely waiting maid are all very smart." Miss French recorded that the garden had a central rectangle of grass surrounded by a raised border of tulips, lilies, jessamine, violets, daffodils, pansies, verbenas, and cosmos.[12]

Garden writer Frances Duncan was charmed by the overgrown quality of the Pringle garden with its arbor-covered path. The view of the Augustine Smythe garden, used as one of the illustrations in her article on Charleston gardens for *Century* magazine, suggests the lush planting that was so appealing. Miss Duncan mentions a hedge of sweet bay; old roses, poppies, cornflowers, hollyhocks, and daffodils along paths; and arbors wreathed in wisteria and honeysuckle.[13]

New gardens made in Charleston at this period tended to follow this pattern, a notable exception being the garden made by artist Elizabeth O'Neill Verner at 3 Atlantic Street. Elizabeth Hamilton, Mrs. Verner's daughter, has amusingly attributed the artistic renaissance in Charleston in the first years of this century to the fact that any money available in good Charleston families went toward educating sons. After study at Harvard, Princeton, or Yale, the young men invariably married the sisters of their wealthy Yankee classmates, leaving several generations of young Charleston women unmarried. Careers as artists or craftswomen were socially acceptable alternatives. In any event, after two years' study at the Pennsylvania Academy, Elizabeth O'Neill did marry and have two children. She continued painting and was a founding member of the Sketch Club and a member of the Charleston Art Association.

In 1913 the Verners moved to 3 Atlantic Street and began a garden there by building a patio and walk with discarded paving stones from Charleston streets. Instead of a lawn or geometric beds, the central area was paved and used for out-of-door living and entertaining. The patio was shaded by a bay tree (*Laurus nobilis*) that was depicted on a greeting card sent to friends. Beds against the encircling wall held nasturtiums, mignonette, sweet alyssum, La France roses, syringa, yupon, and altheas.[14]

Following the lead of Alice Smith, Elizabeth Verner began to learn etching and was a founding member of the Etchers' Club.

The unexpected death of her husband in 1925 made her a professional artist and the sole support of herself and her children. Her husband's garden workshop became a showroom for her etchings of Charleston houses and gardens, with their inhabitants and ways of life.

Eola Willis, one of an earlier generation of women artists, in the early 1890s had gone with her sister and Sabina Wells, a cousin of Alice Smith, to study with American impressionist William Merritt Chase at the Art Students' League of New York. The League, founded in 1875 by painters disgruntled with National Academy classes, was run by its students. There women were given equal treatment and privileges. Miss Willis returned to Charleston and specialized in paintings of gardens, not just well-known ones like Middleton Place and Magnolia Gardens but imaginative evocations with titles such as "The Dream Garden" or "L'Heure exquise."[15]

Perhaps the best known South Carolina painter of gardens was Blondelle Malone. Born in Columbia, she grew up in a commodious house surrounded by a lush, old-fashioned garden. Miss Malone's father, the owner of a piano and music store, could afford (and chose) to pay for his daughter's education at Converse College, followed by two years of painting study at the Art Students' League with Chase and John Twachtman. After a stay at home, during which she painted her own and neighbors' gardens, Miss Malone persuaded her father to finance a two-year stay in France. In Giverny in 1904 she met Monet and was allowed to paint his garden.

Blondelle Malone was vivacious and attractive, with red hair and a piquant profile that many well-known artists seemed to have wanted to draw. Although she was always careful to provide herself with a chaperon, either a fellow woman artist or a married couple, in her lodgings and travels, she enjoyed greater freedom of movement than a young lady in the South. At last forced to come home, she wrote her mother, "We must have the garden so people cannot see in when I return, for I expect to live in it and paint it when I return. If you can plant a high hedge all around it would suit me exactly." The garden became her refuge as well as the subject of many paintings. She never felt at home in the restricted society of Columbia and longed for the freedom and congenial

14. The artist Blondine Malone in her studio garden in Columbia, South Carolina, c. 1908. Photograph courtesy of South Caroliniana Library.

painting colleagues she had had in Europe. As she wrote to her mother from France, where she was staying with the family of Jean Millet, "Here I am in my element but in Columbia I am burying my talents."[16]

After her mother's death in 1915, Miss Malone moved to Aiken, where she had a cottage surrounded by roses. Yankees in increasing numbers made towns like Aiken and Charleston fashionable wintering places. Here, following the lead of the residents, new owners avoided professionally designed gardens for more informal, old-fashioned ones; it was these gardens that Miss Malone preferred to paint.

Blondelle Malone managed to return to France occasionally, and her paintings, including one of impressionist Camille Pissarro's garden, were shown in the Paris Salon. She specialized in garden portraits, which she painted in fashionable vacation spots on the East Coast as well as in Europe, but never received the fame she sought; she was always more or less dependent on support from her father. Following his death, she settled in Alexandria, Virginia, where she became involved in historic preservation. She never married.

Another South Carolina native became better known as a garden writer than as a painter, though she practiced both professions. Hanna Rion was born in Winnsboro in 1875, the daughter of prominent lawyer Colonel James Rion and Mary Weir Rion, who had written the first American gardening book addressed to women, *Ladies' Southern Florist* (1860). Before her marriage, Mary Rion had lived for some years with William Preston's family in the Hampton-Preston house in Columbia and thus had intimate knowledge of a very fine old garden.

The appearance of Mary Rion's own garden is suggested in part by advice from her book. She advised that the main walk be the width of the house's front steps. Her own walk of this width led to a decorative iron gate ornamented with an "R" and was lined with boxwood. She believed that beds should never be square or triangular, but oval, circular or irregular with edgings of dwarf box, violets, lavender, pinks and lemon or vanilla grass. She felt the over-all design ought to be symmetrical and preferred no hedge in front, as she put it, "unless you wish to conceal your garden." In that case she suggested osage orange, privet, euonymous, or box.[17]

Hanna Rion, in her book *The Garden in the Wilderness* (1909), recalled visiting the garden after her mother's death. "I stood outside the fence an exile. Gazing past the straggling, aged box borders, my eyes sought in vain the beautiful old traceries of paths— the curves of symmetrical beds. Alas! beds and paths had intermingled in an universal neglect."[18]

Hanna Rion had gone to the Columbia College for Women, at

that time located in the Hampton-Preston House. Her education was interrupted when she eloped with her music teacher, Winfield Abell, in 1894. Her one child Teresa was a result of this marriage. She was to marry three more times in her relatively brief life. With her third husband, artist Frank Verbeck, she made the garden in the Catskill Mountains of New York state that was the subject of *The Garden in the Wilderness.*

The garden there had grown haphazardly, Miss Rion confessed, with none of the beds especially designed. Rather she sought inspiration in old gardening magazines and books, including her mother's, and nursery catalogues. Her garden had begun with hardy plants rescued from abandoned farms or given from neighbors' gardens. She added old-fashioned annuals and perennials, making, as she put it, a "beautiful chaos." She noted that "some old-timey flowers are like patch quilts—the more indiscriminate the mingling of color, the more consistently traditional they seem."[19]

Eventually there were many garden areas linked by narrow paths through clumps of native pines and cedars. There was one very large bed planted with masses of goldenrod, wild purple asters, feverfew, black-eyed Susans, and ferns with a border of hepaticas. A more conventional rose garden was underplanted with dianthus. There was a moon garden of pale flowers designed for fragrance and night viewing, and a border along the central walk with hollyhocks, perennial poppies, and Shasta daisies. Another garden area, deliberately old-fashioned, centered on a sundial surrounded with spring bulbs, phlox, and sweet peas.

Hanna Rion felt that "Garden making is creative work just as much as painting. . . . Music, painting and gardening are based on the same laws of color, harmony, composition." She seems to have made her garden as she would have done a landscape painting, on the spot, reacting to local conditions. For Miss Rion gardening, like painting, was an art of process rather than a finished idea laid out on paper. "It is only by means of constant shifting and rearrangement that we can come nearer, or even keep pace with, an ever-growing ideal of perfection." She added encouragingly, "Above all we have a right to be frankly ourselves in our own home surroundings, and the less the personal garden suggests the professional perfection, the more does it hold of loving intimacy."[20]

Like Blondelle Malone and several of the Charleston artists, all over the South young women of Hanna Rion's generation began to travel North for art study, often to New York's Art Students' League. One of these, Catherine Wiley, grew up in Knoxville and entered the University of Tennessee in one of the first classes to admit women students. In 1903 she traveled to New York and the Art Students' League where she studied illustration, a branch of the fine arts traditionally hospitable to women—as was the League itself.

At the League Miss Wiley encountered William Merritt Chase, whose gentlemanly demeanor and impeccable appearance made his classes a haven for genteel young women who had serious talent but could not abandon the constraints of their upbringing. He was a gifted teacher and his brilliant technique in portraiture, still lifes, and out-of-door landscape painting proved an inspiration. The subject matter of his art held nothing objectionable. Indeed, his paintings seemed to infuse glamour and beauty into the daily life of gently nurtured people like themselves.

Miss Wiley absorbed Chase's subject matter, if not a fully impressionist style. In 1905 she returned home to teach art in the home economics department of the University of Tennessee, where she remained for nearly twenty years, with occasional forays North to summer painting classes. She achieved local success with her paintings of young women in the house and garden, suitable settings for a Southern lady.[21]

A more nationally known painter, Helen Turner, was born in 1858 in Louisville but brought up in New Orleans by an uncle. Although a generation older than Catherine Wiley, her career began at nearly the same time, and she spent most of it teaching art. As she pointed out in a later interview, "Ladies in those days did not go out into the world to make money." It was only in 1895 after the death of her uncle when she was thirty-seven that she was able to move to New York with a younger sister to study art.[22]

Miss Turner spent four years at the Art Students' League and then earned a certificate in art from Teachers College of Columbia University. At forty-four she began a seventeen-year career in the Art School of the YWCA. About the same time she began spending summers with her sister in the art colony at Cragsmoor, New York. Here she was able to paint and garden full-time while her sister did the housework. Her garden climbed in three rock-bordered terraces beyond the porch of her cottage. Its masses of peonies, delphiniums, phlox, and foxgloves form a brilliant blur in the background of many of her paintings done on the porch. Unlike Catherine Wiley, Helen Turner remained in New York in touch with other artists and the art scene. Her return to New Orleans after her sister's death in 1923 signaled the end of her career.

Kate Freeman Clark was born in Holly Springs, Mississippi, in 1875 and was brought up by her widowed mother and formidable grandmother in the house built by her great-grandfather, one of the original settlers of the town. Both her mother and grandmother supported Miss Clark's desire to study art, and both accompanied her to New York where she enrolled in the Art Students' League in 1894.

After meeting Chase at a visit to his Shinnecock, Long Island, summer school of landscape painting, Miss Clark enrolled in his new school that had just opened in New York. She remained under his wing until 1903 and learned from him that it was possible to paint in oils and yet remain immaculate. She wrote that he looked, even when giving painting demonstrations, like "a tastefully dressed millionaire."[23]

Miss Clark received a great deal of encouragement as one of Chase's most talented pupils and began to send paintings to exhibitions. Unfortunately she was pressured by friends and family to give up her art, which was keeping both her mother and grandmother far from home, and return to Holly Springs. In any event, she was never able to paint full time; she was never allowed to have a studio and was distracted by a social life suitable to a young Southern lady of her background and wealth.

After the deaths of her mentor Chase and her grandmother, and then her mother in 1922, Miss Clark returned to Holly Springs and abandoned painting. After her own death twenty-five years later, the town's inhabitants were astounded to discover that she was an accomplished artist who had left all her paintings and the money to endow a museum to them. The will specified that the building be surrounded by "flowers, masses of color, flowering trees and shrubs and bulbs in quantities," evidencing their importance both in her painting and her life.[24]

Gardens drew the attention of photographers as well as painters in the 1880s and 1890s. Photography was seen as a suitable pastime for women, particularly after the development of a low-cost glass dry-plate negative that could be developed at leisure in the home. Books instructing women in fancy work for home decoration often included information about photography; amateur women photographers began to write of their experiences as gardeners had.

The perils as well as pleasures of learning photography were amusingly recorded by Alice French, who under the pseudonym of Octave Thanet wrote *An Adventure in Photography* (1893). Born in Massachusetts in 1850, brought up in Iowa, and educated at Vassar College, she became known in the 1890s for her colorful stories of the Arkansas delta. Her life companion, Jane Allen Crawford, had inherited the plantation "Clover Bend" in Arkansas, where they spent sixteen winters and springs beginning in 1883. Miss French used earnings from her best-selling books to build a frame mansion there with a vine-covered porch and expansive garden. Here she could indulge her passions for photography, carpentry, cooking, and entertaining lavishly, as well as gardening.

Alice French's illustrated newsletter, the *Clover Bend Poke Root,* published sporadically and sent to friends all over the country, gave a vivid picture of the garden. The issue of May 25, 1905, for example, recounted the never-ending battle against weeds, specifically ragweed. "Bro Thanet has used salt, lye, hoes, spades, hands, and profanity with but slender results: the conqueror of the Poke Root, the narrow dock and the army worm declares himself at the end of his wits."[25] Intended for winter and spring use, the grounds included a kitchen garden, flowering shrubs, a peony bed, an old-fashioned formal garden, and a rose garden with climbers on iron frames, all enclosed in a privet hedge.

In Nesho, Missouri, Ida Woodside Dougan, a divorced woman with three children, began a garden in a house bought for her by her father. On a restricted town lot she created a charming old-fashioned garden that was recorded in many photographs taken by herself and her daughter Kathleen, who became a professional photographer. The garden was meant to be enjoyed from the vine-covered porch; many photographs show friends gathered there. A wide gravel path led from the side of the porch across the lawn, through a grape arbor furnished with seats, and on to the

15. Ida Dougan in her garden in Nesho, Missouri. Photography courtesy of Michael
B. Dougan.

barn. To the right a vegetable garden was hidden behind a lush
growth of vines and hardy flowers, nicotiana being a particular favorite. Flowering shrubs, roses, and perennials surrounded the
house and masked the property line.[26]

For Ida Dougan, and for so many other women at this time, the
garden was not just a delightful recreation but an essential part of
their lives. It was an extension of their domestic space, a locus for
family and social life, and a very palpable demonstration both of
their artistic flair and their executive ability. The unpretentious
old-fashioned garden with mature shrubs, well-grown perennials,
and annuals used in bold masses within a carefully thought-out
structure sent other signals as well. Along with tasteful home fur-

nishings, styles of entertaining or appropriate dress, such a garden indicated the genteel background of its maker.

Like Kathleen Dougan, many amateur women photographers were able to become more or less professional. Kate Matthews, born and brought up in Peewee Valley near Louisville, Kentucky, began taking photographs of friends and relatives in 1886. She followed the accepted wisdom of the time that photographs should be artistic rather than mere snapshots; they should elevate, tell a story, or embody some ennobling sentiment. Some of her carefully posed photographs were published in popular magazines like *Youth's Companion.* Many illustrated *The Land of the Little Colonel,* the autobiography of her friend Annie Fellows Johnson, who wrote the popular *Little Colonel* series of children's books.[27]

Another friend was painter Patty Thum. Born in Louisville, she was educated at Vassar College and studied at the Art Students' League. Upon returning home, she specialized in flower painting, both of still lifes and flowers in the garden. Her painting *The Lady of the Lilies* used as a model Annie Johnston's step-daughter Mary, who also appears in Miss Matthews' very similar photo. The garden filled with lilies was that of the Johnston house "The Beeches" in Peewee Valley, the subject of many of Miss Matthews' photographic compositions.

Many of Miss Matthews' posed photographs are reminiscent of American paintings done at the same time. American artists had been painting women in gardens since mid–century, and their paintings tell us a great deal about the position of women at the time. Eastman Johnson's *Hollyhocks* (1876) enclosed elegantly clad ladies in a walled garden. In Hamilton Hamilton's *Hollyhocks* (c. 1885), the young woman is the equivalent of the flowers she stands among, both in her dress and flesh tones. The figure in Frederick Frieseke's *Iris* (c. 1910) is nearly indistinguisable from the flowers, while Robert Reid's beautifully dressed lady in *The Garden* (1900) doesn't seem capable of gardening at all. It was precisely at this moment, however, that a phenomenon called the "New Woman" made her appearance.

In a tongue-in-cheek self-portrait, the noted photographer Frances Benjamin Johnston shows herself enjoying all the shocking things the New Woman espoused: smoking, drinking, and short skirts that allowed masculine freedom of movement. Miss

Johnston was born in West Virginia in 1864 and grew up in Washington, D.C., where her father worked for the Treasury Department. In 1883 she traveled to Paris for two years of art study. On her return to Washington, she and several artist friends organized the Art Students' League, modeled on the one in New York. At the same time she began to study photography and by 1889 was supplying articles and illustrations for the Associated Press and popular illustrated magazines.

By 1894 Frances Johnston was well enough established to build her own six-room studio and office building in the rose garden behind her parents' house. Here she concentrated on portraiture of prominent Washingtonians and on documentary subjects. In 1899 she submitted a photograph of her studio and rose garden to a *Ladies' Home Journal* gardening contest, where it took second prize.

Miss Johnston began to concentrate on photographing gardens around 1909 when she entered into partnership with photographer Mattie Edwards Hewitt in New York. Here they specialized in architectural photography, including many newly built estates and their gardens. The partnership dissolved in 1917, and Miss Johnston returned to Washington to photograph Southern houses and gardens. By 1920 she had amassed enough hand-colored glass slides to lecture on American gardens to garden clubs across the country. When Miss Johnston retired to New Orleans in 1940, the garden she created behind her house there was as innovative as Elizabeth Verner's had been—simply a large, square lily pool beautifully occupying nearly the whole space.[28]

All of the women discussed above came from established families, and many went to college and were encouraged to develop their talents by pursuing professional training. Almost to a woman, however, they were discouraged from careers. The exceptions were those who were forced to support themselves and their families. Few seem to have been able to maintain the professional commitment of Helen Turner or Frances Johnston.

In 1893, just as Frances Johnston began her career, Mrs. Potter Palmer, director of the Woman's Pavillion of the Chicago World's Fair, addressed the dignitaries gathered at its opening. Recognizing the increasing opportunities for women to pursue higher education and professional training, she declared optimistically, "We may confidently await . . . the first blooming of the flower of womanhood. After centuries of careful pruning into conventional shapes, to meet the requirements of an artificial standard, the shears and props have been thrown away. We shall learn by watching the beauty and vigor of the natural growth in the open air and sunshine, how artificial and false was the ideal we had previously cherished."[29]

May Brawley Hill writes on American art and gardens. She is the author of Grandmother's Garden: The Old-Fashioned American Garden 1815–1915 *(Abrams, 1995).*

NOTES

1. Anna Lea Merritt, *An Artist's Garden* (London: George Allen and Sons, 1908), 22–23.

2. Anna Bartlett Warner, *Gardening by Myself* (New York: Anson D. F. Randolph, 1872), 19, 64.

3. Mariana Van Rensselaer, *Art Out-of-Doors: Hints on Good Taste in Gardening* (New York: Charles Scribner's Sons, 1893), 58, 63.

4. Helen Ashe Hays, *A Little Maryland Garden* (New York: G. P. Putnam's Sons, 1909), 7.

5. Candace Wheeler, *Yesterdays in a Busy Life* (New York: Harper and Brothers, 1918), 16.

6. Alice Morse Earle, *Old-Time Gardens* (New York: Macmillan, 1901), 48.

7. "Old-Fashioned Gardens," *Atlantic Monthly* (June 1908), 860.

8. "Moving Old Box to New Gardens," *Country Life in America* (November 1905), 56.

9. Roberta Seawell Brandau, ed., *History of Homes and Gardens of Tennessee* (Nashville: Garden Study Club, 1936), 241; and "Art and Artists," *Nashville Banner* (13 November 1886), 3.

10. Elizabeth Patterson Thomas, *Old Kentucky Homes and Gardens* (Louisville: Standard Printing Company, 1939), 101 and 108.

11. See Martha R. Severens, *Alice Ravenel Huger Smith* (Charleston: Carolina Art Association, 1993).

12. Alice French, Alice French diary (19 February 1916), in the Newberry Library, Chicago, Ill., 51

13. Frances Duncan, "Charleston Gardens," *Century* (May 1906), 710.

14. I am indebted to Elizabeth Hamilton for much information about her mother's garden. Photographs of the garden are in the collection of the South Carolina Historical Society, Charleston.

15. Eola Willis and Sabina Wells papers, in the collection of the South Carolina Historical Society, Charleston.

16. Blondelle Malone diary, papers, and photographs in the collection of the South Caroliniana Library, Columbia. See also Louise Jones DuBose, *Enigma: The Career of Blondelle Malone in Art and Society 1879–1951* (Columbia: University of South Carolina Press, 1963), 68.

17. Mary Rion, *Ladies' Southern Florist* (Columbia: Peter B. Glass, 1860), 15–16.

18. "A Hermit," in *The Garden in the Wilderness* (New York: Baker and Taylor Co., 1909), 203.

19. Hanna Rion, *Let's Make a Flower Garden* (New York: Robert M. McBride, 1912), 40.

20. *Ibid.,* 49{EN}50.

21. See Estill Curtis Pennington, *Southern Impressionist: The Art of Catherine Wiley* (Nashville: Tennessee State Museum, 1990).

22. Lewis Hoyer Rabbage, *Helen M. Turner, N.A.* (Cragsmoor, New York: Cragsmoor Free Library, 1983), 4.

23. Cynthia Grant Tucker, *Kate Freeman Clark: a Painter Rediscovered* (Jackson: University Press of Mississippi, 1981), 34.

24. *Ibid.,* 88.

25. Octave Thanet, *An Adventure in Photography* (New York: Charles Scribner's Sons, 1893). Issues of the *Clover Bend Poke Root* are in the Newberry Library, Chicago.

26. I am indebted to Michael B. Dougan for photographs and information about his grandmother's garden.

27. Dolinda Buie at the Ekstrom Library, University of Louisville, kindly sent me information about Kate Matthews. The Photographic Archives of the Ekstrom Library contains a collection of Miss Matthews' photographs. Patty Thum's *The Lady of the Lilies* is in the collection of the J.B. Speed Art Museum, Louisville.

28. A photograph of Frances Johnston's studio and garden appears in the *Ladies' Home Journal* (February 1899), 18. The Prints and Photographs Division of the Library of Congress, Washington, D.C., owns a collection of Miss Johnston's photographs. See fig. 8, a photograph of Prestwould for the Carnegie Architectural Survey of the South in the 1930s. See also Pete Daniels and Richard Smock, *A Talent for Detail: The Photographs of Miss Frances Benjamin Johnston 1880–1910* (New York: Harmony Books, 1989).

29. *History of the World's Fair* (Philadelphia: Standard Publishing Co., 1893), 114.

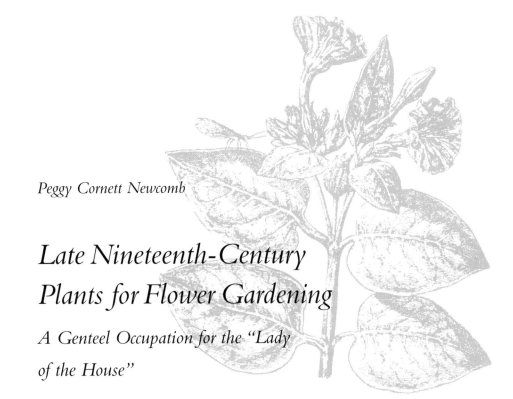

Peggy Cornett Newcomb

Late Nineteenth-Century Plants for Flower Gardening

A Genteel Occupation for the "Lady of the House"

By the second half of the nineteenth century, the unprecedented technological and cultural changes of the Industrial Revolution profoundly affected the development of horticulture in America. Many transformations in garden flowers were achieved through more refined and scientific breeding techniques. These novelties were quickly marketed to an eager gardening public through popular gardening books and periodicals of the time. By the turn of the twentieth century, an astounding selection of "new and improved" ornamentals were being developed and promoted by a burgeoning American seed industry. Companies such as James Vick's in Rochester, New York; David Landreth's of Philadelphia; and Peter Henderson's in New Jersey flourished in this period. The W. Atlee Burpee Company, one of today's mega-seed industries, saw its beginnings in this time as well.

16. "Gardening," from Washburn and Co.'s *Amateur Cultivator's Guide to the Flower and Kitchen Garden*, Boston, 1869.

Late Nineteenth-Century Plants for Flower Gardening

Gardening styles also dictated the types of plants most commonly used. The ornate carpet-bedding vogue of the mid-Victorian era featured dwarfed, stiff plants with large, brightly colored flowers. Gardeners sought plants that were uniform, durable, vigorous, and relatively easy to cultivate. Many "bedding annuals" were developed during this period, including zinnias, marigolds, cockscombs, and the like.

With the onset of a new audience of middle-class consumers, there evolved a cult of domesticity that conceived of the home as an orderly and secure place where the family could concentrate on the socialization of its children. The Victorian image of womanhood included notions of her place in the home, and her role in planning her flower garden. Flower gardening during this late Victorian era was particularly promoted as the genteel occupation for "the lady of the house." Whether it was the (predominantly male-controlled) seed industry writing to women or women gardeners themselves (who often wrote under pseudonyms or veiled identities), the feminine aspects of flower gardening were a constant theme throughout.

A basic familiarity with the types of flowers cultivated during this era is critical for those attempting accurate restorations of period gardens. It is often the case that plants selected for restored gardens either reflect earlier periods (such as the "colonial herb garden") or were not even available during that time. A good example of this is the annual *Impatiens wallerana*. The impatiens we commonly grow in shady gardens today was introduced very late in the nineteenth century and was probably not a standard garden plant until well into the twentieth. On the other hand, the old salmon-colored, single flowered balsam (*Impatiens balsamina*) was considered too old-fashioned by the 1870s. People were more interested in the double rose- or camellia-flowered sorts. Streaking and variegation in the flowers was all the rage. Therefore, in a proper late Victorian flower garden, it would be inappropriate to grow either the modern impatiens or the old, single balsam.

Large, doubled forms of the old garden standards were popular during this period. The blossoms of marigolds (both African and French), China asters, zinnias, verbenas, and even petunias were developed to nearly monstrous proportions. Burnside, the Hillsborough, North Carolina, home of Paul and Anne Ruffin Cameron, is but one example of a mid-nineteenth-century Southern garden that included vibrant 'Giant of Battles' verbenas and multi-colored and doubled 'Red Cross Banner' petunias. While the advent of the 'California Giant' petunias in the 1890s was heralded as a major triumph for America's plant breeders, not all shared this opinion. British garden writer and critic William Robinson despaired of these developments in 1891, writing: The tendency now-a-days with most subjects is to get the flowers as large as possible, and the petunia is no exception . . . indeed, it is one in which this character is strongly marked, for the huge lumpy blossoms composed of a mass of flimsy petals are totally wanting in any pleasing feature, while out of doors they are easily spoiled by wind and wet."

At the same time, dwarfing of the plant was also a desired quality, especially for the bedding-out style of garden design. Again, Anne Cameron's 1859 list of flowers for the Burnside gardens in Hillsborough included classic bedding plants such as dwarf, free-flowering 'Tom Thumb' geraniums. Dwarfed and non-trailing forms of nasturtiums were epitomized also by the 'Tom Thumb' strains, while scentless, dwarfed, non-climbing sweet peas such as 'Cupid' were promoted as the latest craze. Although sweet peas were extremely popular by the end of the nineteenth century, with literally dozens of varieties listed in seed catalogues in both America and England, many garden writers were beginning to lament their loss of fragrance. Gertrude Jekyll said it best when she observed that the old hedge of sweet peas was once the sweetest thing in the garden.

Another very different trend that developed during this period was a fascination with the American West. New wildflowers introduced from these regions were greeted with the enthusiasm associated with the latest cultivar of zinnia. Many flowers brought from these regions were better suited to the climate of Great Britain than they were to the eastern United States. Nevertheless, flowers such as abronias, clarkias, and collinsonias were listed in nearly every seed catalogue of the time. The California poppy (*Escholzia californica*) and the annual Drummond's phlox (*Phlox drummondii*) are two flowers that have continued in popularity even in gardens on the Eastern Seaboard, while most of the others have vanished from popular seed magazines.

As the Victorian era waned, a strong eclecticism crept into gardening and reached a zenith by the beginning of the twentieth century. As a result, garden designs that emerged ranged from highly architectural to modest and informal. These styles reflected European, English, and even Asian influences. Anti-Victorian sentiments, coupled with a renewed American sense of patriotism, led to many stylistic revivals. Interest in the "old-fashioned" flowers of the cottage garden and of the traditional styles of the early republic ultimately led to the full-blown Colonial Revival movement of the early twentieth century. Although many of the same carpet-bedding plants reappeared in these very different gardens, cultivars with freer habits increased in popularity. Nonetheless, loyal proponents of the Victorian bedding-out style remained through the nineteenth century. Seedsmen, such as Peter Henderson of New York, maintained this interest through effusive floral depictions in their catalogues and books. Indeed, feeble remnants of this style are still evident today, especially as focal points in the lawns of our public parks and institutions. It is rare, however, to find precisely executed re-creations of these elaborate and labor-intensive Victorian displays.

Peggy Cornett Newcomb is the director of the Thomas Jefferson Center for Historic Plants at Monticello and the editor of Magnolia, *the bulletin of the Southern Garden History Society.*

SELECTED BIBLIOGRAPHY

Early Plant Books

Bailey, L. H. *The Standard Cyclopedia of Horticulture,* vols. I–III. New York: Macmillan, 1915.

Bourne, Hermon. *Flores Poetici: the Florist's Manual.* Boston, 1833.

Breck, Joseph. *The Flower Garden: or, Breck's Book of Flowers.* New York: C. M. Saxton, 1861.

Bridgeman, Thomas. *The Young Gardener's Assistant.* New York, 1847.

Buist, Robert. *American Flower Garden Directory.* Philadelphia, 1839.

Cobbett, William. *The American Gardener.* London: C. Clement, 1821.

Earle, Alice Morse. *Old Time Gardens Newly Set Forth.* New York: Macmillan, 1901.

Furber, Robert. *Twelve Months of Flowers.* London, 1730.

Gerard, John. *The Herball or General Historie of Plants.* London, 1633.

Henderson, Peter. *Henderson's Handbook of Plants and General Horticulture.* New York: Peter Henderson & Company, 1890.

Loudon, Jane. *Gardening for Ladies.* New York: Wiley and Putnam, 1843.

McMahon, Bernard. *The American Gardener's Catalogue.* Philadelphia: B. Graves, 1806.

Miller, Philip. *The Gardener's Dictionary.* London, 1769.

Parkinson, John. *A Garden of Pleasant Flowers (Paradisi in Sole, Paradisus Terrestris).* London, 1629; reprint, New York: Dover, 1976.

Paxton, Joseph. *Paxton's Botanical Dictionary.* London: Bradbury, Evans, and Co., 1868.

Squibb, Robert. *The Gardener's Calendar for South-Carolina, Georgia, and North-Carolina.* Charleston, S.C., 1781; reprint, Athens: University of Georgia Press, 1980.

Thornton, Robert. *Temple of Flora.* London, 1812.

Modern Publications with Historic Plant Lists

Beales, Peter. *Roses.* New York: Henry Holt, 1992.

Bender, Steve, and Felder Rushing. *Passalong Plants.* Chapel Hill: University of North Carolina Press, 1993.

Coats, Alice M. *Flowers and Their Histories.* London: Adam & Charles Black, 1956.

———. *Garden Shrubs and Their Histories.* New York: E. P. Dutton, 1965.

Cothran, James R. *Gardens of Historic Charleston.* Columbia: University of South Carolina Press, 1995.

Dutton, Joan Parry. *Plants of Colonial Williamsburg.* Williamsburg, Va.: Colonial Williamsburg Foundation, 1979.

Favretti, Rudy J., and Joy P. Favretti. *For Every House a Garden.* Hanover, N.H.: Univeristy Press of New England, 1990.

———. *Landscapes and Gardens for Historic Buildings.* Nashville, Tenn.: Association for State and Local History, 1978; revised edition, 1991.

Gardener, Jo Ann. *The Heirloom Garden.* Pownal, Vt.: Storey Communications, 1992.

Hedrick, Ulysses Prentice. *History of Horticulture in America to 1850.* New York: Oxford University Press, 1950; reprint, Portland, Ore.: Timber Press, 1988.

Leighton, Ann. *Early American Gardens: "For Meate or Medicine."* Boston, Mass.: Houghton Mifflin, 1970; reprint, Amherst: University of Massachusetts Press, 1986.

———. *American Gardens in the Eighteenth Century: "For Use or for Delight."* Boston, Mass.: Houghton Mifflin, 1976.

———. *American Gardens of the Nineteenth Century: "For Comfort and Affluence."* Amherst: University of Massachusetts Press, 1987.

Martin, Tovah. *Once Upon a Windowsill.* Portland, Ore.: Timber Press, 1988.

Newcomb, Peggy C. *Popular Annuals of Eastern North America, 1865–1914.* Washington, D.C.: Dumbarton Oaks, 1984.

Ogden, Scott. *Garden Bulbs for the South.* Dallas: Taylor Publishing, 1994.

Stuart, David, and James Sutherland. *Plants from the Past.* New York: Viking, 1987.

Sturtevant's Edible Plants of the World, edited by U. P. Hedrick. New York: Dover, 1972.

Taylor, Geoffrey. *The Victorian Flower Garden.* Essex: Anchor Press, 1952.

Welch, William. *Antique Roses for the South.* Dallas: Taylor Publishing, 1990.

Welch, William, and Greg Grant. *The Southern Heirloom Garden.* Dallas: Taylor Publishing, 1995.

Whiteside, Katherine. *Antique Flowers.* New York: Villard Books, 1989.

———. *Classic Bulbs.* New York: Villard Books, 1991.

Susan Haltom

"Where Wonder Expresses Itself"

Flowers in Eudora Welty's Garden and Prose

Women have shaped the Southern landscape in many ways, both direct and indirect. Whole landscapes, gardening traditions, and individual plants have been handed down from generation to generation. Southern prose also has served a garden preservation role by describing in words the unique sense of place that characterizes our land.

To give you a feeling for Mississippi and its people through plants, I'm going to use the words of the twentieth century's greatest short-story writer, Miss Eudora Welty (fig. 17). The following quotes are but a few examples of how she uses plants and plant imagery in her work; closer examination of her writings reveals a sense of place that is deep and true. Flowers, plants, and gardens color her work with the varied hues of her home state, so that any Mississippian who reads Welty will immediately conjure up that image. In her characters, regardless of race, gender, or age, her expressions of

17. Eudora Welty's fascination with the living world led her to use Mississippi plants and flowers as backgrounds to her stories. Her actual work in the family garden gave her first-hand experience and sharpened her famous eye for detail. Photograph by Terry James; courtesy of Mississippi Department of Archives and History.

our better nature are evoked by comparison with the world around us.

Although known for her literature, Miss Welty has long thought of herself as a gardener, rooted in reality. In 1977, garden writer Henry Mitchell wrote an article for the *Washington Post* entitled "Eudora Welty: Rose-Gardener, Realist, Storyteller of the South," and the October 1995 issue of *Southern Living* contains a wonderful story on "Miss Eudora" by Willie Morris. He says:

Through the corpus of her work and in her own life, Eudora has touched many people. In an American age in which blitzkrieg best-sellers are marketed across the land like TV dinners, she in her quiet, comprehending, and, yes, passionate words is right here with us as she has always been. She is the real thing.[1]

Eudora Welty likes to feel part of the outdoors; only one room in her house is air conditioned, and she keeps her sitting-room windows open to the north breeze and the sights and sounds and smells of the outdoors. She wrote,

The outside world is a vital component to my inner life. My work, in the terms in which I see it, is as dearly matched to the world as its secret sharer. My imagination takes its strength and guides its direction from what I see and hear and learn and feel and remember of my living world.[2]

Eudora Alice Welty was born in 1909 in Jackson, Mississippi, then a town of about 7,000 people. Her parents, Christian and Chestina Welty, had met in West Virginia and moved South to start married life. Their first house was located near the new state capital building (Eudora and her friends used to roller skate through the State House's marbled halls to reach the city library); families still kept their own milk cows and chickens out back.

In her later writings, Eudora would often describe the natural world from a child's point of view. This world was a place full of power and mystery, yet accessible to all:

It kept her from eating her dinner to think of all she had caught or meant to catch before the time was gone—June bugs in the banana plants to fly before breakfast on a thread, lightning-bugs that left a bitter odor in the palms of the hand, butterflies with their fierce and haughty faces, bees in a jar.[3]

Since her parents had family in Ohio and West Virginia, the Weltys took many summer trips to the home places. Miss Welty told me about the bright flowers in the yards of her great aunts, whose Victorian flower beds looked like bites in the grass. "No one ever spoke of planting a garden, it was just something they did," she said. A 1917 photograph showed Grandpa Jefferson Welty with Eudora and her brothers on the Ohio farm. Feathery cosmos, cannas wrapped to protect them from the chickens, and barrel-sized peony bushes dotted the yard. She later wrote in a short story,

All the children came running and jumping out. She went along chewing nasturtium stems and sucking the honey from four o'clock stems, out for

whatever figs and pomegranates came to hand. She floated a rose petal dry in her mouth, and sucked on the spirals of honeysuckle and the knobs of purple clover. She wore crowns.[4]

In 1925 her father, then president of Lamar Life Insurance Company, built the city's first skyscraper and used the same architect to design a new home for the family on the outskirts of town. Eudora was sixteen when her mother began to plant the garden that was to be a major influence on her body of work. "I was my mother's yard boy," Miss Welty told me. A Welty scholar said that Eudora has conceivably spent more time in the garden than at the typewriter. The "salubrious pine trees," which her mother thought would contribute to her family's good health, and the iris border, the bulbs, and old-fashioned flowering shrubs all benefitted from the loving care of these two genteel Southern ladies.

Eudora was encouraged by both her parents to develop her writing skills, and to also study business in order to make a living. When her father died in 1931, Eudora returned home from her studies at Columbia University to help out. Her two younger brothers were still in school, so she took various local jobs in journalism, including a position in public relations with the WPA. The three years she spent traveling across Mississippi by bus and train acquainted her with the terrain and later provided a background for her fiction.

We have heard it said that deep levels of meaning may underlie our connection with the landscape. We also know that many cultures think of the earth as a mother and its contours as sacred. In *Sacred Groves and Ravaged Gardens,* Louise Westling writes that this is especially true of Eudora Welty, "whose fertile Delta cotton fields, baptismal rivers of life and sexuality and death, mysterious bayou woods, and carefully tended flower gardens all glow with feminine sacredness." Her women are far from incidental, nor do they exist in mere supporting roles. Westling continues, "Welty's women move freely and comfortably across the landscape, at the center of a world which affirms them and denies male pretensions of control."[5]

Whether or not she means to portray women as the real power holders is debatable. I think she naturally uses a female point of view, and she is a confident, funny, witty, well-educated woman. In

1970 Miss Welty was interviewed for a book entitled *Open Secrets: Ninety-four Women in Touch with Our Times*. Her replies to the following questions on matters of male and female roles in society give evidence to her matter-of-fact openness:

Men a help or hindrance?—*Writing is a profession outside sex.*
Men treat you as equal?—*As far as I know.*
Must a woman sacrifice femininity in career?—*No.*
Meaning of "male chauvinism"?—*No idea.*
Mother oppressed?—*Not at all.*
Brought up to believe a woman's place was in the home?—*I don't believe I was ever told where it was.* [6]

This female strength of character sifts over into descriptions of the landscape. Whether described from a little girl's point of view as she looked out the window of a train, or from the all-knowing heart of the matriarch, Miss Welty's landscapes are unforgettable.

Thoughts went out of her head and the landscape filled it . . . The land was perfectly flat and level but it shimmered like the wing of a lighted dragonfly. It seemed strummed, as though it were an instrument and something had touched it. Sometimes in the cotton were trees with one, two, or three arms—she could draw better trees than those were. Sometimes like a fuzzy caterpillar looking in the cotton was a winding line of thick green willows and cypresses, and when the train crosses this green, running on a loud iron bridge, down its center like a golden mark on the caterpillar's back would be a bayou. [7]

In contrast to the open Delta fields were the bayous, thick with mystery, danger, and daring (fig. 18):

There is something Gothic about the vines, in their structure in the trees— there are arches, flying buttresses, towers of vines, with trumpet flowers swinging in them for bells and staining their walls. . . . Muscadine vines along the stream banks grow a hundred feet high, mixing their dull, musky, delicious grapes among the bronze grapes of the scuppernong. . . . The passionflower puts its tendrils where it can, its strange flowers of lilac rays with their little white towers shining out, or its fruit, the maypop, hanging. Wild wistaria hangs its flowers like flower-grapes above reach, and the sweetness of clematis, the virgin's-bower which grows in Rodney, and of honeysuckle, must fill the highest air. [8]

18. Swamps and bayous in southwest Mississippi, with a rich variety of vines and flowers, remind Eudora Welty of the sinuous lines found in Gothic architecture. S. Haltom photograph.

When little girls at a summer camp ran off into the bayou, it was the orphan Easter who showed the others a forbidden pleasure:

Easter lifted to her lips a piece of cross-vine cut back in the days of her good knife. She brought up a kitchen match from her pocket, lighted up, and smoked.

They sat up and gazed at her.

"If you count much on being a singer, that's not a very good way to start," said Jinny Love. "Even boys, it stunts their growth. . . ."

Easter once more looked the same as asleep in the dancing shadows, except for what came out of her mouth, more mysterious, almost, than words.
    "Have some?" she asked, and they accepted. But theirs went out.[9]

Notice how Miss Welty uses the following suggestions of scent to evoke an unmistakably Southern atmosphere:

Set here and there in this country will be a mimosa tree, with its smell in the rain like a cool melon cut, its puffs of pale flowers settled in its sensitive leaves. . . .
    Spanish moss invariably hangs from the live oak branches, moving with the wind and swaying its long beards, darkening the forests; it is an aerial plant and strangely enough is really a pineapple, and consists of very, very tiny leaves and flowers, springy and dustily fragrant to the touch; no child who has ever "dressed up" in it can forget the sweet dust of its smell.[10]

Though sense of place is crucial to her writings, Miss Welty once observed that "place is one of the lesser angels, feeling wears the crown." When she wished to convey feelings of fecundity and family responsibility, she used a garden setting with its fall cleanup duties. From *Delta Wedding,* set in the 1920s, for the expectant mother in the dry Mississippi September there is a feeling of overripeness, and too little time.

A Dainty Bess that wanted to climb held a cluster of five blooms in the air. "I can't reach," Ellen remarked firmly. She needed to take up some things that would go in the pit for winter, she wanted to flower some bulbs, too. When, when? And the spider lilies were taking everything . . . She looked at the tall grass in her beds, as if it knew she could no longer bend over and reach it. What would happen to everything if she were not here to watch it, she thought, not for the first time when a child was coming. Of all the things she would leave undone, she hated leaving the garden untended—sometimes as much as leaving Bluet, or Battle.[11]

Miss Welty is a connoisseur of names—she loves their origins and hidden meanings. When I asked her about Bluet, the baby's name, she said she had gotten this name from a friend of her father's, who had named his own baby Bluet. "That's something only a man would do, don't you think?" she asked me. We have talked about botanical names and their meanings, like *Amaryllis advenum* and the *zephranthes,* which she collected in her garden.

She told me what fun she had imagining the result if the Jackson lady named Vashti Ishee married Atlee Burpee.

Although Miss Welty used plants to reflect what a particular character was growing, she used them to describe the character's physical appearance. Consider these images:

Ellie Morgan was a large woman with a face as pink and crowded as an old-fashioned rose.[12]

She was old and fair as a doll. Up close, her yellowish hair was powdery like goldenrod that had gone forgotten in a vase.[13]

Miss Eckhart pushed herself to quite another level of life for it. A blushing sensitivity sprang up in her every year at the proper time like a flower of the season, like the Surprise Lilies that came up with no leaves and overnight in Miss Nell's yard.[14]

Solomon had a lightish face, with eyebrows scattered but rugged, the way privet grows.[15]

The face was set now, and ugly with that rainy color of seedling petunias, the kind nobody wants.[16]

Virgie carried the magnolia bloom like a hot tureen, and offered it to Miss Eckhart, neither of them knowing any better: magnolias smelled too sweet and heavy for right after breakfast.[17]

Flower names in Welty prose have a down-home connotation that rings true. The novel *Losing Battles* is set in the rugged hills of northeast Mississippi during the Depression. Miss Welty had been reading the *Mississippi Market Bulletin* for years, so she had a stash of information that provided a suitable setting, using country flowers with homespun biblical names: milk and wine lily, Jacob's ladder, angel trumpet. *Gardening for Love* tells how Miss Welty introduced her friend Elizabeth Lawrence to these periodicals, and years of correspondence ensued.

In Miss Welty's short story, "The Wanderers," Mrs. Katie Rainey's confused mind races through her *Market Bulletin* list of flowers, trying in desperation to keep count of her list and the places things grew as she slipped away from this life:

Dying, Miss Katie went rapidly over the list in it, her list. As though her impatient foot would stamp at each item, she counted it, corrected it, and yet she was about to forget the seasons, and the places things grew. Purple althea cuttings, true box, four colors of cannas for 15 cents, moonvine seed by teaspoonful, green and purple jew. Roses: big white rose, little thorn rose, beauty-red sister rose, pink monthly, old-fashioned red summer rose, very fragrant, baby rose. Five colors of verbena, candlestick lilies, milk and wine lilies, blackberry lilies, lemon lilies, angel lilies, apostle lilies. Angel trumpet seed. The red amaryllis.

Faster and faster, Mrs. Rainey thought: Red salvia, four o'clock, pink Jacob's ladder, sweet geranium cuttings, sword fern and fortune grass, century plants, vase palm, watermelon pink and white crape myrtle, Christmas cactus, golden bell. White star jessamine. Snowball. Hyacinthus. Pink fairy lilies. White. The fairy white.[18]

The novel for which she won the Pulitzer Prize, *The Optimist's Daughter*, proved to be the most autobiographical. In it Miss Welty speaks of the indomitable spirit of Laurel's deceased mother through images of Becky's tough old rose:

"I'd give a pretty to know what exactly that rose is!" Laurel's mother would say every spring when it opened its first translucent flowers of the true rose color. "It's an old one, with an old fragrance, and has every right to its own name, but nobody in Mount Salus is interested in giving it to me. All I had to do was uncover it and give it the room it asked for. Look at it! It's on its own roots, of course, utterly strong."[19]

Though she has lived in the house alone for some thirty years now, Miss Welty still speaks of the garden as "my mother's garden." Her mother, Chestina Andrews Welty, was born in the mountains of West Virginia where the rivers always seemed to be in a hurry. Life was hard. She was an only daughter with five younger brothers, and like so many young ladies of her time, she pursued the life of a teacher. Throughout her life, scholarship was uppermost in her mind. Miss Welty told me, "It was a perfectly simple matter of fact; the garden was to be a learning experience. The last thing on my mother's mind was to make it a show garden. But she thought of it as a living picture, always changing. Not a competition. She had a schoolteacher's love of accuracy. She would look up everything so there would be no mistakes made and no foolishness. She knew every blade of grass in the garden." Chestina Welty started the first garden club in Jackson, to be called "The Garden Diggers," with the intention that it be a club for the study and swapping of plants. But when it became apparent that most of the ladies were meeting to gossip and drink tea, Chestina dropped out.

Miss Welty recently told me, "To get Jackson interested in flowers we had competitions at the State Fair. We had ribbons of red, blue, and white. I know this because I did the publicity. My mother always won 'Best of Other Than Named,' which was a funny category."

I asked her, "But wouldn't you rather win in that category? It means that you cannot be pinned down."

"Yes," she replied. "Mother complained about the contest; she knew that growing things was not competitive. They were grown for their own sake. But she was a judge. She would rather judge other people because she knew the standards she held."

Chestina was a great saver of things, seeds and cuttings; they had a cold frame and rooted roses and grafted camellias. Tender plants were covered against the cold with soldier hats made of newspaper. Miss Welty sat up at night sewing slipcovers out of croker sacks to clothe the camellias. And if anyone doubts that they were day-to-day gardeners, listen to Eudora's words in *Delta Wedding*:

The camellia bushes had all set their buds, choosing the driest and busiest time, and if they did not get water they would surely drop them, tempermental as they were. . . . The eleagnus had overnight, it seemed, put out shoots as long as a man. . . .

"Howard, remind me to ask Mr. Battle for three or four loads of fertilizer tomorrow." . . . She wanted to separate the bulbs again, too, and spread the Roman hyacinths out a little under the trees—they grew so thick now they could hardly bloom last spring. "Howard, don't you think breath-of-spring leans over too much to look pretty?"[20]

Although Chestina was adventurous in the garden, she did not believe in forcing things, and as her daughter recalls, "Fashion meant zero to her." Chestina kept a journal in a black composition book, arranged for detailed photographs of her beds, and read garden literature like Sackville-West, not the ladies' magazines because they were "too boring." Southern garden writer Elizabeth Lawrence was a friend to both Weltys; one time she stopped in Jackson to see Eudora only to discover that Eudora was out of town. Miss Lawrence accepted Chestina's hospitality and ended up staying six weeks.

After her husband's untimely death in 1931, Chestina spent every day in the garden. Her favorite flowers were the roses, which included 'Mermaid,' 'Lady Banks,' 'Silver Moon,' 'Crimson Glory,' 'The Doctor,' 'Étoile de Holland,' and many others. The garden evolved as a typical Depression-era landscape with irregular curving beds and garden rooms filled with flowers.

Time passed, and the garden so lovingly cared for aged along with the gardeners. Chestina Welty's eyes grew dim. She still wrote in her journal, but then she couldn't read what she had written. When nematodes caused all the roses in the bed to up and die overnight, Miss Welty removed them and never told her mother. Arthritis of the hands also debilitated Chestina, and many years later it plagues her daughter. All garden tasks must now be performed by someone else.

In 1986 Miss Welty deeded her home to the state with the wish that it not become a shrine or mausoleum. When I was called in by the Mississippi Department of Archives and History to help pull out some of the choking honeysuckle and poison ivy, I was both humbled and grieved by what I saw. Miss Welty wished she could get out and help; she felt personally responsible for the garden's degeneration. "I can't bear to look out the window and see what has become of my mother's garden," she said.

I spoke to the Board of Trustees, and they recognized our opportunity to research this garden with Miss Welty's input. An advisory committee is now seeking to understand the garden's significance to Miss Welty's life and work and develop a realistic approach for its current use and transition to public garden status later. A base plan has been drawn up according to survey notations (fig. 19), and the garden has been stabilized. Interviews with Miss Welty and further research are proceeding; we hope to find Chestina's garden records and more photographs.

Miss Welty is anxious for the garden. After my work in the garden I have pricked her memory from time to time about the way it once was, and she enjoys our discussions. But she doesn't want the garden made into something it never was. She said, "I think that people have lost the working garden. We used to get down on our hands and knees. The absolute contact between the hand and

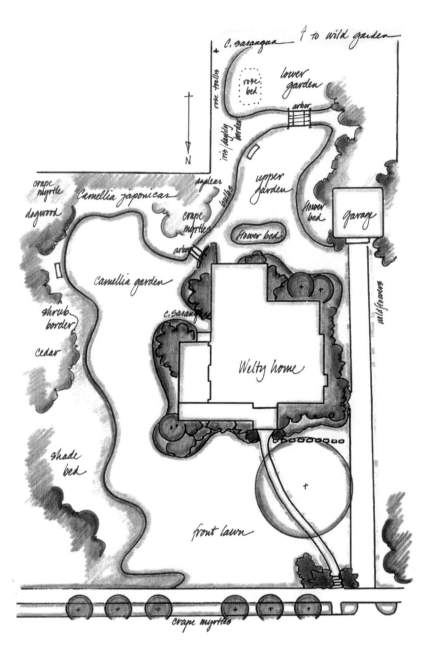

C. sasanqua → to wild garden

rose bed

lower garden

arbor

rose trellis

N

iris/daylily border

azaleas

bushes

upper garden

crape myrtle

Camellia japonicas

crape myrtles

dogwood

arbor

flower bed

flower bed

garage

Camellia garden

wildflowers

shrub border

C. sasanqua

cedar

Welty home

shade bed

front lawn

crape myrtles

19. A plan for the restoration of the gardens at the Welty Garden Trust, Eudora Welty's home, in Jackson, Mississippi. S. Haltom.

the earth, the intimacy of it, that is the instinct of a gardener. People like to classify, categorize, and that takes away creativity. I think the artist—in every sense of that word—learns from what's individual; that's where wonder expresses itself."

Susan Haltom is the project director for the Welty Garden Trust in Jackson, Mississippi.

NOTES

1. Willie Morris, "Miss Eudora," *Southern Living,* October 1995. Quoted comments by Miss Welty are taken from interviews and conversations between Miss Welty and the author.

2. Eudora Welty, *One Writer's Beginnings* (Cambridge, Mass.: Harvard University Press, 1984), 76.

3. Eudora Welty, "The Winds," from *The Wide Net and Other Stories* (New York: Harcourt, Brace and Company, 1943), 125.

4. Welty, "The Winds," 122.

5. Louise Westling, *Sacred Groves and Ravaged Gardens: The Fiction of Eudora Welty, Carson McCullers, and Flannery O'Connor* (Athens: University of Georgia Press, 1985), 179.

6. Peggy Whitman Prenshaw, ed., *Conversations with Eudora Welty* (Jackson: University Press of Mississippi, 1984), 36.

7. Eudora Welty, *Delta Wedding* (New York: Harcourt, Brace, 1946), 4.

8. Eudora Welty, "Some Notes on River Country," from *The Eye of the Story* (New York: Random House, 1978), 295.

9. Eudora Welty, "Moon Lake," from *The Golden Apples* (New York: Harcourt, Brace, 1947), 119.

10. Welty, "Some Notes on River Country,", 297.

11. Welty, *Delta Wedding,* 225.

12. Eudora Welty, "The Key," from *A Curtain of Green and Other Stories* (Garden City, New York: Doubleday, Doran, 1941), 56.

13. Eudora Welty, "June Recital," from *The Golden Apples* (New York: Harcourt, Brace, 1947), 53.

14. Welty, "June Recital,", 62.

15. Eudora Welty, "Livvie," from *The Wide Net and Other Stories* (New York: Harcourt, Brace, 1943), 160.

16. Welty, "Moon Lake," 134.

17. Welty, "June Recital," 36.

18. Eudora Welty, "The Wanderers," from *The Golden Apples* (New York: Harcourt, Brace, 1947), 207.

19. Eudora Welty, *The Optimist's Daughter* (New York: Random House, 1969), 114.

20. Eudora Welty, *Delta Wedding,* 224.

Sherold D. Hollingsworth

Women Landscape Architects and Their Influence on Southern Gardening

Landscape architecture is a young profession that is just becoming aware of itself and is just beginning to record its history rather than just the components of the profession. When I was in graduate school in the Landscape Architecture program at the School of Design of North Carolina State University during the mid-1980s, the only woman landscape architect I was taught anything about was Beatrix Farrand, the sole female founding member of the American Society of Landscape Architects. She was, to my mind, the greatest landscape architect who ever practiced.

But what about Elizabeth Lawrence, whom all of you know about, and who many of you knew, and with whom some of you even traded flowers? She was the first female graduate in landscape architecture at North Carolina State University. She was never even mentioned. Nor, of course, were the other women we will talk about today.

The most important single thing that I discovered during this research is that not much is known about female landscape architects. In the past few years several books have been published about Beatrix Farrand, and one each about Marian Coffin and Florence Yoch. But the great majority of landscape architects, female and male, remain undocumented. The careers of many of them probably never will be recorded because their offices were dismantled and their files thrown away when they died.

In 1989, the National Trust for Historic Preservation and the American Society of Landscape Architects, realizing that it was time to begin documenting and analyzing the profession in an organized fashion, published a book, *American Landscape Architecture: Designers and Places,* which memorialized some of the best known landscape architects in America. Ellen Shipman and Beatrix Farrand are the only two women who are the subject of articles, but four other women are mentioned in the text.

Ellen Shipman, whose garden for Dewitt Hanes in Winston-Salem is fairly well known, is listed as having "practiced from Texas to Michigan and North Carolina to New Hampshire." Her largest North Carolina garden, the Sarah Duke Memorial Garden at Duke University, is mentioned,[1] but not the other fourteen North Carolina gardens of which I am aware. Luckily a book on her work, *The Gardens of Ellen Biddle Shipman* by Judith B. Tankard, is being published by Sagapress.

This discrepancy in the available information about Ellen Shipman was my first intimation that I might have taken on more than I was expecting with this research. At that point I began to realize that I would not simply be showing pictures of gardens of important landscape architects who happened to be female, but would be trying to present the names of women who have not been researched and inspire others to document women's contributions as they come across their work.

If gardens as important to the career of Ellen Shipman as her North Carolina gardens have not been documented, who knows what other gardens in the South designed by women were also unrecorded and forgotten? Many of the women who are listed as practicing in other parts of the country may have designed lovely gardens all over the South and we may never know it. Gardens are ephemeral, and blueprints crumble. Documenting this work needs to be undertaken community by community, garden by garden, before it is too late.

By 1993, when the National Park Services published *Pioneers of American Landscape Design: An Annotated Bibliography,* the number of women about whom articles had been written had increased to eleven.[2]

In magazines and books of the period as well as secondary sources, I have found references to 149 women who practiced between the founding of the American Society of Landscape Architects in 1899 and the beginning of World War II (see appendix A). I found ten women whose main offices were in the South (see appendix B), but I am sure that this list is not comprehensive.

These lists do not include the names of women who influenced others though their writings because of the difficulty of determining the influence of the written word, but writing was important to many of them. Of the 149 women landscape architects from this period, I discovered that thirty-four of them wrote books or articles for contemporary magazines. In addition, the gardens of many of these women appeared in the "shelter magazines" of the day. Undoubtedly they did influence Southern women through their writing and through their designs of gardens in other parts of the country that were published in the magazines Southern women read.

Landscape architecture includes more than simply garden design. It has been defined in various ways, but one of my favorite definitions is by Charles Eliot, an early practitioner, partner of Olmsted, and the son of the founder of the landscape architecture program at Harvard, the first landscape architecture degree program in the country. Mr. Eliot said, "Landscape architecture is primarily a fine art, and as such its most important function is to create and preserve beauty in the surroundings of human habitations and in the broader natural scenery of the country."[3]

In their famous 1917 textbook, *An Introduction to the Study of Landscape Design,* which I feel sure the majority of these women read, H. V. Hubbard and Theodora Kimball defined it as

primarily a fine art whose most important function is to create and preserve beauty in the surroundings of human habitations and in the broader natural scenery of the country; but is also concerned with promoting the comfort, convenience and health of urban populations, which have scanty access to rural scenery and urgently need to have their hurrying workaday lives refreshed and calmed by the beautiful and reposeful sights and sounds which nature, aided by the landscape art, can abundantly provide.[4]

Garrett Eckbo, a contemporary landscape architect, goes further when he defines it as covering

that portion of the landscape which is developed or shaped by man, beyond buildings, roads, or utilities and up to wild nature, designed primarily as space for human living (not including agriculture, forestry). It is the establishment of relations between buildings, surfacing, and other outdoor construction . . . but with primary emphasis on the human content, the relationship between people and landscape.[5]

The American Society of Landscape Architects goes further and requires that all practicing landscape architects consider themselves to be "stewards of the land."[6] Norman Newton may have given the best definition of all in his *Design on the Land* when he wrote that landscape architecture is "the art—or science, if preferred—of arranging land, together with the spaces and objects upon it, for safe, efficient, healthful, pleasant human use."[7]

The first known use of the term *landscape architect* was in 1858 when Frederick Law Olmsted and Calvert Vaux signed their plan for Central Park, using the new term.[8] In the 1890's, landscape architecture was not yet organized as a profession; there was no systematic method of formal training, other than through apprenticeship, and the number of practitioners was small. Nevertheless, some of these few began to feel the urgent need to unite in some form of organization. In 1899, in New York, the American Society of Landscape Architects (ASLA) was founded. Of the eleven charter members, only one, Beatrix Farrand, was a woman.[9]

However, there were apparently women who practiced before Beatrix Farrand. Elizabeth Bullard of Bridgeport Connecticut, is sometimes referred to as "the first woman practitioner." She was the first woman actually elected to membership as a fellow after the founding meeting.[10] John Olmsted, nephew of Frederick Law Olmsted, wrote of her, "Miss Bullard had been an assistant to her father who had practiced as a landscape architect for many years . . . after her father's death she was forced by circumstances to carry on his work."[11] (You can hear the faint underlying notion that he really didn't think that she should be doing it. She had to earn a living some way—too bad she thought it was in landscape architecture! Although 55 percent of landscape architects today are women, they were not welcome in the early days.)

Mable Parsons, another early practitioner, was born in 1872. The daughter of Samuel H. Parsons, Jr., she carried on his practice after he died and wrote extensively of her father and his work. She was also a strong supporter of Parson's decision to push for a professional organization of landscape architects.[12] However, she was not one of the founding members of ASLA. Indeed, I am not sure that she ever was a member.

During these early days there were few organized courses in landscape design, and until 1900 there were no organized courses in landscape architecture. Harvard was the first to offer such a program but refused to admit women until 1942, when decreased enrollment because of World War II made it economically attractive to do so.[13]

Because many schools barred women, it was inevitable that schools devoted to the training of women for the profession would be established. The three most notable were the Pennsylvania School of Horticulture for Women, outside Philadelphia; the Cambridge (Massachusetts) School of Architecture and Landscape Architecture; and the Lowthorpe School of Landscape Architecture, Gardening and Horticulture for Women in Groton, Massachusetts."[14] Of the women I have identified in Appendix A, fifty-three attended either the Cambridge School or Lowthorpe. There may have been more; I could not find the names of the schools of a great number of them.

Among the Southern practitioners who attended one of these two schools were Edith Harrison Henderson, who practiced in Atlanta beginning in 1935; Rose Isabel Greely, who practiced in Washington, D.C.; Clermont Hugger Lee who practiced in Savannah, Georgia; Ruth London, who practiced in Houston; and Mary Louise Speed, who practiced in Louisville, Kentucky.[15]

Even after the schools were established, women still had to struggle to be able to enjoy the benefits of training for the full profession. For example, although Lowthorpe offered courses in engineering design and drawing for those women who wanted to go beyond gardening and horticulture, Harvard president emeritus Charles W. Eliot stated in a fundraising letter, "It is my belief that the future of the School will be best assured by serving to the utmost women who desire to study landscape beauty, garden design, and planting rather than the engineering and architecture embraced in the general term 'landscape architecture.'"[16]

Although a woman had been a founding member, in 1913 some considered membership in the ASLA to be a right that should be enjoyed exclusively by the male sex. At that time, Charles Downing Lay, then secretary, received the following note from a member: "I have a blank form stating that a young lady is being considered for Junior membership in the ASLA. I think it is a mistake to encourage women to enter the Society. I hope some action will be taken in this matter."[17]

Rather than belabor the difficulty women had in entering the profession, it is more interesting to discuss the women themselves. Beatrix Farrand, Marian Coffin, and Florence Yoch were important figures, but since books have been written about their lives for you to read in much more detail yourselves, I will discuss them briefly and move on to a few of the others whose careers have not yet been documented.

According to Donna Palmer, "The most notable accomplishments of a woman during this period, were those of Beatrix Jones Farrand. She was a charter member and original fellow of the ASLA while still in her twenties. As a young woman, Miss Jones overcame the prejudices of late Victorian standards of what became a 'lady.' She studied with Professor Charles Sprague Sargent at the Arnold Arboretum. After leaving Professor Sargent, her early works included the design and implementation of small and large gardens, forestation, and designing and unifying various university campuses—Princeton, Yale, and Chicago in particular."[18]

Beatrix Farrand first practiced in New York City and then later in Bar Harbor, Maine, but her greatest garden was in the South: Dumbarton Oaks, the home of Mildred and Robert Woods Bliss in Georgetown (figs. 20, 21). Beatrix Farrand was fortunate in her choice of clients. They were rich and interested in their gardens, and they allowed her to spend many, many hours getting everything exactly right. The moon gate of the Abbey Aldrich Rockefeller Garden is a good example of this process. Miss Farrand de-

20. This detail of a bench that was constructed as an essential part of a railing at Dumbarton Oaks, Washington, D.C., illustrates Beatrix Farrand's remarkable facility with construction detailing and materials. S. Hollingsworth photograph.

veloped drawings of two different designs for the client to choose from, as well as a full-size mock-up of the gate that allowed both the client and designer to make needed modifications. (The gate was simplified in the final design.)[19]

Frederick Law Olmsted, Jr., the son of the founder of landscape architecture, is reported to have said about Beatrix Jones Farrand that she was "inclined in some way to dabble in landscape architecture."[20] [I'd vote for her work over his any day of the week.]

Another outstanding designer was Marian Coffin. She once said that she had heard of the work of Beatrix Farrand and decided to become a landscape architect because of it.[21] Miss Coffin studied at MIT, graduating in the 1904 class. There were four women students, two of whom were in landscape architecture, in her class at MIT. She joined the ASLA in 1906 (in the same class as Thomas Sears, the landscape architect who worked on Reynolda Gardens), becoming its third woman member.

Most of Marion Coffin's 130 known clients were in the Northeast, but she did have clients in the South: H. Rodey Sharpe in Boca Grande, Florida; Charles T. Ballard, Alexander Humphrey, and William Marshall Bullitt (her first important commission) in Glenview, Kentucky;[22] Russell Campbell in Lynchburg, Virginia; and the Foxcroft School in Middleburg, Virginia. Her most famous garden was, of course, Winterthur, Henry du Pont's garden in Delaware. She was known for her use of color and her choice of plants, creating gardens with an effect of delicate naturalism. Careful in the use of form and texture, she used shrubs and trees for vivid accents.[23] She had a logical, highly organized approach to design. Like Ellen Shipman and Beatrix Farrand, she often used "a

21. Beatrix Farrand's masterful use of texture and form is evident in this detail of an arbor at Dumbarton Oaks, Washington, D.C. S. Hollingsworth photograph.

profusion of flowers tumbling over the hard edges of the formal structures of her flower gardens."[24]

Florence Yoch, who practiced in California, is the last of the three women to have had books published about them to date. During most of her career she worked with Lucille Council. Miss Yoch designed the gardens, and Miss Council contributed planting schemes. Florence Yoch's style is somewhat different from the other designers discussed. In the words of her cousin James Yock, she "was boldly utilitarian in analyzing the actual needs of her clients, emphasizing comfort and practicality in the gardens of even her wealthiest employers. She discarded the ideal of a lazy country house, maintained by a vast gardening staff. Instead she assumed that busy owners wanted their gardens to be easy to keep and to enjoy."[25] Her creations of low-maintenance landscapes that used minimum space and care became the model for later gardening developments that spread from California to the rest of America during the 1930s and 1940s.[26]

Though few of their gardens were outside of California, Florence Yoch and Lucille Council probably influenced more people in the South than all of the other designers combined. Through designing gardens for people in the movie industry, they began almost a second career of designing movie sets. *The Garden of Allah* (1936), *Romeo and Juliet* (1936), *The Good Earth* (1937) and their most acclaimed movie, *Gone with The Wind* (1939).

The first unresearched designer we will discuss is the extremely talented Annette Hoyt Flanders. She trained at the University of Illinois, graduating in 1918 and going on to practice in both New York and her native Milwaukee. After 1920 she was in practice with Helen Swift Jones. They were instrumental in training other female landscape architects. Among the people who trained in their office were Iris Ashwell, Alice Bauhan, Margaret Eaglesfield Bell, Hellen Bullard, Delores Hoyle Richardson, Mary Elizabeth Sprout, Tina Valen, and Nelva Weber.[27] Miss Flanders taught at the Milwaukee Art Institute and contributed design articles to such magazines as *House and Garden, Country Life in America*, and *Good Housekeeping*. In 1932, she won the Gold Medal in Landscape Architecture of the Architectural League of New York for her work at the Charles E. F. McCann estate in Oyster Bay, Long Island.[28]

Some of her gardens in the Chicago-Milwaukee area are still in existence.[29] Her practice spread from Canada south to North Carolina, and from the eastern seaboard to Texas and New Mexico.[30]

Rose Isabel Geely, another designer who has scarcely been researched, conducted the majority of her practice in the South. She graduated in the first class of the Cambridge School. After graduation, she worked as a garden writer at *House Beautiful* and with Fletcher Steele in his office. In 1926 she was licensed to practice both architecture and landscape architecture and opened her own practice in Washington, D.C. She won a number of regional awards and was the only female member of the ASLA's Advisory Committee of the Williamsburg Restoration Project. She specialized in residential design, where she emphasized the integration of both home and garden. Most of her more than 500 clients were in the Washington metropolitan area of Virginia and Maryland.[31]

Virginia G. Cavendish worked for Rose Greely. She also studied at the Cambridge School off and on between 1919 and 1928. In 1935 she became an instructor in landscape design at the Lowthorpe School. She also maintained an independent practice in Huntington, West Virginia, where her practice included both small gardens and large estates in West Virginia and the surrounding states. She was known up and down the eastern seaboard for her lectures on flower arrangements.[32]

Other women who may have developed contacts in the South and designed gardens here after opening their own practices were the women who worked in Ellen Shipman's office. They were Dorothy Mae Anderson, Agnes Selkirk Clark, Mary Parsons Cunningham, Cary Millholland Parker, and Elizabeth Leonard Strang.[33]

Appendix B lists other women who practiced in the South, about whom I could find no additional information than what the list contains. I hope that others who live in the areas where these women had their practices will be interested enough to research and document them.

Common threads run though the careers of these women. Some of them worked in governmental agencies and some taught, but most of them worked in private practice.[34] Indeed, in the early years they worked almost exclusively in either their own offices or the offices of other women because they were not welcome in the offices run by men. As Marian Coffin reported, male landscape architects said to her so frequently, "My dear young lady, what will you do about supervising the work on the ground?" She said, "The only thing seemed to be to hang out my own shingle and see what I *would* do about it."[35]

Because of the difficulty in finding training and offices in which to work, it may have been that only the superior designers and the unusually dedicated were able to even begin to pursue a career. Many of these women had a quite extraordinary mastery of design principles and applications. Their use of color and texture was especially well done. They frequently used rigid geometries and classical details in laying out their basic plans and then softened them with a varied and sensitive use of plant materials. They paid strict attention to the culture of the plants they specified, giving exact guidelines to clients concerning their planting and culture. Many grew up in educated, socially prominent families. Their schooling was long and grueling, preparing them well to meet the demands of their chosen profession.

I would like to close by quoting something Ellen Shipman told a journalist in 1938, "Until women took up landscaping, gardening in this country was at its lowest ebb. The renaissance of the art was due largely to the fact that women, instead of working over their boards, used plants as if they were painting pictures, and as an artist would."[36]

Appendix A. Women in Landscape Architecture, 1899–1942

Alma Alison
Nellie Beatrice Allen (1869–1961)
Dorothy Mae Anderson
Edith Greaves Antognollia
 (1912–   )
Julia H. Andres (1933–   )
Mai K. Arbegast (1922–   )
Iris Ashwell (1897–   )
Mabel Keyes Babcock c. 1883–   )
Anne Baker (1890–1943)

Hariet Rodes Bakewell (1904–   )
Helen Mackenzie Barnes (1907–   )
Katherine Bashford (1885–1953)
Alice M. Bauhan (1902–1962)
Margaret Eaglesfield Bell (1888–   )
• Marie M. Berger (1907–   )
Faith Florance Jones Block
 (1907–   )
Betty Blossum

• Denotes that at least part of her practice was in the South.

Alice J. Bourquin (1909–   )
Jessie I. Bourquin (1909–   )
Eunice Cottrell Brandt (1917–   )
Catherine R. Brown
Marie H. Browning (1906–   )
Elizabeth Bullard, FASLA
    (1847–1916)
Helen Elise Bullard (1896–   )
Mary Franklin Bunting (1910–   )
• Theodosia Burr
Genevieve Caldwell (1893–   )
Harriet Carter (1909–   )
Marjorie Sewell Cautley
    (1891–1954)
Hannah Champlin
Elenor H. Christie, FASLA
    (1890–   )
Agnes Selkirk Clark, FASLA
    (1898–1983)
Clara Stimpson Clark
Elizabeth Books Clark
Edith Cochran
Clara Stimson Coffey (1894–)
• Marian Cruger Coffin
    (1876–1957)
Mirian W. Cook (1910–   )
Lucille Council
Mary Parsons Cunningham
    (d. 1934)
Janet Darling (d. 1966)
Marianne Dean (1908–   )
Ruth Bramley Dean (1880–1932)
Alice Lindsley Dustan
• Beatrix Jones Farrand (1872–1959)
Barbara W. Fealy (1903–   )
Frances V. Finletter
• Annette Hoyt Flanders, FASLA
    (1887–1946)
Rosalind Spring Fontaine
Adeline Frederick

Anna Biddle Frishmuth
Florence Gerke
Elsetta Gilchrist
Genevieve Emma Gillette, FASLA
    (1898–1986)
Druscilla Pratt Gjeroff
Margaret Olthof Goldsmith
Dorothy Butler Graves (1904–   )
• Rose Isabel Greely, FASLA
    (1887–1969)
• Ann Bruce Haldeman
Mirian Lucille Hall (1912–   )
Dorothea Harrison
Ethelwyn Harrison
Elizabeth Sears Harrold
Ruth M. Havey (1899–   )
• Edith Harrison Henderson
    (1911–   )
Mary McGovern Hendrick
• Agnes R. Hornbeck (1908–1979)
Beatrice C. Horneman (1906–   )
Elizabeth Howerton (1903–   )
Elizabeth F. Hume (1912–   )
Martha Brookes Brown Hutcheson
    (1872–1959)
Alice Recknagel Ireys, FASLA
Mary Rutherford Jay
Helen Swift Jones, FASLA
    (1890–   )
Grace Hight Kirkwood (1906–   )
Lucille Teeter Kissack
Gertrude Deimel Kuh (1893–   )
Rosalind Spring Lafontaine
    (1892–   )
Mary Deputy Lamson
Carole H. Lawrence (1898–   )
• Elizabeth Lawrence (1904–1985)
Ruth Layton
Elvisina Lazanby
• Clermont Huger Lee (1914–   )

- Ruth London (1895–1966)
Judith E. M. Low
Elizabeth Lord (1887–1976)
- Elizabeth Johnson Marshall
  (1912–)
Ruth S. May (1908–)
May Elizabeth McAdams
  (1881–1967)
Jean P. McDaniel
Elizabeth Meade (1905–)
June Meehan (1916–)
Louise Klein Miller
Jeanette Minturn (1909–)
Dorothy R. Morris (1900–)
Mary Frances Nearing (Mrs. Rom-
  ney Spring)
Rose Standish Nichols
Marion V. Packard, FASLA
Cary Millholland Parker (1902–)
Mabel Parsons (1872–)
Mary A. Pascoe (1911–)
Janet Patt (1909–)
Elizabeth Patee (1893–)
Sarah Lewis Pattee
Louise Payton
Isabella Pendelton
Constance Peters
Helen Marquise Pope
Eloise Anderson Ray (1905–)
Eleanor Raymond
Elsa Rehmann (1866–)
Dolores Hoyle Richardson
  (1914–)
Florence Bell Robinson
Maude Sargent (1909–)
Edith Schyver (1901–1984)
Geraldine Knight Scott (1904–)
Gladys Ross Sebold (1902–)
Ruth Patricia Shellhorn (1909–)

- Ellen Biddle Shipman (1870–1950)
Julia Jane Silverstein (1909–)
Alice Orme Smith (1891–)
Alice Upham Smith
Mary Parsons Sovers (1907–)
- Mary Louise Speed (1891–)
Mary Elizabeth Sprout (Mrs.
  Gilmore Clarke) (1906–)
Katherine M. Stevenson (Mrs. Holly
  W.) (1910–)
Elizabeth Leonard Strang
  (1918–1948)
Grace Tabor (1872–1972)
Melita Taddiken (1907–)
Margherita Tarr (1903–)
Alberta Williams Taubert (1909–)
Catherine Jones Thompson, FASLA
  (1897–)
Kitty Thompson, FASLA
Helen A. Tilapaugh (1912–)
Amy F. Tripp
Cornelia Turrell (1906–)
Tina Valen (1902, Russia)
Jean Walton (1910–)
Helen Blish Warner, FASLA
Janet Darling Webel, FASLA
  (1913–1966)
Nelva Weber (1908–)
Roberta A. Wightman (1912–)
Cynthia Wiley (1898–)
Helen Van Pelt Wilson
Harriet B. Wimmer, FASLA
  (1899–1981)
Grace Campbell Wing (1912–)
Margaret Winters (1907–)
Florence Yoch (1890–1972)

Appendix B. *Women Landscape Architects with Offices in the South: Miscellaneous Notes on Their Careers*

Marie M. Berger (1907–   )
Oregon State College
Worked in office of Thomas Church
Independent practice, 1943, Dallas, Texas, with husband Arthur Berger

Theodosia Burr
Worked in office of Robert Fowler
ASLA member, 1931
Home (1981) Hendersonville, North Carolina

Rose Isabel Greeley FASLA (1887–1969)
Cambridge School
Independent practice, Washington, D.C.
Her papers may be in the University of Virginia archives

Ann Bruce Haldeman
ASLA member, 1937
Independent practice, Glenview, Kentucky

Edith Harrison Henderson (1911–   )
Born in Charlotte, North Carolina
Lowthorpe School, 1934
Independent practice, Atlanta, Georgia, 1935–
Writes weekly newspaper column
Work frequently published in *Southern Living* magazine

Agnes R. Hornbeck (1908–1979)
B.L.A., University of Pennsylvania, 1932
Worked in the offices of A. D. Taylor and Cary Milholland Parker
Worked with the New York Department of Parks
Was an instructor at the University of Georgia

Elizabeth Lawrence (1904–1985)
First female graduate of the North Carolina State University program in
    Landscape Architecture
Published numerous magazine articles in the 1930s
Wrote a column for Raleigh and Charlotte newspapers

Published several books on gardening:
A Southern Garden
Gardens in Winter
The Little Bulbs

Clermont Huger Lee (1914–   )
M.L.A., Cambridge School, 1939
Independent practice, Savannah, Georgia, 1949

Ruth London (1895–1966)
Certificate, Lowthorpe School, 1928
Worked in offices of Agnes Selkirk Clark and Isabella Pendelton
Independent practice, Houston, Texas, 1932

Elizabeth Johnson Marshall (1912–   )
Studied at the Pennsylvania School of Horticulture for Women, 1930–1932
Certificate, Cambridge School, 1935
Worked in office of James Bush-Brown
Independent practice, Washington area, from 1935

Sherold D. Hollingsworth, ASLA, is a landscape designer in Winston-Salem, North Carolina, specializing in garden design and in historic landscape restoration.

NOTES

1. William H. Tishler, ed., *American Landscape Architecture: Designers and Places* (Washington, D.C.: Preservation Press, 1989), 90.

2. Charles A. Birnbaum and Lisa E. Crowder, eds., *Pioneers of American Landscape Design* (Washington, D.C.: National Park Service, 1993), iii–v.

3. Charles W. Eliot, *Charles Eliot, Landscape Architect* (Boston: Houghton, Mifflin and Co., 1902).

4. H. V. Hubbard and Theodora Kimball, *An Introduction to the Study of Landscape Design* (New York: Macmillan, 1917).

5. Garrett Eckbo, *Landscape for Living* (New York: Architectural Record, 1950), quoted in Michael Laurie, *An Introduction to Landscape Architecture,* 2d ed., (New York: Elsevier, 1986), 10.

6. Lane L. Marshall, *Landscape Architecture: Guidelines to Professional Practice* (Washington, D.C.: American Society of Landscape Architects, 1981), 7.

7. Norman T. Newton, *Design on the Land* (Cambridge, Mass.: Belknap Press of Harvard University, 1971), xxi.

8. *Ibid.*

9. *Ibid., 385–387.*

10. Catherine R. Brown, *Women and the Land* (Washington, D.C.: American Society of Landscape Architects, 1981), 69.

11. Donna Palmer, "An Overview of the Trends, Eras, and Values of Landscape Architecture in America from 1910 to the Present, with an Emphasis on the Contributions of Women to the Profession," unpublished master's thesis, School of Design, North Carolina State University, 1976, 3.

12. *Ibid.*

13. *Ibid., 4.*

14. *Ibid.*

15. Hollingsworth, original research.

16. Palmer, 5.

17. *Ibid., 13.*

18. *Ibid., 4.*

19. Diana Balmori, Diane Kostial McGuire, and Eleanor M. McPeck, *Beatrix Farrand's American Landscapes: Her Gardens and Campuses* (Sagapanack, N.Y.: Sagapress, 1985), 49.

20. Tishler, *American Landscape Architecture,* 90.

21. Nancy Fleming, *Money, Manure, & Maintenance: Ingredients for the Successful Gardens of Marian Coffin, Pioneer Landscape Architect 1876–1957* (Weston, Mass.: Country Place Books, 1995), 7.

22. *Ibid.,* 15.

23. *Ibid.,* 25.

24. *Ibid.,* 34.

25. James J. Yoch, *Landscaping the American Dream: The Gardens and Film Sets of Florence Yoch, 1890–1972* (New York: Abrams and Sagapress, 1989), 3.

26. Fleming, 60.

27. Brown, *Women and the Land.*

28. William A. Mann, *Landscape Architecture: An Illustrated History in Timelines, Site Plans, and Biography* (New York: Wiley, 1993) 329.

29. Rosemary Verey and Ellen Samuels, *The American Woman's Garden* (Boston: Little, Brown & Company, 1984), 17.

30. Palmer, 32.

31. Birnbaum and Crowder, 54–55.

32. Palmer, 37.

33. Brown, *passim.*

34. Palmer, 39.

35. Fleming, 8.

36. Mac Griswold, "Carolina Grown," *House and Garden* (Sept. 1988): 180.

Sue Anne Ware

The Sisterhood of Gardens

African-American Women's Gardens, from the Backwoods to the Cul-de-sac

As several generations of Southerners move from rural to suburban lifestyles, it is important to document which land practices migrate with them. More importantly, the ideas and patterns that distinguish these landscapes as uniquely African American or feminine must be explored. This examination includes a series of personal profiles which at the very least will give designers, academics, and other interested conference participants an insight into cultural landscapes in suburban settings. The transformation of culture within the landscape can not only serve as a framework for design of distinct communities, but it can inform us of aesthetic and intrinsic values toward the land. To set the stage for this exploration of cultural expression in the landscape and to establish "typical" suburban land practices, a brief synopsis concerning the development patterns of the American suburb follows.

The Development and Origins of American Suburbia

Many historians have explored the evolution of American suburbs and have commented on the "new landscape form"—the
single-family house surrounded by grass—that began to develop
after the Civil War and spread throughout the nation in the twentieth century. This new residential landscape developed in connection with three major suburban movements in our history. The
first suburban communities were encouraged by the expansion of
railroad, street car, and trolley lines. The public park movement
begun by Frederick Law Olmsted also directly influenced this
suburban development. Further, late nineteenth-century suburban
communities were modeled after parks with rolling hills, well-
placed trees, and carefully maintained lawns. These upper middle-
class suburbs became the models for later twentieth-century suburban developers. The second great expansion into suburbia came
in the 1920s with the rapid adoption of the automobile by middle-class Americans. This time, suburban development was also influenced by the recent introduction and growing popularity of
the game of golf and the notion of building houses with yards that
were an extension of the golf course. The third and by far the
most widespread impetus to suburban development came after
World War II. It was financed by the federal government through
low-cost mortgages for veterans and by government funding of
highways.[1] During all three episodes, and particularly during the
latter, Americans saw extensive deconcentrations of urban populations and substantial transformation of the landscape around their
metropolitan areas. Any sharp distinction between city and country remaining from prior urban settlement was quickly obliterated
and replaced by a middle landscape of suburban and exurban development.[2]

However, as Peter Rowe notes, the stereotypical image of the
American suburb, a vestige of an earlier stage of development, no
longer applies. Contemporary suburban life is simply not a case of
"white, middle-class homeowners, single-family homes, men
commuting to city jobs, women at home caring for the children,
stable neighborhoods and safety." Within the middle landscape
shaped out of the suburban mosaic, society is becoming as hetero-
geneous and life is becoming as diversified as it once was in the

city. In a remarkable transformation, it is as if the city has gone into the suburbs, just as the suburbs left the city shortly after the turn of this century.[3] More specifically, Rowe found that the suburban black population increased by nearly 40 percent during the 1970s, moving African Americans much farther into the suburban mainstream than the marginal locations they occupied only a decade earlier.[4]

With the population of suburbia becoming more diversified, the suburban landscape often takes on new cultural meanings. These meanings for African Americans have origins that may date back to slavery and most certainly date back to rural traditions.

History of African-American Female Slaves and Their Gardening Practices

Various descriptions of slave quarters and plantation life document garden plots in which the slaves raised produce to supplement their diets. According to Charles Ball, a noted writer who traveled throughout the South, "On every plantation, with which I ever had any acquaintance, the people are allowed to make patches, as they are called—that is gardens, in some remote and unprofitable part of the estate, generally in the woods, in which they plant corn, potatoes, pumpkins, melon and cucumbers, for themselves. These patches they must cultivate on Sunday or at night, or let them go uncultivated."[5] Paul Finkleman documents this further through the diary of Emily Weston, a plantation holder's wife: "Many of them use part of their day-off time to cultivate their own plots and raise livestock, both for their own consumption and to sell to the planters. Such purchases are contrary to South Carolina law, as the planters clearly understand; but they are part of the body of rights asserted successfully by the slaves even in the face of specific legislation to the contrary."[6] The evidence of subsistence gardening is consistent throughout accounts of slave life. The availability of a plot for their own gardens obviously depended greatly on their master's or the overseer's judgment.

Women slaves are often cited as the caretakers of these plots and even small ornamental beds. According to historian Deborah White, "The fact that marriage did not yield traditional benefits for women, and that "abroad Marriages" existed, does not mean that women did not depend on slave men for foodstuffs beyond weekly rations, but since additional food was not guaranteed, it probably meant that women along with men had to take initiatives in supplementing slave diets."[7] Other aspects of the female slave's life suggest that her world was independent of the male slave's and that slave women were rather self-reliant. It has long been recognized that slave women did not derive traditional benefits from the marriage relationship, that there was no property to share, and that essential needs like food, clothing, and shelter were not provided by slave men.

In addition to vegetable plots, early accounts of antebellum women's and "free women's" homes often include descriptions of ornamental or flower gardens. George Rawick in his research recorded descriptions of many Southern blacks' homesteads. The following excerpts are from his work where he quotes interviews by Mary Hicks, a social reformer at the turn of the century, who was concerned with the "Black Condition":

Here, in 1856, was born a Negro girl, Betty, to a slave mother. Here, today under the friendly protection of this same Jones family, surrounded by her sons and her son's sons, lives this same Betty in her own little weather-stained cottage. Encircling her house are lilacs, althea, and flowering trees that soften the bleak outlines of unpainted out-buildings. A varied collection of old-fashioned plants and flowers crowd the neatly swept dooryard.[8]

Further, Mary Hicks also reported about Minnie and Maybelle Beckett, free women of color in South Carolina. "Minnie Beckett and her sister are 'free issues,' who live a few miles north of Furman, SC. Their house is painted, and their front yard is full of flowers. Vegetables are at the side in the same inclosure with the flowers."[9]

While these findings may seem insignificant, they are the precursors to African-American vernacular gardens. Slave traditions were undoubtedly carried on throughout the rural South, and although specific plans and practices were not well documented, oral transmission accounts for many of these practices and traditions being passed on today.

Vernacular Gardens

The term vernacular or common garden denotes gardens that did not come into being as a result of the powerful intervention on a site of a wealthy patron or well-known designer. John Hunt describes them as "small scale, not monumental; they could also in more recent times be mass-produced, products of the garden center or of new technology like the lawn mower, which enabled far more people than ever before its invention in 1830 to have what previously were prized as bowling greens."[10] Vernacular gardens might also be those where maintenance and management were privileged over making, and where aesthetics was never a primary concern. Inasmuch as the vernacular garden belongs to a specific group or subgroup that changes within as the larger society around it changes, then vernacular gardens are to be understood—even more than elite examples—as a process. Peirce Lewis, a cultural geographer, states, "The basic principle is this: all human landscape has cultural meaning—no matter how ordinary that landscape may be. Our human landscape is our unwitting autobiography, reflecting our tastes, our values, and our ideas, in tangible, visible form. All our cultural warts and blemishes are there and our glories too, but above all, our ordinary day-to-day qualities are exhibited for anybody who wants to find them and who knows how to look for them."[11] With this in mind it is important to understand what roles women, and more specifically African-American women, may have in shaping vernacular gardens, for their gardens may tell us much about their culture and its expression through the landscape.

The working garden was generally the domain of the woman of the house. She was the one who controlled the planting, cultivation, and the eventual distribution of the produce. According to J. B. Jackson, "Ancient Roman law acknowledged that relationship, and so for that matter does the name 'Hildegard,' which means 'She who protects the garden.'"[12] Anthropologists and agricultural historians have several explanations for the role of women in the traditional garden. The theory that the vernacular garden first evolved during a remote prehistoric time when matriarchal rule prevailed, along with the worship of the Earth Goddess or Earth Mother, has received much attention in feminist literature and among deep ecologists. Jackson offers another explanation: "Our remote ancestral Indo-European agriculture was based (largely for climatic reasons) on the propagation of plants by means of seeds, whereas in tropical regions propagation was by means of roots and cuttings. Seeds can be, and often are, planted in the early winter, and the seedlings are taken care of and provided with an artificial climate in the house, then transplanted in the spring. This protective role was taken over by the woman of the house, who also assumed the same responsibility for young animals on the farm, thereby domesticating them."[13] Further, Jackson states, "I suspect that the only truly vernacular gardens in Colonial America—gardens which supplemented the food produced in the fields—were those of the Black slaves. That is not to say that small-scale domestic gardens were not common in the colonies, yet they seemed to have been planted more for medicinal purposes, and later for aesthetic satisfaction, especially when people learned to appreciate the beauty of flowers instead of concentrating on their fragrance."[14] Because vernacular gardens tend to be seen as common or ordinary, much of their history and relevance to current gardening practices has been lost. The evidence that has survived, however, suggests that since the colonial period, African-American customs—and more specifically, the contributions of African-American women—influenced rural African-American gardening practices. Rural African-American gardens most certainly descended directly from traditions in slavery, vernacular practices, and working gardens.

Before the African-American suburban garden can be examined, an accurate analysis of its rural antecedents must be explored.

Patterns of African-American Gardens

Three major functions of African-American rural gardens include their contribution to subsistence; their utility as a kitchen extension for household chores; and their use for entertainment, recreation, and display. Richard Westmacott, the author of *African-American Gardens and Yards in the Rural South*, reports that typical rural yards include crops, livestock, ornamental plants, enclosures, plants for structure (hedges, foundation plantings), manufactured

and found objects used for edges (bricks, snuff bottles, jugs), manufactured and found objects used for plant containers and plant
stands (tires, pots, washing machines), and yard art.[15] Mr. Westmacott also describes what he considers as collective expressions of
values, ideas, and beliefs in the landscape; these include family and
community importance, private property and security of tenure,
self-sufficiency, self-reliance, independence, resourcefulness, work
and play, privacy and sanctuary, fatalism, and nostalgia. More
specifically, he interprets the following as symbols embodied into
these landscapes:

1. The homestead as it embodies the values of home, family,
ownership, and self-reliance;

2. Gatherings of family and friends in the yard as symbolic of
commitment to family and community;

3. The vegetable garden as a demonstration of self-sufficiency,
resourcefulness, and hard work;

4. The yard, floral displays, and shaded decorated areas within
the yard are visible from the road as gestures of welcome and an
invitation to stop in;

5. The peaceful, beautiful sanctuary of the yard, despite other
pressures, offering an escape;

6. The use of discarded items such as tires or washing machines
as expressions of individuality and resourcefulness;

7. Finally, these families saw all the things that they did—their
homes, their way of life—as symbolic of their devotion to God.[16]

Westmacott's study defines what he observed and learned about
cultural landscape patterns of African Americans in the rural
South. His work was used as a precedent for this study, to compare
and contrast what patterns or land uses are transferred directly, im-
provised upon, or disregarded when examining African-American
women's suburban landscapes.

Case Studies

African-American relationships to the Southern landscape are
deeply ambivalent, arising on one hand from the rich legacies of
African culture, gardening expertise, and community ties, and on
the other hand, under the shadow of European or European-

American rationalizations for slavery and—after Emancipation—disenfranchisement, land grabbing, and Ku Klux Klan terrorism. The expressive arrangements of plants and objects in yards are not so much "results" of these forms of oppression, as they are contributions to the network of activities through which members of the diverse African-American population make sense of, and generate positive countercurrents from, their history. The following case studies will introduce you to six extraordinary African-American women. They were all raised in the rural South and now reside in suburban Greensboro, North Carolina. While they share common themes among their land practices and what they draw from rural Southern traditions, they also have their own personal improvisations that demonstrate that the expression of culture through the landscape is a dynamic, ever-changing process.

Shirley Clegg

Shirley Clegg is a native of Vidalia, Georgia. She remembered her mother's garden as a blanket of flowers in all colors in both front and back yards. She recalls that in the back of the house, there was a vegetable patch with peas, collards, corn, squash, "anything you ever wanted to eat." Shirley's family survived by canning and growing vegetables, in a community of people who cared about each other. If you didn't have fruit, others in the community with an orchard would share their harvest. Shirley remembered working hard in the garden patch with a rake and a shovel, while fetching buckets of water from the well and watering plant by plant.

Shirley has lived at her home in Greensboro for thirteen years. She says that "she didn't much like the house but she had a vision when she was a child about living out next to a lake, so she purchased the house and the lot." She misses the family, nice neighbors, and that "you can't grow tomatoes as good here" as in the country. But she also recalled that country people have junk around their house like old cars, wood, and metal. She felt that she is a very neat person and she didn't like that stuff: "In the suburbs I don't have to see it." Shirley grows tomatoes in her shrubbery in the front yard; they seem to do better in the bushes. Pots line the walk to welcome people. She has a lot of potted plant material, and she switches it out when she doesn't like something or changes her mind about her yard. She doesn't do much vegetable gardening anymore: "The ground is too hard and I don't miss the hard work." She continues to can a lot of things that people give to her, and she also composts, and she burns leaves even though it is illegal. She states, "Some country things like burning and piling just make too much sense to give them up, and besides it reminds me of the bonfires in the pecan orchards when I was a young 'un." Her favorite part of her own garden is the deck looking at the potted plants and the lake, where she can relax at the crack of dawn. Gardening makes her feel like her mother, whom she describes as being kind, caring, and very good with nature.

One significant aspect of Shirley's garden is how she continues her mother's flower-planting tradition of improvising using potted containers. Her tomato plants provide another unique aspect; she plants them where they will grow the best, which happens to be in the front yard, an area usually reserved for lawn and foundation plantings. Leaf burning provides her with a significant memory of the country and her community, so this process symbolizes another important tie. Shirley's garden is one of subtle improvisations and cultural differences, but her connection to the country through her present landscape and her individual expression within it show that suburban landscapes can evolve into diverse reflections of their owners.

Janie Davis

Janie Davis is from Wilmington, North Carolina; she developed an appreciation of nature from visiting her grandparents in a rural area. Her mother did not garden much, so most of what she knows she learned from her grandparents or by her own experimentation. The two pine trees in the front yard are native of the Carolina coast and difficult to grow in Greensboro, but they remind her of home, so she cares for them tenderly. She has different ideas every year for her garden: "It depends on the mood I am in; I had a rough year last year. This year I said I would not focus on the past. I had mixed feelings and mixed emotions, so everything in my yard is mixed. It was rough, but through it all I learned to be patient and meditate. My flowers help me out to find peace." She likes to mix colors that people would not normally put together. Mrs. Davis states, "I make the design up in my head, early in the morning when the dew is out, mounds of flowers, and mounds of plants." She is very knowledgeable about plant names and blooming times, and prefers plant material that looks good year-round. Further, she grows most her plants from cuttings, and she often uses plants given to her to create remembrance areas.

Mrs. Davis also expresses her sentiment through her garden with significant objects. She keeps a pumpkin left over from last Halloween to remind her of her granddaughter, and she has a frog from her mother-in-law. She always wanted that frog, and her mother-in-law gave it to her when she died, so she glued it together and keeps it as a sentimental reminder of her mother-in-law's kindness. Janie Davis also enjoys a connection to nature and God through her garden. She plants species that will attract a variety of birds. She says she entertains herself by observing nature, and finds it very relaxing to see how God works himself. She even talks to her plants: "Me and my plants talk, we have a good time!" Unfortunately, she suffers from chronic pain, but she feels that "it helps you to see the simple things in life, like nature. For instance, a simple plant from my son when I was in the hospital I have given away many cuttings from. . . . All that happiness from that one plant." She spends a lot of her time in the "Florida Room," where she meditates. This room blends the inside with the outside of the house; it allows nature to part of her interior world.

Mrs. Davis's garden represents an emotional, introspective approach to landscape. She sees nature as connection to God and a soothing influence. While she lives in an everyday neighborhood, she is able to personalize and commemorate important aspects in her life through her landscape. Similar to Ms. Clegg's landscape, the expression is subtle but the emotion, thought, and result is powerful.

Luise Wilson

Luise Wilson is originally from a rural area outside of Plockton, North Carolina. She remembers, "Mama had a garden with all sorts of flowers and everything in the garden. She grew everything!" They were a very self-sufficient family. She had three brothers who did a lot of the work in the fields and slaughtered their own meat. Growing up, she recalls that she was a tomboy and loved to play outside. Her mother still gives her advice for her garden: "She knows how to use plants and so she always tells you which ones to buy and where to put them." Mrs. Wilson and her husband live in a house he built thirty-two years ago.

Mrs. Wilson loves to garden, and she sees each plant as an individual. Further, she states, "I see something, whatever is pretty, and put it in some kind of coordination. To me everything is pretty. I like things to look natural, kind of wild." Like Mrs. Davis, she uses her garden to help her cope with illness. She finds that in the yard she doesn't think about her asthma: "It relaxes me and makes me feel good about myself." She enjoys using a lot of colors throughout the garden to brighten the day. And she moves things around the yard because she gets bored with looking at the same thing all the time. She states very simply, "I never finish in the yard!"

Mrs. Wilson, like the other women, uses plants in her garden to keep memories alive. She planted rose bushes in the front to remind her of her mother's yard. When she was thirteen years old, she planted a magnolia tree with her aunt. She now has a magnolia tree, which she cares for tenderly by protecting it from the sun with a basket, that she planted to remember the other tree. Mrs. Wilson found the plants in her "wild garden" at an old house where they farm. Her mother used to have all the same old plants; everything she saw with a bloom on it, she put in her garden. She also was very fond of sunflowers: "Mama had loads of them. When I was kid, I just thought it was pretty so I put them in my garden to think about the sunshine Mama brings to us all."

Like Ms. Clegg, Mrs. Wilson mixes her vegetable plants with her flower beds. At the base of an old stump she planted some flowers to shade her collards. And in her granddaughter's strawberry patch, she mixes berry plants and annuals. "The flowers keep us interested until the fruit comes." She and her husband also have quite an extensive vegetable garden from which she cans and gives away things to friends who might need them. Further, Mrs. Wilson resourcefully uses discarded objects for planters and decorations within her garden. A lady out in the country gave her the washtub she uses for a planter, her husband made another planter out of a tire, and a seashell decoration on the tree was a souvenir of a trip to Atlanta.

Mrs. Wilson's garden begins to establish a pattern of common elements or themes throughout the case studies seen thus far. Plants and objects are often used for commemoration or memorials. Vegetables and flowers are not always grown in separate beds, and are usually placed where they can benefit the most in the landscape. Gardening is often used to help heal or soothe a person's suffering. What is probably the most significant finding in terms of suburban design is that these women are able to take a fairly homogenized landscape, alter it, and create personal, emotional expressions in the land.

Geneva Bayles

Geneva Bayles (fig. 22) is from outside Chesterfield, South Carolina, where she grew up on a large farm of about 250 acres. She remembered the hard work that farming was and how she always wanted to work in town. She has lived in Greensboro for the past forty years. Mrs. Bayles is a deeply spiritual woman who proclaims that the Bible and scriptures are the inspiration for her garden. Mrs. Bayles states, "I love the Bible. I live the Christian life day by day. Praise the Lord! I use the ideas that God gives me for my garden. The Lord loans it to me to enjoy and give back beauty to others."

One of the most striking things about Mrs. Bayles' garden is her use of color. "Pink is my favorite color. White is pure and symbolizes the Virgin Mary. My house and yard are always pink and white." She had the house painted to match the yard. The dogwood tree is her favorite because of its beautiful pink blooms. She always gardens in pink or blue clothes to match the garden.

Mrs. Bayles also enjoys placing objects within her garden that attract attention and symbolize her connection to God. Most of her "garden things" are now given to her, but in the beginning they were things that she found. For example, she reuses an old well for a planter of wishes, old wheels form a border meaning "the circle of life," and an old washtub she used to boil clothes in is now a planter representing purity. Her porch area is filled with objects that remind her of her late husband and his active involvement with the Freemasons. Mrs. Bayles states, "Nobody told me to put the stuff here, the Lord brought the idea to me in a dream." Her porch is decorated with a shovel to represent the cornerstone, a lamp for wisdom, the star for a guiding force, and various

22. Geneva Bayles beside a ligustrum bush in her front yard in Greensboro, North Carolina. S. Ware photograph.

other objects, including shoes, a hat, and a yoke, whose meanings she says she would rather keep secret. A few of the objects share both aesthetic and practical purposes. The poles and rocks add a border to the yard while keeping cars from crashing into the house. The mailbox allows "the Lord to bless us with news from loved ones far away." And the blue ducks and pink swans welcome those who come to visit.

Mrs. Bayles has a vegetable patch where she grows string beans, zucchini squash, watermelons, tomatoes, bell peppers, corn, and cantaloupes. She also grows cotton to remind her of home. She says, "I give the extra to people who are ailing or need it; better to give than receive."

Mrs. Bayles's garden is notably different. Her spirituality helps her to define the physical forms of her environment, and her use of color and spiritual objects helps proclaim her ideas and individuality through the landscape. Like Ms. Clegg, she relies on visions for inspiration and ideas. Almost everything in her garden has meaning and symbolism, and much of it has her story of strength behind it.

Lucy Sligh and Clara Shoffner

Lucy Sligh and her sister Clara Shoffner (fig. 23) are the final case study. Although Lucy and Clara live together in Lucy's house to care for their elderly mother and to help each other out, Clara still maintains a garden at the home she shared with her late husband. Lucy and Clara are from Northhampton County, in northeastern North Carolina. They grew up in a large family on a small farm. The farm produced cotton, corn, and peanuts, while their household garden yielded "as many fruits and vegetables as you can name." They grew their own meat: hogs, chickens, and cows. Lucy states, "Mama was too busy to keep the yard with nine kids, but we kids had our own yard. Our family lived very independently, lived very comfortable and with very little money. We lived off the land." Lucy has lived in her Greensboro house since 1960.

Lucy and Clara's large backyard garden carries on their family tradition of independence and subsistence from the land. They grow such a large selection and a large quantity of vegetables and fruits that they never have to purchase produce from the store. Further, Lucy states, "When everybody visits, nobody smokes and nobody drinks, so everybody eats! We have to put up a lot of food." The two sisters spend a lot of time in the summer and fall canning. In addition, Lucy says, "We can come out in this garden and work for about two hours, then take a nap, and grow all the veggies, squash, pole beans, cucumbers, corn, kale, etc. Make fruit wines and preserves from our orchard of apple trees, peaches, and plums. I enjoy this so much that right before my husband passed, he said he was not worried 'cause I was a survivor." He was right.

Lucy's yard, like the other women's, is filled with symbolism and personal meaning. The large circular flower bed that she created in 1966 is a memorial for the son she lost in Vietnam. The flowers are always red, white, and blue, with a calla lily in the center. She planted hemlock trees, a fig tree, dogwood trees, and roses to support her belief in the Bible and God's vision. She cleverly reuses objects, such as the grapevine trellis that used to be a

23. Clara Shoffner picking peaches in her garden in Greensboro, North Carolina. S. Ware photograph.

clothes line. She likes to add statues, like ducks and chickens, to keep the wild animals company. She keeps the birdhouses and birdbaths because she and Clara enjoy watching and listening to nature. Lucy likes to use red to make things stand out in her yard.

Clara Shoffner's house may be unoccupied, but she continues to plant and care for her yard and gardens. Clara states, "This neighborhood used to be white but now it's black. As soon as it turned black, they put housing projects in it. My husband was a mason and he worked on brick houses for whites. Well, when this neighborhood changed, we moved right in because it was our dream to live in one of those brick houses." She left the house to help her sister take care of her mother and because it was nice to have some company. Clara says that she and Lucy picked up gardening after their husbands died: "It helped us both stay busy when we retired and it helped me sort out being sad about my husband's death."

Clara, like Lucy, plants her garden with inspiration. She explains this when she says, "I like variety and all different colors in my gardens. I love it all. I love the flowers, the yard, the garden. I love working in it, one hundred percent. Everything here is love, it is my world. Life inspires me. That old tree there died, so I cut it down and I shaped the bed like a heart. It's my heart, so all people who pass by can share my heart. It was a large tree so it needed to be remembered." In addition, she also planted a memorial bed for her husband. Clara explains that she always feels her husband's presence at her home: "I have enjoyed my place even though I lost my husband. I put a calla lily in his memorial because he loved all flowers, and an evergreen for eternal life, so he knew his memory would be here forever." She also has an extensive collection of vegetable garden plots to supplement the larger garden at Lucy's house.

Clara's and Lucy's gardens symbolize their strength and self-reliance. They proclaim both their independence and emotions throughout their landscapes. Each woman has been able to personalize her yard and create a living memory to a loved one. They both share with the other women in the case study the use of objects and individual plant species as important keys to understanding their gardens, as well as a spiritual belief in and inspiration from God that is reflected in their gardening.

Conclusion

This study begins to examine what effects gender and culture may have on personal expressions in the landscape. Alice Walker writes of a woman similar to those introduced here,

Whatever she planted grew as if by magic, and her fame as a grower of flowers spread over three counties. Because of her creativity with her flowers, even my memories of poverty are seen through a screen of blooms—

*sunflowers, petunias, roses, dahlias, forsythia, spirea, delphiniums, verbena
. . . and on and on.*

*And I remember people coming to my mother's yard to be given cuttings
from her flowers; I hear again the praise showered on her because whatever
rocky soil she landed on, she turned into a garden. A garden so brilliant
with colors, so original in its design, so magnificent with life and creativity,
that to this day people drive by our house in Georgia—perfect strangers
and imperfect strangers—and ask to stand or walk among my mother's
art.[17]*

All of the women in this study use the landscape to express
their emotions, find gardening to be therapeutic, and personalize
their space so it would reflect much of who they are and what
they believe. For this group of participants, gardening encompasses
activities that purposefully invest the landscape with visual and
material testimony to moral, ethical, and spiritual values. These
same values inform appropriate relations with people who pass in
and out of the yard, including strangers, neighbors, kin, and the
dead.

I do not suggest that these women are typical or representative
of what all African Americans do; the making of personal landscape is a specialized activity. Moreover, I offer that this activity is
better understood as a mixture of African, European, and American philosophical and cultural precedents; it is clearly a highly cre-
olized tradition. However, because these African-American women's aesthetic preferences and symbolic meanings differ from
gardening practices commonly utilized in American popular culture, this separates them from other ethnic groups. The diversities
of cultural landscapes prevalent in today's society deserve a more
thorough and thoughtful understanding by designers, historians,
and academics alike. The expression of culture and gender through
the landscape is a rich and integral part of both modern and historic landscapes, and it merits further attention.

*Sue Anne Ware is assistant professor of landscape architecture at North
Carolina A & T State University in Greensboro, North Carolina.*

1. Virginia Jenkins, *The Lawn: A History of an American Obsession* (Washington, D.C.: Smithsonian Institution Press, 1994), 3–4.

2. Peter Rowe, *Making a Middle Landscape* (Cambridge, Mass.: MIT Press, 1991), 3.

3. *Ibid.,* 30.

4. *Ibid.,* 37.

5. Paul Finkleman, *Women and the Family in a Slave Society* (New York: Garland, 1989), 82.

6. *Ibid.,* 243.

7. Deborah White, "Female Slaves: Sex Roles and Status in the Antebellum Plantation South," *Journal of Family History* 6, no. 12 (Fall 1983), 255.

8. George Rawick, ed., *The American Slave: A Composite Autobiography,* vol. II, *North Carolina and South Carolina Narratives* (Westport, Conn.: Greenwood Press, 1977), 15.

9. *Ibid.,* 59.

10. John Hunt and Joachim Bulmahn, eds., *The Vernacular Garden* (Washington, D.C.: Dumbarton Oaks, 1993), 3.

11. Peirce Lewis, "Axioms for Reading the Landscape: Some Guides to the American Scene," *Material Culture Studies in America* (Nashville, Tenn.: The American Association for State and Local History, 1982), 43.

12. J. B. Jackson, "The Past and Present of the Vernacular Garden" in John Hunt and Joachim Bulmahn, eds., *The Vernacular Garden,* 11–12.

13. *Ibid.,* 12–13.

14. *Ibid.,* 15.

15. Richard Westmacott, *African-American Gardens and Yards in the Rural South* (Knoxville: University of Tennessee Press, 1992), 35–50. Also see Grey Gundaker, "African-American History, Cosmology and the Moral Universe of Edward Houston's Yard," *Journal of Garden History* 14, no. 3 (July–Sept. 1994).

16. *Ibid.,* 112–13.

17. Alice Walker, *In Search of Our Mothers' Gardens* (New York: Harcourt, Brace, Jovanovich, 1967), 241.

Davyd Foard Hood

"To Gather Up the Fragments that Remain"

Southern Garden Clubs and the Publication of Southern Garden History, 1923–1939

In March 1923, Edith Tunis Sale sat down at her work table at Tuckahoe in Goochland County, Virginia; her task that morning—or perhaps it was in the afternoon—was to write a foreword for a book that has become a landmark in American garden history. In seven short paragraphs, she described the background of efforts leading to its publication and the collaborative work of many women whose essays she had edited and was now seeing into publication.

The revival of interest in old-fashioned gardens, the enthusiasm which has recently developed for their restoration and preservation; the passion for the past which is in the air and is having a marked influence on landscape architecture, encouraged our Historic Committee to make a study of the old gardens of Virginia. This manifestation has led to our research with historical and horticultural intent.

Until now, the state possessing more colonial and early Republican gar-
dens than any other has made no attempt to preserve their histories, though
it must be remembered that the oldest were planned and planted before the
corner-stone of America was firmly laid in Virginia soil . . . This is the
only book which has undertaken to tell the stories which should possess
deep significance for every American, as they have more than a mere local
interest.

A large part of this material has never before been made public. Many
of the illustrations are entirely original and were made expressly for this
book and all but four of the garden plans were drawn especially for it.

It has been with a desire of lifting the latch of some of the old gates
and, through the courtesy of their owners, inviting the reader to enter the
gardens that the James River Garden Club has undertaken, before it is too
late to "gather up the fragments that remain."[1]

Those "fragments" were published in 1923 as *Historic Gardens of*
Virginia, with a title page by Lila L. Williams (fig. 24).[2]

Today, some seventy-two years later, we may find the sentiment
expressed in these words to be decidedly old-fashioned and romantic, a part of myth-making in Virginia that might even be em-
barrassing from a scholarly point of view. Nevertheless, in these
lines and others penned for the introduction, Edith Tunis Sale and
Mary Johnston, respectively, clearly set forth certain values, as-
sumptions, and representations that would influence garden writing in Virginia to the present. As events proved, their view of garden history, incorporating genealogy, architecture, and the decorative arts with horticulture, was a potent and persuasive argument.
Then as now, it evokes a sense of place and place-making in Virginia in which the garden is a part of the greater whole—and its
symbol.

This essay builds upon the cornerstone laid by the publication
of *Historic Gardens of Virginia* and explicates the role of Southern
women and garden clubs in the documentation and publication of
Southern garden history. It was the women of the South who associated themselves in garden clubs in the 1910s and the 1920s: in
the 1920s and the 1930s these same women and their garden clubs
produced statewide surveys of gardens that have remained largely
unexampled in the six decades to the present. Within the space of
seventeen years, between 1923 and 1939, seven particular books
were published that both represent "the passion for the past" that

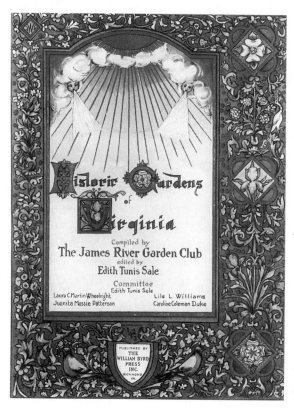

Title page of
*Historic Gardens of
Virginia,* designed by
Lila Lefebvre Isaacs
Williams (1874–
1963), the wife of
prominent Rich-
mond financier
John Skelton
Williams. She gar-
dened at their estate,
Paxton, on Cary
Street Road in Rich-
mond. Mrs. Williams
was also responsible
for many of the gar-
den plans in the
Virginia garden
anthology.

was in the air in the interwar period, and the era of estate and
garden making that represents a part of the renaissance in Southern cultural life in the opening decades of the twentieth century.[3]

As a group these books have no parallel in American garden
history, and they stand as an unrivaled accomplishment by Southern gardeners and garden writers. In all of America, there is no
other such series of statewide garden surveys, either from the interwar period or later days to the present. The existence of these
books confirms the traditions of the garden history of the South
which is the focus of the Southern Garden History Society: in
their discussion of "modern gardens" they illustrate the extraordinary wealth of garden-making in the South that awaits further—
and necessary—research and interpretation. These books should
not be considered as ends in themselves, as some type of final
word, nor can large claims be made for their literary merit.
Rather, they vivify the mindset of garden-makers in the South,
they provide a perspective on the values of gardeners, club wom-
en, and writers in that period, and they form the important cor-
nerstones upon which much of the fabric of Southern garden history can be built.[4]

Whether in fact the Ladies Garden Club, organized in Athens, Georgia, in January 1891, is the oldest garden club in America is a question whose answer was long assumed by Southerners. It was formed in the Victorian parlor of Mrs. E. K. Lumpkin and survives today as the Garden Club of Athens.[5] The claim has been challenged by an earlier, similar club in Massachusetts. Nevertheless, the fact that it was the first known garden club organized in the South remains a truth we can hold to the present. It was also the only garden club in the South for many years. On the larger national level, the formation of garden clubs was a phenomenon of the early twentieth century. It coincided with the formation of the American Society of Landscape Architects in 1899 and the rise of women within that profession. It was a period when women gained an important status as writers and photographers. The names of Alice Morse Earle, Frances Benjamin Johnston, Helena Rutherford Ely, Louise Shelton, and Mrs. Francis King are becoming increasingly well known. They are among the most prominent of a long list of women who achieved significance in a period that saw a virtual explosion in the number of books and magazines available to the gardening public.

In the years of the late nineteenth and early twentieth centuries, large fortunes were made and displayed in the development of town and suburban houses and country estates such as Maymont in Richmond. At the same time, old eighteenth- and early nineteenth-century plantations and estates were acquired, expanded, and rebuilt by members of old families or the newly wealthy. William du Pont, recently returned from a stay in England, acquired Montpelier at the turn of the century; he renovated the house and its grounds in the style of a great English country house and renewed its garden. Another important development of this period, particularly to garden historians, was the construction and use of winter and summer houses by a small but growing segment of the population. Camden, Augusta, and Aiken were the locations of significant winter colonies: gardens such as Francis Hardy's at Augusta were developed as complements to the winter home. Jeptha Wade of Cleveland, Ohio, hired Warren Manning to design the gardens and grounds of his winter estate, Millpond, near Thomasville, Georgia, which remains a family retreat.

In the South, the garden club movement made its strongest showing in the 1910s and early 1920s. The earliest group of garden clubs was probably the series formed in Virginia between 1913 and 1919. Mrs. Samuel A. Appleton was the driving force behind the organization of the Warrenton Garden Club in spring 1913. The Albemarle Garden Club was organized in the autumn of that same year.[6] The year 1913 is also celebrated as the date of the founding of the Garden Club of America. On 30 April, representatives of some eleven garden clubs met in Philadelphia and organized themselves as the Garden Club of America. Two of those eleven clubs were from the South. Mrs. Appleton represented the Warrenton Garden Club, and Mrs. John Ridgley of Hampton appeared on behalf of the Amateur Gardeners Club of Baltimore. Mrs. Appleton's sister, Ernestine Goodman, together with Elizabeth Price Martin, had founded the Garden Club of Philadelphia in 1904, and it was this club that hosted the organizational meeting. Mrs. Martin was elected the first president and remained in office until 1920.[7] Mrs. Francis King, the popular garden writer and a club woman, also attended that meeting.

Largely through the auspices of Mrs. Ridgley, the third annual meeting of the Garden Club of America met in Baltimore in May 1915. Among the gardens opened for the tour was Hampton, Mrs. Ridgley's pride. The Albemarle Garden Club joined the national association at this meeting.[8] In Virginia, in 1915, three garden clubs were organized. The Norfolk and James River garden clubs were organized in the spring: in late November the Fauquier and Loudoun Garden Club was organized. Mrs. Fairfax Harrison, who gardened at Belvoir, was elected president of the Fauquier and Loudoun club and remained president until 1930. During this period she was a force in both the Garden Club of America and the Garden Club(s) of Virginia. The organization of the James River Garden Club in Richmond on March 1, 1915, proved to be the more important event in Southern garden history. On that day, Juanita Massie Patterson (Mrs. Malvern Courtney Patterson), invited a group of friends to Hillcrest, her early-twentieth century estate on the James River just outside Richmond. A friend of Mrs. Francis King, she was elected the club's first president and would remain an important figure in the association until her death in 1932. *Historic Gardens of Virginia* was dedicated to her in 1923. The James River Garden Club was two years old in 1917 when the Danville Garden Club was formed. Two years later, in

1919, the Dolly Madison and Augusta garden clubs brought the total number of organized garden clubs in Virginia to eight.[9]

Cognizant of the growth and accomplishments of the Garden Club of America as a national organization, Mrs. Patterson and the members of the James River Garden Club saw the potential of a similar statewide association of garden clubs in the commonwealth of Virginia. In spring 1920, Mrs. Thomas Wheelwright, then president of the James River Garden Club, invited the presidents and one delegate from each of Virginia's other seven garden clubs to a meeting in Richmond on 13 May 1920. That afternoon a federation, first called the Garden Clubs of Virginia, was organized, and the ladies concluded the day at Hillcrest. Mrs. Malvern Courtney Patterson was elected the first president of the Garden Clubs of Virginia and served to 1922. In that same year, 1920, the James River Garden Club joined the Garden Club of America.[10]

In retrospect, it becomes clear that Mrs. Patterson and other Virginia gardeners in the new organization patterned many of their activities and programs after those of the national association. The Garden Club of America's committee structure proved successful in handling its business, and that practice would be implemented in Virginia. One of the earliest committees formed by the Garden Club of America was the Historic Gardens Committee. In 1914, Mrs. H. C. Groome of Warrenton was named chairman of the committee charged with gathering documentation on the nation's historic gardens for eventual publication. It appears that relatively little was accomplished under her charge; however, the effort gained momentum in the 1920s. In 1925, the success of the undertaking was sealed when Alice Gardner Burrell Lockwood, known to garden historians as Mrs. Luke Vincent Lockwood, was named chairman of the renamed Special Publications Committee. During her tenure as chairman, until 1937, she successfully saw through publication both volumes of *Gardens of Colony and State*.[11] Volume I, published in 1931, was a survey of northern gardens. Volume II, on Southern gardens, appeared in 1934 and included articles of gardens in Delaware and California as well. Lavishly printed in a large folio format that enabled the inclusion of handsome photographs, these two volumes reflect a level of scholarship and erudition that was exceptional in their day: the marshalling of data for literally hundreds of gardens was an extraordinary task. As editor of the two volumes, Mrs. Lockwood had tremendous energy and also the foresight and skill to seek and obtain information from the most knowledgeable sources. While later research has altered our understanding of certain places and their gardens, her work as a survey of eighteenth- and early nineteenth-century American gardens remains impressive and unequalled sixty years later.

While the publication of volume I of *Gardens of Colony and State* was still a decade away, the members of the James River Garden Club determined to compile a history of Virginia's gardens and pleasure grounds. As the producers of the first statewide garden survey published in the United States, the members of the James River Garden Club had no specific prototype to consider. They were left to follow their intuition; one of their best decisions was to employ Edith Tunis Sale as the editor of the book that would come to be called *Historic Gardens of Virginia*. Mrs. Sale had become a well-known and respected writer on Virginia places. Her *Manors of Virginia in Colonial Times* was published by J. B. Lippincott in 1909. For it she had produced historical sketches of old Virginia places: these were illustrated with photographs showing houses like Gunston Hall in their pre-restoration, "as found" condition. In 1916, she and her family moved into Tuckahoe.[12]

Manors of Virginia in Colonial Times was one in a series of architecture, gardening, and decorative arts books produced by Lippincott and other publishers in the opening decades of the century that shaped perceptions of life in eighteenth- and early nineteenth-century America. As events proved, *Manors* was something of a bridge between the lavish folio volumes consisting mostly of large scale plates with little text and the like books of the 1920s where illustrations were in the service of the text. It was in that first group of books that Southern gardens were initially brought to the attention of the American public. One such book, *American Country Homes and Their Gardens,* appeared in 1906. It included large plates of the newly constructed Biltmore Estate at Asheville, as well as handsome photographs of the gardens at Hampton, in Towson, Maryland, and the garden at Mount Vernon. Lesser known gardens like that at Holly Hedge in Camden, South Carolina, and Lausanne, also in Camden, recalled garden-making on a different but no less successful scale.[13] Successive editions of Louise Shelton's *Beautiful Gardens in America,* first published in 1915, also featured Southern gardens both old and modern. Preston Garden at Columbia, South Carolina, appeared together with a view of the Ross garden (Rostrevor) at Knoxville, Tennessee, and the Greek Revival style garden walls at Longview in Nashville. A year earlier, in 1914, the same photograph appeared as the frontispiece of Mrs. Alex Caldwell's *Your Garden and Mine.* Some of its contents had earlier appeared in the *Southern Woman's Magazine.* Modern garden-making was seen at its finest in Virginia at Meadowbrook, designed by James L. Burley for Thomas Jeffress.[14]

Historic Gardens of Virginia contains sketches, half-tones, color engravings, and often plans of some seventy-nine historic gardens. The well-known gardens of the commonwealth were favored in text and image. Mount Vernon was illustrated by one of the earliest aerial photographs of the estate, which provided a bird's-eye view of the spatial relationship of the house, its grounds, and component gardens. At the same time, many lesser-known gardens also appeared in the book. The image of a long dense avenue of boxwood leading up to the door of Oak Hill in Pittsylvania County was a common experience for Virginia gardeners; this welcoming landscape was one that appeared throughout the South, and like photographs would appear in the subsequent books on Georgia, Tennessee, and North Carolina gardens. The book was organized into seven geographical regions that reflected a shared history, design background, general climate, and location. The sketches compiled by the James River Garden Club were written by James River club members, other garden club women, wives and daughters of these ancestral places, or Mrs. Sale herself when necessary. Mary Mason Anderson Williams prepared the sketch of her family's town garden on Franklin Street in Richmond: it was swept away about 1895 for the construction of the Jefferson Hotel. The published photograph of that garden is important for two reasons. First, it handsomely illustrates the character and scale of old gardens in Virginia which were being lost in the physical expansion and rebuilding of the capital and other parts of the state. The other reason, of course, is that after the 1920s, Victorian gardens with such lavish plantings of elephant's ear would be banished from the pages of Virginia garden publications. The gardens of Shirley and

Westover were illustrated in color paintings by Ashton Wilson; the gardens of both plantations were represented also by two of the many plans prepared for the book by Lila Isaacs Williams.[15]

The insistent symmetry of the garden plans published in *Historic Gardens of Virginia* drew the strongest criticism in an unsigned review appearing in the January 1924 issue of *Landscape Architecture,* the journal of the American Society of Landscape Architects.

In those cases where the reviewer has access to plans of the same places known to be accurately drawn, the plans in this book differ in proportion and in detail, and differ in a way tending to straight lines, right angles and balanced dimensions, giving an effect of stiff formality which the reviewer believes to be seldom characteristic of these gardens, either now or in the past.[16]

It is surprising that the reviewer, having made those remarks, did not call attention to the fact that *Historic Gardens of Virginia* contained illustrations of work by three important architects and landscape architects working in the South in the early twentieth century. The garden at Horse Shoe Farm was designed by Charles F. Gillette. The subject of a recent monograph, Gillette was the principal landscape architect in Virginia in the 1910s and 1920s and had a career that extended into the 1960s. Warren H. Manning designed the grounds and gardens of Carter Hall, at Millwood (Clarke County), which were partially implemented by the Burwell family before 1930 when the estate was sold to Gerald Lambert. Charles Barton Keene, long recognized for his work in Winston-Salem, North Carolina, designed the colonial revival seat at Red Hill, the Charlotte County plantation of Patrick Henry. The house burned in 1919; however, portions of the large boxwood garden survive to the present.[17]

The writer in *Landscape Architecture* concluded his review with well-chosen words:

The book is excellent reading for one who knows and loves Virginia—particularly the Virginia of 'before the war.' It is not the last word as a technical book of reference on Virginian gardens for the landscape architect and garden designer.

The reviewer laid the book down feeling that he had been in the best of company—perhaps better than his critical spirit deserved.[18]

Historic Gardens of Virginia was reprinted in 1930 in a revised edition on the bicentennial of George Washington's birth. More than a dozen gardens were added to the book for the new memorial edition. The book might well have enjoyed subsequent reprintings except for the fact that its role as an anthology of Virginia gardens was quickly taken by a new work associated with the Garden Club of Virginia. During the late 1910s and 1920s, the federation and its associated clubs had been involved with a few small but influential garden restoration projects. Over the course of time, these became increasingly larger and more expensive. To raise funds for the restoration of the gardens at Kenmore, the Garden Club of Virginia undertook the sponsorship of a tour of gardens in the Old Dominion. Historic Garden Week was first held in the spring of 1929 and it remains an annual event. In anticipation of the tour two members of the club prepared a hard-bound guide book for tour participants. The *Descriptive Guide Book of Virginia's Old Gardens* was written by Mrs. William Russell Massie and Mrs. Andrew H. Christian. While the guide book was originally produced for the 1929 garden week tour, it was immediately expanded and reprinted in 1930 in a larger format as *Homes and Gardens in Old Virginia*. It was reprinted several times in the early 1930s; a revised edition was issued in 1950 on the twentieth anniversary of the original edition.[19]

Meanwhile, in other parts of the South, there was a growing interest in nineteenth-century town and plantation gardens: gardening, garden and estate making, and garden writing were increasing as well. This was particularly so in Georgia and Tennessee. *The Blossom Circle of the Year in Southern Gardens,* one of the earliest twentieth-century books on gardening for the South, was published in 1922. Its author, Julia Lester Dillon, was a native of Augusta, Georgia, and a garden designer by study and experience. In the 1910s she had developed a large clientele among the owners of winter estates in Augusta: photographs of those gardens made up over half of the illustrations in *The Blossom Circle*. The cover showed a color photograph of the garden at The Hill, the estate of Francis A. Hardy. While not an official publication of a garden club, *The Blossom Circle of the Year in Southern Gardens* provides insight into the character of gardening in Georgia in the opening decades of the century.[20]

Another indication of the wide-scale gardening movement in Georgia occurred near the end of the decade, in 1928, when the Garden Club of Georgia was formally organized in Atlanta. In 1920, when the Garden Club(s) of Virginia was organized, there were only eight garden clubs in the commonwealth. In June 1928, twenty-nine garden clubs in Georgia had representatives at the meeting at the Biltmore Hotel. Mrs. Robert L. Cooney was elected chairman of the meeting and held this temporary post until Mrs. Phinizy Calhoun was elected the first president of the Garden Club of Georgia.[21] Among the many topics discussed at the organizational meeting was one that appertains to an account of early twentieth-century garden history. Mrs. Edgar P. McBurney informed the club members of the work of the Garden Club of America toward a publication on the history of American colonial and early Republic gardens. She also requested the submission of material on gardens that had been established in Georgia prior to 1840. In retrospect, it would appear that this announcement and the subsequent research on Georgia gardens for volume II of *Gardens of Colony and State* must have planted the seed that grew into the *Garden History of Georgia*. The 1931 publication of volume I of *Gardens of Colony and State* also influenced this effort. *The Garden History of Georgia* was planned as a part of the celebration of the bicentennial of Georgia in 1933. It was compiled and published under the auspices of the Peachtree Garden Club of Atlanta whose president, Mrs. Robert L. (Loraine) Cooney, served as chairman. Hattie C. Rainwater, who supervised gardening and nature study for the Atlanta public school system, was the editor.[22]

The Garden History of Georgia is, despite their common topic, a book unlike *Historic Gardens of Virginia* in many ways. The book was introduced by an essay on Georgia garden history by Florence Marye. Part 1, comprising some 120 pages, was an account and survey of the state's early gardens dating to 1865. Among them were Esquiline Hill near Columbus, which survived, then, as a fragment of its antebellum glory. The Ferrell Gardens at La Grange, nurtured by Sarah Coleman Ferrell, were prominently featured. Gardens that were lost or compromised, including Rose Hill Plantation (fig. 25), were illustrated by unusually handsome drawings by P. Thornton Marye. Marye's beautiful drawings placed the garden within the context of the house, its outbuildings, the

25. The inclusion of plans like this one of Rose Hill plantation in Elbert County, Georgia, which illustrates the relationship of pleasure gardens and house grounds to the plantation seat and its outbuildings, is one of the important contributions to garden history of *The Garden History of Georgia*. The plan of Rose Hill and many others in the book were drawn by Atlanta architect P. Thorton Marye (1872–1935.)

lawn and yards, fields and roads: they answered the complaints which landscape architects had raised over Lila Williams's drawings for *Historic Gardens of Virginia*. While they, too, were given to an overriding symmetry, they probably represent a truer picture of antebellum places in Georgia. Antebellum life in Georgia repre-

sented a sophisticated culture and manner of living. Many planters, like those in other Southern states, placed their plantations
under the supervision of resident overseers and established residences in towns like Columbus and Madison, where they lived in
handsome state and entertained frequently. In Madison, Wildes
Kolb erected an impressive house with parterre gardens to the
front and rear and with outbuildings and a service yard to the side.
Marye skillfully recreated these gardens on paper as believable ex-
emplars of high-style garden design.[23]

Mr. Marye also drew a plan of Mimosa Hall, at Roswell, Cobb
County, Georgia, that forms one of the bridges between the nineteenth-century gardens of the Peachtree State and those of the
twentieth century. Mimosa Hall had been acquired by Neel Reid
in 1916. As an architect and landscape architect, Neel Reid would
create some of the most beautiful places in Georgia in a brief career cut short by death in 1926. Another of the important Georgia
gardens whose importance stretches through two centuries is
Greenwood, near Thomasville. An imposing Greek Revival mansion was built as the seat of a plantation house and it later came to
serve as the winter home of the Payne and Whitney families. The
turn-of-the-century garden and improvements to the house are
attributed to Stanford White.[24] In the 1950s, when the estate was
dismantled, the garden ornaments were donated to the Garden
Club of North Carolina and installed in the Elizabethan Gardens
at Manteo, designed by Innocenti & Webel.

While the Virginia garden publications had included a few
twentieth-century gardens in their pages, over two-thirds of the
contents of *The Garden History of Georgia* was devoted to the
sketches, plans, and photographs of modern, early twentieth-century gardens in Georgia. In this way, the Peachtree Garden Club
produced one of the two finest representations of early twentieth-
century garden and estate making in the South. Many of these
places were the homes of members of the Peachtree Garden Club
or their friends. The gardens and grounds of Lane's End, the estate
of Mr. and Mrs. Cam D. Dorsey, were designed by William C.
Pauley. Mrs. Dorsey served as the secretary at the organizational
meeting of the Garden Club of Georgia in 1928. Pace's Ferry
Road was the location of several large suburban estates with important gardens. The bowl garden at Woodhaven was a part of the

property of Mr. and Mrs. Robert Foster Maddox. The sunken gardens at Broadlands was the principal feature on the much larger estate of Mr. and Mrs. Hugh Richardson.[25]

These gardens and others in Atlanta and Georgia were the work of nationally known landscape architects, including Robert B. Cridland, the Olmsted brothers, Ellen Shipman, and Herbert, Pray & White, as well as Warren H. Manning and Stanford White who have already been noted. However, it was a local firm, Hentz, Reid and Adler and its successor Hentz, Adler and Shutze, which created suburban estates in Atlanta that are still remarkable for their integration of house, gardens, and grounds into places of great and poetic beauty. Inspired by Italian villa design and the work of Charles Platt, these estates owe their genius to Neel Reid and Philip Trammell Shutze. Reid had designed a lavish stucco-covered villa for Fuller Callaway at La Grange in the Ferrell Gardens in the 1910s: a principal work of the early 1920s was the design for Trygvesson for Mr. and Mrs. Andrew Calhoun. Swan House, like Trygvesson, comprised an elegant Italian villa with steps descending to a great lawn which stretched in front of the house.[26]

The early twentieth-century gardens of Augusta also form one of the important chapters in the *Garden History of Georgia*. The garden of Alfred S. Bourne at Morningside featured a series of terraces rising up to a wisteria-covered trellis and, farther on, a pavilion. Cypresses, arborvitae, and other evergreens frame the vista in this Edwardian garden. Italian cypresses also form the architectural framework of the garden at Green Court, which belonged to H. P. Crowell. Another of the important Augusta gardens was Sandy Acres which, like many of the gardens in the *Garden History of Georgia,* was refined and expanded by a sequence of owners. At Sandy Acres, Mr. and Mrs. Rodney Cohen, who acquired the property in 1921 from the Loyless family, built a series of parterres outlined with boxwood. Published photographs of this garden, clearly showing plantings of different generations, are invaluable in understanding the evolution of place in the turn-of-the-century Southern landscape.[27]

A History of Homes and Gardens of Tennessee was released at a breakfast meeting of the Garden Study Club of Nashville on March 25, 1936 (fig. 26). As had been the case with both the Virginia and Georgia books, this state garden history reflected the collaborative efforts of a leading garden club in the state's capital, one in which the governor's wife was a member. It was compiled by the Garden Study Club under the direction of the club president, Roberta Seawell Brandau, with the assistance of Mrs. John Trotter Moore, the State Librarian of Tennessee. Of the books discussed here, it is the closest in format, documentation, and organization, to the *Garden History of Georgia*. The assistance of Mrs. Cooney, the editor of the Georgia book, is acknowledged together with the help of Mrs. Thomas Wheelwright of Virginia. Mrs. Cooney was a guest of honor at the breakfast celebration that morning.[28]

An editorial published in the *Tennessee Banner* that same day provided its readers with the larger context of events leading to its publication.

Since the revival of interest in gardens began and states and communities generally were brought to realize the material as well as the aesthetic importance of emphasizing beautiful homes and gardens as community resources as well as private assets, there have been a number of state garden books issued. The Tennessee garden book, as it comes from the hands of the Garden Study Club via the Parthenon Press, is comparable both in appearance and in contents with any of those from other localities which have found their way to Nashville, even those of older states the boxwood of whose gardens is older than the Declaration of Independence.[29]

In her foreword, Mrs. Brandau noted the events that had encouraged the production of the book: the loss of most of the state's early gardens, the destruction of antebellum gardens during the Civil War and Reconstruction, and the ongoing loss of places to burgeoning economic and civic development. These events and the broad-scale construction of new paved highways across the South were a concern in Tennessee as they had been to garden club members in Virginia, Georgia, and other Southern states. As Mrs. Brandau wrote,

All of which was an added incentive for expediting the effort to collect data, to search for lost or forgotten records, to verify traditions, and to list and compile descriptions of the early gardens of the state. All material, together with drawings, photographs, and plans, were to be placed in the Tennessee Archives as a gift to the state.

26. Images of impressive plantation seats standing at the head of a long boxwood alley appeared in virtually every Southern garden history published in the interwar period, including *History of Homes and Gardens of Tennessee*. Meux Place in Haywood County, Tennessee, is said to have been built in 1836 by John Oliver Meux; his wife planted the boxwood in 1840.

As research progressed it was realized that the history of Tennessee gardens was so closely interwoven with the history of Tennessee homes that to separate them was to lose something very precious, and so the original plan was expanded to include both. There are houses of historic interest still standing whose gardens have vanished—unrecorded. These houses were also included in the hope that accounts or descriptions of the gardens which grew and blossomed around them might yet be found. . . .

It was the judgement of the Garden Study Club that the book should not only be a history of the past, but a living record of the present. . . . Tennessee gardens of today not only are recording a history in the making, but the far sweeping development of the garden spirit throughout the state has found expression in the creation of gardens of such beauty and charm as to entitle them to a place in this volume.[30]

A review of *A History of Homes and Gardens of Tennessee* by Leon Henry Zach appeared in *Landscape Architecture* in January 1937.

In Part I, on the "Old Homes and Gardens," the photographs are more often of the house, rarely of the garden, for often little remains of the garden to photograph. Exceptions occur, and the gardens that are shown reveal beautiful great specimens of box and crapemyrtle and fine vistas along paths lined with rich box hedges. When no garden photographs were possible, enough of the garden often remains so that plans could be drawn to show the actual or probable subdivisions of the garden and its chief horticultural interests. Nearly forty such layout plans of varying degrees of excellence—the best by Alma A. Alison, Landscape Architect—amply serve to give the garden archaeologist a good idea of estate design in Tennessee from the early decades of the last century to the Civil War.[31]

As might be expected, there was an extended discussion of the history and garden of the Hermitage, the home of General Andrew and Rachel Jackson, outside Nashville. Belmont, the estate of Adelicia Hayes Acklen, was also a particular focus of attention in the section on "Old Homes and Gardens." The federal and antebellum gardens at Clifton Place were illustrated in a half-dozen photographs and a plan.

Although the Tennessee book was divided into two main sections, "Old Homes and Gardens" and "Modern Homes and Gardens," many of the places illustrated reflected sequential generations of garden-making. One of these estates was Rotherwood, at Kingsport in Sullivan County. The house and initial gardens were built for Dr. Frederick A. Ross; however, the garden photographs used as illustrations showed the extensive work undertaken by John Bartlett Dennis, the founder of Kingsport, and his wife Lola Anderson, a landscape architect. The grounds and gardens of Two Rivers Farm at Nashville reflected the work of succeeding generations of the Harding-McGavock family, who lived there since 1802. The seat of Annesdale, in Memphis, was also an antebellum house, but Tuscan Revival in design, while Two Rivers was Italianate. The modern garden installed at Annesdale, with beds encircled with new box borders, could well have provoked Mr. Zach's description of Tennessee gardens' new box hedges as "rows of oversized cannon balls."[32]

"Modern Homes and Gardens" comprises the final third of *A History of Homes and Gardens of Tennessee;* the pages of this section illustrate some seventy-nine suburban and country estates developed largely in the early twentieth century. Many of these are unusually handsome places; however, some reflect a "stiff newness" that Mr. Zach found unappealing. Within the group of important places, the work of Bryant Fleming is exceptional and stands above convention. Fleming was educated at Cornell and worked for a period in Warren H. Manning's office before he established his own firm. In Nashville, as elsewhere, he sought projects where he would design house, gardens, and grounds; he found in Tennessee—and particularly in Nashville—a small group of clients who responded to his talent and his vision. At Treetops, one of his first commissions in Nashville, Fleming was called in to design the grounds and gardens for a substantial Colonial Revival house built in 1912 for Mr. and Mrs. George A. Shwab. At Watersmeet, he again designed the grounds for a Colonial Revival brick house. However, in the design of Cheekwood for Mr. and Mrs. Leslie Cheek, Bryant Fleming was given the commission for the entire estate. It was his finest achievement and one of the most lavish estates created in the South in the late 1920s and early 1930s. The centerpiece in the elaborate tableau of house, gardens, grounds, greenhouses, quarters, and outbuildings was a massive three-story stone Georgian Revival mansion. Because of the topography, Fleming was able to create a dramatic terraced garden on the south elevation that incorporated a series of stairs linking the terraces in their rise from the pool to the main level of the house. Cheekwood was completed in 1932 and is contemporary with Fleming's other major commission in Nashville, the Burlington estate of Mr. and Mrs. Bruce Shepherd, where he also designed the house and gardens.[33]

While the events of the 1930s and the national Depression brought the great era of garden-making in the South to a virtual end, they did not appreciably slow the work of writers and historians who took eighteenth- and nineteenth-century gardens and old places as their topics. Three books on Southern garden history were published in 1937 and 1939. *Old Homes and Gardens of North*

Carolina was a project of the Garden Club of North Carolina: the other two books—*Carolina Gardens* and *Old Kentucky Homes and Gardens*—were individual efforts by two authors who had developed a long interest in the history of places and pleasances in their native states.

Carolina Gardens was first published in 1937 and reissued in 1939 in a "garden club edition" by the University of North Carolina Press. Edward Terry Hendrie Shaffer, a native of Walterboro, South Carolina, who wrote as E. T. H. Shaffer, was a farmer and a journalist. The research for the book was completed over a long period of time and, in part, while Shaffer was working on magazine articles in which parts of it first appeared. As the book's endpapers suggest, it focused on the gardens of South Carolina, with short excursions into Wilmington for Orton and Airlie, and the mountains of North Carolina where many South Carolinians had summer houses, particularly at Flat Rock and Cashiers. Although *Carolina Gardens* cannot be considered a scholarly work, it is extremely valuable for the wealth of information Shaffer uses to describe the evolution of the South Carolina landscape and particularly the changes wrought by those who came to the state to establish winter homes, hunting lodges, and equestrian facilities. William Shannon's Camden house and garden became the Hobkirk Inn, which catered to northern clients. In Aiken, Mrs. C. Oliver Iselin remade the Charles Burckhalter place and named it Hopelands, her namesake. The wealth generated by the textile industry centered in Greenville and Spartanburg found its expression in gardens there, including Cohasset, the garden of Mr. and Mrs. A. Foster McKissick. Shaffer's discussion of North Carolina places included The Boxwoods, together with the Burnham S. Colburn garden in Biltmore Forest; Colburn was a founding director of the Biltmore Estate Company, which developed a large tract of George Vanderbilt's residual property as Biltmore Forest, a residential park adjoining the estate.[34]

While members of the Garden Club of North Carolina were surely cognizant of the earlier statewide garden histories produced in Virginia, Georgia, and Tennessee and in *Gardens of Colony and State,* in *Old Homes and Gardens of North Carolina* they did not set out to emulate those works. Instead, they selected a group of nearly one hundred houses and/or gardens as the subjects of short historical sketches of a paragraph or two: these places were illustrated with a single photograph of each property. The sketches, frankly, tell one little of the place or the people who made and occupied it. The photographs Mrs. Bayard Wootten produced for the book, on the other hand, are its chief value. They follow the example of Frances Benjamin Johnston and convey a period atmosphere that evokes a world on the edge of change. The book was compiled by a small committee consisting of Mrs. Charles A. Cannon, Mrs. Lyman Cotten, and Mrs. James Latham, all of whom were active in the Society for the Preservation of North Carolina Antiquities. Maude Moore Latham underwrote most of the expenses for the production of the book; she is best remembered as the benefactor of the restoration of Tryon Palace in New Bern. Ruth Coltrane Cannon, the wife of the president of Cannon Mills, established the fund that awards the Cannon Cup for historic preservation in North Carolina each year. Elizabeth Brownrigg Henderson Cotten (1875–1975) was a historian and the first curator of the Southern Historical Collection at the University of North Carolina, Chapel Hill. She was the sister of Professor Archibald Henderson who contributed an introduction, "The Place, The People, Their Homes and Gardens," to the book's catalogue of historic places.[35]

The places illustrated in *Old Homes and Gardens of North Carolina* are mostly of the late eighteenth and early nineteenth centuries. Woodlawn, a Georgian house in Granville County, in 1939 stood at the head of a typical boxwood avenue, but it stands no more. Hill Airy, built for Dr. Francis Gregory in the 1840s, was also the seat of a plantation in Granville County. It stood at the head of an expansive T-shaped arrangement of edging boxwood (*Buxus sempervirens* 'Suffruticosa') and flanking avenues of tree boxwood (*Buxus sempervirens* 'Arborescens'). Today this sophisticated landscape stands virtually abandoned. Granville County was the center of an important plantation community that thrived on the profits of tobacco.

Warrenton was another important plantation community on the Virginia–North Carolina border. William Eaton built Eaton Place in Warrenton about 1842; the boxwood gardens on its front lawn are said to have been added later by the second Mrs. Eaton. The house and garden survive today; however, its red brick elevations have been painted.

The best-known boxwood garden in North Carolina was planted in the late 1840s and 1850s at a plantation overlooking the

Dan River in Rockingham County. First known as Rural Retreat, it eventually came to be called The Boxwoods. Another of the state's important antebellum gardens, composed chiefly of boxwood, was Beallmont in Davidson County, which also survives to the present. The later nineteenth-century garden of Dr. Richard Dillard at Beverly Hall in Edenton was probably the most important late Victorian or Edwardian garden represented in the North Carolina book. The 1930s view of the garden, by Mrs. Wootten, conveys a somewhat less elaborate landscape than that seen in turn-of-the-century photographs of Beverly Hall.[36]

Although not a publication of a garden club, *Old Kentucky Homes and Gardens* belongs in this discussion of the era's publications. In its focus on families and their shaping of place, mostly during the nineteenth century, the book shares certain similarities to *Historic Gardens of Virginia*. Its author, Elizabeth Patterson Thomas, was the daughter of a Methodist missionary to Mexico and the wife of the chief justice of the court of appeals in Kentucky. Like its predecessors in other Southern states, *Old Kentucky Homes and Gardens* is divided into chapters representing physical divisions within the state. There is no separation of old and modern gardens. Most of the book's pages are given over to the houses erected in the first half of the nineteenth century, including residences like Castlewood, said to have been built in 1826 by James Estill. Its late Federal appearance also reflects influences of the Greek Revival style which in mid-century would dominate Kentucky architecture.[37]

There are far fewer illustrations of gardens in *Old Kentucky Homes and Gardens* than its title and text would indicate and necessitate. Among them is a view of the garden at Montrose Farm in Jefferson County where modern plantings are laid over the house's nineteenth-century garden. Oxmoor, also in Jefferson County, had been a property of the Bullit family since the 1780s. In the early twentieth century, William Marshall Bullit returned to the long-unoccupied house and set about making improvements to the house and its grounds. These occurred in the 1910s and 1920s; between these efforts, Marion C. Coffin designed the garden featuring circular beds within a rectangular frame. Prior to this, Jens Jensen had designed the large grounds of Airdrie, the estate of William E. Simms in Woodford County. Unfortunately, this

garden received little attention from Mrs. Thomas and was illustrated by a somewhat indifferent photograph. A lesser place, the
garden of Frederick A. Wallis at Paris, Kentucky, was the principal
representative of the modern garden in Kentucky.[38]

In 1923, when Edith Tunis Sale described the desire to "gather
up the fragments that remain," she expressed feelings of regret for
the loss of old Virginia places that she and her fellow garden club
members had felt for many years. Numerous gardens, remembered
from childhood visits to family and friends, had long since vanished. In 1901, Alice Morse Earle had voiced similar concerns in
Old Time Gardens in her chapter on "Garden Furnishings."

*A quaint and universal furnishing of old Southern gardens were the trel-
lises known as garden lyres. Two are shown in this chapter, from Waterford,
Virginia; . . . Garden lyres and Rose bowers are rotting on the ground in
old Virginia gardens, and I fear they will never be replaced.*[39]

They were not! Not one of these "universal furnishings" appears in *Historic Gardens of Virginia* or in *Homes and Gardens of Old
Virginia*. However, that relatively minor lamentation and other
concerns cannot diminish the tremendous accomplishment and
legacy represented by those two books and the histories of Georgia, Tennessee, Carolina, and Kentucky gardens. Had those books
and their illustrations not been published, we, too, would have
larger regrets for the loss of old gardens from the Southern landscape. Likewise, our comprehension of the renaissance of Southern gardening in the early twentieth century might have been
thin or incomplete. For our understanding of both, we are indebted to Southern garden clubs and the women of the South.

*Davyd Foard Hood of Vale, North Carolina, is an architectural and land-
scape historian.*

NOTES

1. Edith Tunis Sale, ed., *Historic Gardens of Virginia* (Richmond, Va.: William Byrd
Press, 1923), 3–4.
2. The members of the publication committee were listed on the title page: Mrs.

Sale, Laura C. Martin Wheelwright, Juanita Massie Patterson, Lila L. Williams, and Caroline Coleman Duke.

3. Davyd Foard Hood, "The Renaissance of Southern Gardening in the Early Twentieth Century," *Journal of Garden History* 16, 2 (April–June 1996).

4. Notice should also be paid to a series of smaller guidebooks published for the Federated Garden Clubs of Maryland in the 1930s which were issued, under several titles, in conjunction with garden pilgrimages in Maryland. These are similar to the original 1929 hardbound guidebook prepared for the first Historic Garden Week in Virginia and issued by the Garden Club of Virginia.

5. Hattie C. Rainwater, ed., *Garden History of Georgia* (Atlanta: Peachtree Garden Club, 1933), 149–151. *Sixty-Year History, the Garden Club of Georgia, Inc.* (Athens: Garden Club of Georgia, 1988), 24–25.

6. Mrs. James Bland Martin, ed., *Follow the Green Arrow* (Richmond, Va.: Dietz Press, 1970), 1–4. This book is a history of the Garden Club of Virginia from its founding in 1920 over a half century to 1970.

7. Ernestine Abercrombie Goodman, *The Garden Club of America* (Philadelphia: Edward Stern & Co., 1938), 7–9.

8. *Ibid.*, 16–18.

9. Martin, *Follow the Green Arrow*, 2–4. Juanita Massie (1864–1932) was born on May 13, 1864, in Chillicothe, Ohio, and spent her childhood in Charlottesville, Virginia. She was married to Malvern Courtney Patterson (1864–1933) in 1894, and in 1906 they built Hillcrest in Henrico County, near Richmond. She died at Hillcrest on October 12, 1932, and was buried in Hollywood Cemetery, Richmond.

10. *Ibid.*, 5–6. At a meeting of its board of governors on October 27, 1925, the name of the federation was changed to the Garden Club of Virginia.

11. Goodman, *The Garden Club of America*, 165.

12. For the role of Mrs. Sale in the architectural and gardening history of Virginia see Royster Lyle, Jr., "Of Manor Houses and Gardens," *Virginia Cavalcade* 34/3 (1985), 126–35.

13. John Cordis Baker, ed., *American Country Homes and Their Gardens* (Philadelphia: John C. Winston, 1906), 38–41, 62–68, 123–26, 191–92, 194–96.

14. Louise Shelton, *Beautiful Gardens in America* (New York: Charles Scribner's Sons, 1916), plates 110, 114–16, 121–22. Mrs. Alex Caldwell, *Your Garden and Mine* (Nashville, Tenn.: Baird-Ward Printing Co., 1914).

15. At present little is known of the career of Miss Ashton Wilson, who also supplied a painting of Mount Airy for the book; she was born in 1880 in Charleston, West Virginia, and appears to have been primarily known as a portrait painter. Lila Lefebvre Isaacs was born in Richmond on January 27, 1874; in 1895 she was married to John Skelton Williams (1865–1926), who achieved prominence and wealth as a financier and banker. She died on August 30, 1963 and is buried in Hollywood Cemetery, Richmond, beside her second husband William Allen Willingham (1872–1945).

16. Unsigned review of *Historic Gardens of Virginia,* in *Landscape Architecture* 14, 2 (1924), 148–49.

17. Sale, *Historic Gardens of Virginia,* 260–64, 287–90, 334–41.

18. *Landscape Architecture* 14, 2 (1924), 148–49.

19. Martin, *Follow the Green Arrow,* 15–16, 113-114. Dorothy Hunt Williams, *Historic Virginia Gardens* (Charlottesville: University Press of Virginia, 1985), 3–8. Susanne Williams Massie was born on February 11, 1861 in Caroline County, Virginia: she was the daughter of T. C. Williams, the founder of T. C. Williams & Co., a tobacco firm, and the wife of William Russell Massie. She lived for many years, until her death, at Rose Hill, an estate near Greenwood, in Albemarle County, Virginia. She died in April 1952 at Rose Hill and was buried in Hollywood Cemetery, Richmond. Frances Williamson Archer was born in Richmond on September 18, 1864: she was the daughter of Major Robert S. Archer, an executive with the Tredegar Iron Works. She was married to Andrew H. Christian Jr. (1859–1913). Long involved in garden club work in Virginia and a leading figure in Richmond society, she died on October 24, 1938 and was buried in Hollywood Cemetery, Richmond. The expenses of publishing the 1929 guidebook and the 1930 printing of *Homes and Gardens in Old Virginia* were met by Mrs. Massie and Mrs. Christian. In 1931 they executed a contract with the Garden Club of Virginia regarding future printings, proceeds from which went to the Massie-Christian Fund that supported the landscape restoration at St. John's Church, Richmond, of 1949–50.

20. Julia Lester Dillon, *The Blossom Circle of the Year in Southern Gardens* (New York: A. T. De La Mare, 1922).

21. *Sixty-Year History,* 28–30.

22. Rainwater, *Garden History of Georgia,* introductory pages.

23. *Ibid.,* 64–65, 86–87, 94–97, 104–105.

24. *Ibid.,* 90–91, 114–15.

25. *Ibid.,* 194–96, 240–43, 255–58.

26. *Ibid.,* 94–97, 176–80, 228–31.

27. *Ibid.,* 284–87, 294–99.

28. Roberta Seawell Brandau, ed., *History of Homes and Gardens of Tennessee* (Nashville: Parthenon Press, 1936).

29. *Tennessee Banner,* Nashville, March 25, 1936.

30. Brandau, *History of Homes and Gardens of Tennessee,* foreword.

31. Leon Henry Zach, review of Brandau, *History of Homes and Gardens of Tennessee,* in *Landscape Architecture* 27, 2 (January 1937), 99–100.

32. Brandau, *History of Homes and Gardens of Tennessee,* 104–8, 131–36, 168–77, 180, 206–11, 324–26.

33. *Ibid.,* 390–95, 404–08, 438–40, 442–43.

34. E. T. H. Shaffer, *Carolina Gardens* (Chapel Hill: University of North Carolina Press, 1939), 146–61, 180, 202, 228–29, 258–60, 299.

35. *Old Homes and Gardens of North Carolina* (Chapel Hill: University of North Carolina Press, 1939).

36. *Ibid.,* plates 28, 42, 44–45, 63, 72.

37. Elizabeth Patterson Thomas, *Old Kentucky Homes and Gardens* (Louisville: Standard Printing Company, 1939), 79–80.

38. *Ibid.,* 56, 72–73, 143–44, 150–53.

39. Alice Morse Earle, *Old Time Gardens* (New York: Macmillan, 1901), 385.

PANEL DISCUSSION

Southern Women, Southern Landscapes

Moderated by Valencia Libby, with

the following panelists: Alice Eley

Jones, Jane Symmes, Davyd Foard

Hood, Greg Grant, Joanne Lawson

Recorded by Betsy Farrell

Panelists introduced themselves as follows:

Alice: Currently African-American history co-ordinator at Historic Stagville in Durham, North Carolina; from Murfreesboro, North Carolina. Her earliest memories are of her father's large garden, the family plot. He allowed each child to cultivate his or her own plots, so she spent her childhood plotting, planning, and weeding a vegetable garden. It was a very meaningful experience.

Jane: She comes to this discussion from many perspectives. Grew up in Atlanta and went to nurseries all her life, even as a child. She wanted to have a nursery of her own, so in 1966 she and her husband bought an eroded plantation in Madison, Georgia, and began selling native plants, an unusual practice in the trade. She developed an interest in the historic preservation of the plantation. Judging from the period interiors, the house was built between c. 1830–50. It was restored and the gardens, which were no longer extant, were re-created to reflect the atmosphere of that time. After the death of her husband in 1973, she ran the operation herself. In 1976, she published a list of plant references and became involved in the formation of the Southern Garden History Society. She recently decided to close down the nursery so that she can have more time to garden.

Joanne: She definitely entered this field because of her grandmother, who was a member of the Garden Club of America. Joanne has practiced landscape architecture for twenty years; her firm is in Washington, D.C. She recently received a master's degree in historic preservation/landscape history. Her thesis topic was Rose Greely, a Washington, D.C.-based landscape architect who practiced between 1925 and 1960.

Davyd: He lives in Vale, North Carolina, seventy miles west of Winston-Salem. He is an architectural and landscape historian. He worked for twelve years at the North Carolina State Historic Preservation Office, supervising surveys of historic places, specializing in the period between 1890–1940. His thesis examined the lives and work of William Morris Bottomly and Charles Gillette. Davyd also collects garden books and is interested in cemetery markers and gravestones.

Greg: A native of Arcadia, near Center, Texas. As a member of the nursery trade, he introduces new plant materials to the industry, including many old species and "heirloom plants." He has gleaned all his garden history from the women in his life, including his first-grade teacher, grandmother, and a woman who lived next door. As a gardener, he has always focused on growing flowers, "something to look at."

Val: What is the gardening tradition of women in the South?

Joanne: Gardening empowered men and women and gave them a break from the daily routine, as well as a way to earn money. It is the original women's movement.

Alice: There are as many different gardening experiences as there are cultures. Gardens were the only public canvases for African-Americans to display their talents. The tradition appears to be more informal, yet it has its own formality with specific roles defined and understood. Gardening was not about books and schooling; more often it was about creating memorials to other people. I would agree that it was empowering for women, but in very different ways.

There is a totally different meaning between saying "plant" and saying "flower" within the context of the African-American community. "Plant" is a horticultural term. Where she grew up, everything was a flower.

Audience: The experience of twentieth-century blacks resembles that of the nineteenth-century middle-class white woman.

Alice: It is not exactly the same. The gardening experience of African-American women is shared with men. Different gender roles go back to Africa; men and women cultivated certain things. For example, cultivating yams was only done by men. This tradition came from Africa and, although it did not arrive completely intact, men's same gusto and pride about yams did.

Audience (Ellen Samuels): I would submit that women did not play a significant role in the Southern landscape until the late nineteenth century, when the land was less productive. Traditionally, as long as the landscape was income-producing, men controlled it. Only when it ceased to be an economic venture did women take over (the plantations, for example).

Davyd: I don't see it as a matter of production. Women were gardeners and exercised influence when they had money and power, usually as daughters and widows.

Jane: Men bought the land and got it started, but I have seen wills in which the land was bequeathed to a woman to manage and pass on to her children. Being a plantation mistress was a lonely, isolated experience, and flower gardens were a means for creative expression; women began to see the flowers as their friends. It was an emotional activity.

Greg: In my family, it was very simple. There have been gardeners for generations, but I am the first male in the family to grow flowers. Men do the vegetables; women grow flowers. The division is very distinct.

Audience (Kay Moss): We can't forget the common folk and the kitchen garden. In the South, the growing tradition was not just flower gardens and acres of crops. There were also medicinal plants that were cultivated.

Alice: There are few cultures which do not cultivate plants and earth "magic" in addition to food production. The superstitions differ, but European, African, and Asian cultures all share this tradition. People are not as aware of the magic of plants today, so this type of gardening has dropped off.

Plant cultivation is also influenced by class. Certain classes grow certain plants. For the rich, gardening is about leisure time. A garden reflects who has time to cultivate what.

In each culture, the lore and law of "plant discrimination" determine our dietary habits. Just as men make time for certain plants, class and ethnic traits shape the gardening and overall human living experience.

Audience: In England, most gardeners are men. When European colonists came to America, the men were busy with other matters. Women took over the planting and managed gardens for food and survival, medicine and beauty.

Val: Throughout the conference, we have moved back and forth between the present and the past. Is this a problem for preservation? Have we crossed the line between what we think is historic into contemporary issues?

Alice: If you read the history of Jamestown, the reason why the colonists were starving was because nobody was growing anything. In this country, they had to grow things or die. It was a hard practical reality and they would have to start to learn out of necessity. The Native Americans hadn't taught them how to work with the climate and soil here yet.

Audience (Gail Wagner): Putting present values on the past is a problem. For example, the medieval mind set was very different; people ate out of troughs.

Audience: The Benedictine monks had monastic gardens out of necessity but the grape arbors, fruit trees, and other plantings provided pleasure, medicine, and religious connections as well.

Alice: White men only worked together when they had to. The image of yeomen farmers working side by side with enslaved Africans is purely sentimental. The gentry class hoped to get enough money to buy enslaved Africans and then remove themselves from the labor of gardening. White people came here to get rich off tobacco and cotton, to mine gold and make a fortune, then return to England.

Val: What is the role of women in garden history?

Davyd: In the early literature of the Garden Club of America (GCA), half the activities of the Virginia chapter had to do with maintaining and restoring land, basic preservation. The GCA was concerned with what was happening in landscapes at large. They were responding to appearances of bulldozers, laying down tarmac and road construction, the development of billboard advertising.

Alice: The irony is that the women of the GCA with a passion for organizing a garden club were usually the wives of the capitalists, robber barons. The clubs were funded by the railroad profits of their husbands.

These activities would filter down to the middle and working class and became part of a woman's Christian duty, that she could pass on to her children. No one in my neighborhood belonged to a garden club, but my neighbors knew about what was going on at the formal teas even though they weren't members. There was a gardening competition at my school as a child, so being a gardener was part of being a good citizen and part of the community.

Audience: Is it possible that women choose to garden because gardening was the crumb that was left over for them?

Audience: As a garden designer, I would say no. I have both male and female clients, many of whom work outside the home and do not have time for gardening. However, outside employment may not meet a person's aesthetic needs and some people choose to buy the services of professionals. Interest in garden clubs is dropping, since gender roles are not the same.

Joanne: Today, women between the ages of thirty-five and forty-five feel guilty about not having beautiful gardens. It is a big problem.

Audience: In defense of men, the monasteries that were mentioned earlier were beautiful and run by men. Japanese gardens are also done primarily by men.

Alice: The references to nuns and monks are not really relevant to this discussion because they are not typical communities, and they were self-sufficient, single-sex communities.

I never thought of the beauty of gardening as a woman's thing.

Historically, we lived in an agricultural society. Men and women enforced a strict division of labor, a system with important subtleties, which reveal how cultures differ. Transplanting the agricultural traditions of Africa to the Caribbean through slavery resulted in the cultivation of rice and sugar cane.

Val: Shifting the focus to heirloom plants, are there certain plants that are intrinsic to women's gardens?

Greg: Where I live, the gardens have been cultivated continuously over a sixty-year period. My grandmother did not choose to grow the vegetables because it involved using a mule harness and horse-drawn plow. Historically, most women wouldn't have chosen to use a plow if they didn't have to.

Alice: In my community, there are certain things that men do grow—that are more manly. Men like to create a flashy tropical look. In working-class African-American gardens, there would be four o'clocks, hollyhocks, gladiolus. Boxwood and magnolia blossoms don't work for African Americans. The gardens of upper middle-class blacks mirror white people's gardens.

Audience: During the 1980s, the Tallahassee Camellia Club began allowing women into the club and many of the men, the old-timers, dropped out. It was a big upheaval because the camellia is very manly.

Joanne: . . . and roses.

Alice: In the southern Triad, pines, azaleas, camellias, and boxwood are prevalent.

Audience: Men focus on a collection of plants; women prefer variety, like a painting.

Jane: We have neglected the fact that the nursery industry has historically been dominated by men. As a female within the business, I know about the domination. Men determined what was grown in gardens by controlling supply. What we buy is easy to grow because it gets back to greed and money.

Greg: Jane's point is good about nurseries. In graduate school, I conducted a study of all the plants in the community of Arcadia and found that nothing was purchased from a nursery. Everything was handed down, swapped, stolen, whatever. A lot of heirloom plants were growing there.

Val: The trading of plants is an important gardening experience. Gardening enthusiasts often give and swap plants.

Audience (Ellen Samuels): We should keep in mind the distinction between landscape design and flower growing. We are not doing a service to landscape history by confusing it with horticulture.

Joanne: In the United States, landscape design is not considered a fine art. The National Arboretum is not part of the Smithsonian; it is still more often associated with agriculture.

Val: Let's shift back to historic preservation. Is preserving a historic landscape important to a community or are we wasting our time? Is preservation important to the public?

Joanne: There are many reasons why preservation is positive for a community:

1. It provides a sense of history, even though it can be glamorized and adulterated.

2. It protects open space, which is important as a source of inspiration. This is also true of historic buildings.

3. It passes on beauty as a cultural legacy.

4. It addresses larger environmental issues, the landscapes which are extremely valuable to our society, including battlefields, cemeteries, and places which are of a scale or design that have a greater expanse of influence. The Merrit Parkway is an example.

Davyd: This raises a concern about certain artificial parameters set up to define "historic" and "not historic." Places can become too precious with the emphasis on the historic preservation of a part of a place at the expense of the landscape as a whole. Our society is too preoccupied with particular dates and exact places rather than understanding the larger landscapes in which we live.

Jane: I wonder if we would have come to understanding this idea if we hadn't been specific first. The most important feature of Winterthur is often considered the preservation of its open space.

Alice: There is not a great deal of difference between living in Horton Grove now and in the past. Physically, there are still bright flowering plants and the gardens are usually informal. You can see the roots of the same plants today.

Audience: Preservation concern is community stewardship. It is important that members of the community attend the public forums regarding historic preservation. We could also try to develop more uses for gardens and make it economically feasible to protect the environment. In the process, people will develop a love for it.

Greg: The economics of preservation are an important consideration. Much of my hometown of Arcadia has crumbled, and yet there is no interest in historic preservation. People ask, why save a house when you can "rebuild" it with newer, cheaper materials? In poor rural areas, people have no choice.

Alice: It is important to understand the reasons why people grow things. With progress, we don't need to grow just what we need to eat. When we devote time to pulling dead leaves off plants, it is also a spiritual process. When men and women are touching the earth, they could be anywhere. Gardening makes a person peaceful, in touch with spiritual forces. It is an important human thing.

Jane: As with weeding, it is one of the few times that a person can get anything under control.

Audience: Even though I don't live in an old house, I am a historic preservationist. I have to believe that it is important or I'll have no roots.

Joanne: My garden is what my grandmother taught me to do. Like a timeline, I bring forward what I learn from the past into the future.

Audience (Ken McFarland): There would not be a great deal of difference between gardening today or gardening in the past in Horton Grove, the restored slave quarters at Stagville Plantation. Today there would still be bright flowering plants and very informal gardens. At Horton Grove now, you can still see survivors of plants that were grown long ago.

Val: (Drawing the evening to a close) For everyone here, making connections between people is the reason why we are here, and why we do what we do.

Betsy Farrell at the time of the conference was executive director of the Sunnyside Foundation, located in historic Sunnyside Gardens, a planned garden community in Queens, New York City.

Camilla Wilcox

The New
Southern Landscape

*Gardens, Science, Art, and
the Environment*

The year of my college graduation, 1970, was a
time of beginning not only for me but for thousands of young women. There was talk then about
the changes soon to come in American society. We
could see that our lives would be different from
those of the women with whom we had spent our
early years; we would have greater choice in how
we ordered our lives and how we spent the working hours of our days.

We all know the outcome of these young
dreams, having lived or observed them. Choices
have opened for women, helping us to widen our
interest and influence in many areas as we have
gained education and experience. Many women of
my generation developed early interests and were
inspired by influential people, but for us, these
early interests led to vocations and avocations that
were not commonly open to women of earlier
generations. It has been a rewarding but sometimes

difficult passage. While feeling a deep sense of commitment to our work, to fulfilling personal goals, and to contributing to a larger society, many of us still feel frustrated by gender-based constraints and biases.

To help define the influence of women on the new Southern landscape, I looked into the lives of horticulturists, horticultural therapists, landscape architects, landscape designers, community volunteers, mothers, teachers at all grade and university levels, business persons in plant-related fields and others, environmental educators, environmental advocates, artists, and government re-source personnel. Most work in a professional capacity, but not all. Many were interviewed, others read about, heard about, or re-membered.

I will highlight a few of these women, allowing each of them to represent larger numbers of creative and dedicated women whose influence reaches throughout communities across the South. As you read, remember other women who fill similar roles and ask yourself the questions I asked those I interviewed: Who influenced you? Why do you do the work you do? What do you see for the future? Every person who lives in the South, male or female, influences the Southern landscape. We all started some-where, we have reasons for what we do, and we have not yet ac-complished all that we will accomplish in our lifetimes.

The stories of the early influences of a few individuals who now live in the South illustrate a common experience. For them, and others interviewed, the decision to contribute to the body of knowledge and work centered on the landscape was determined in early life by incidents, influential people, freedoms they remem-ber, and discoveries they made themselves.

• Ellen Reynolds' father, a business executive in Ohio, dug in his garden to reduce tension from his work. Ellen began to do this at her home, hundreds of miles away from his, at the time his de-clining health kept him out of his own garden. Now, as she runs her own stressful business, her garden is a haven for wildlife and for her as well.

• Dina Nieuwenhuis grew up on a bulb farm in Holland; her uncle was a noted hybridizer who developed the lily-flowered tulip. As a child, she and her friends made massive garlands of tulips and hyacinths to drape over themselves each year when the flower heads were cut from the farm rows. Retired from banking, she now teaches children about the plants of the North Carolina piedmont.

• Dee Johnson's father, a hunter, walked with her when she was a child in the West Virginia woods and told her the names of all the plants they saw. They still walk together, and he still shows her the ones she hasn't learned yet, even now that landscape designing has been her profession for twenty years.

• Kim Tilley gardens because his mother and her mother gardened. When you ride down Main Street in Bethel, North Carolina, you can see which garden is Kim's grandmother's. As a child, Kim helped his mother gather stones to line flower beds and cut wood for her to build her own arbors, and helped her sell and share at the farmer's market. Now, over 100,000 visitors a year see the influence of these two women on Kim's work at Reynolda Gardens.

All of these people, and all of us, somewhere along the way, found that growing plants and gardens was a part of who we have become. There was always someone, fondly remembered, who opened a door and led the way.

But many women say that early interests, while encouraged, were often tempered by society's expectations of them. At the time when many girls of my generation were forming a view of their role in our culture, females were still expected to be homemakers in their adult lives and males were expected to prepare for careers outside their home grounds. Discouraging experiences, both in educational settings and in the home, often kept girls from following their aspirations. Many of the women I spoke with expressed the same thought—that science or plant study or design had been their real interests, but they were directed firmly away from them, as well as from engineering and architecture. The decision to study or practice in the field often came late in life or even through a back door. It often came after their children were born. The individuals are grateful for those who inspired them and for the freedom they have now to choose their focus.

Even so, today, twenty-five years after women began entering the work force in large numbers, remnants of biases that were once standard in American society still present obstacles to the fulfillment of aspirations; the frustrations many women feel as a result of these biases are important factors in how they view the quality of their lives and work. Women I talked with repeatedly said that they are judged more harshly than the men they work with, that universities and colleges are reluctant to hire them, and if they do, the schools are smaller, their labs are smaller, and, in their departments, their budgets are lower than those of their male colleagues. They feel they have to prove themselves every day, they often feel isolated, they are expected to perform wide varieties of duties outside their training field, and they are paid less than they think they should be. They say they are in a position not to determine policy, but to carry it out, and that often they must develop creative ways to get around established policies and norms.

Why do they do it? Because, despite the problems, each one feels a sense of urgency and commitment, that these are lives well spent, that there will be women following them, for whom they will pave the way.

The influence women exert upon the landscape encompasses, but is not limited to, horticultural areas. Women's art can be a vehicle for expressing a response to their own experience with and observation of the natural world. Art often shows what has been and what might be. It can be a powerful tool for persuasion. When it is large in scale and out-of-doors, art itself can shape and change a landscape. All visual artists and land designers link our soul and our world.

The history of Europe-derived American art has closely corresponded with human's relationship with nature. In the earliest days, many pieces both by amateur and professional artists gave clear indication that the artist was intimately familiar with nature. But with industrial and technological advances, themes have changed. Now a dominate theme might be broadly described as the human response to technology and an impersonal society. In such a climate, one would expect that nature themes had lost their touch to move a viewing public. And for the most part they have, according to the experts. But there are a few female artists who remind us of our close ties to the natural world.

• Maud Gatewood paints large, intensely colored landscapes that demand our attention and then draw us into them.

• Elsie Popkin recreates the beauty she sees in the garden in pastels, reminding us to look closely and cherish flowers and trees and shadows.

• Linda Armstrong explores Cumberland Island, Georgia, and

observes natural forms so closely that she is able to abstract them, causing us to look again and perhaps to reexamine our own relationship with our natural environment.

• Ann Eringhaus's photographs of Ocracoke Island capture the appearance of the Outer Banks island today, a memoir for tomorrow.

Visual art takes many forms across many media. Its form follows its function.

• Diana Balmori grounds us in the earth even as we approach the modern buildings her husband, Caesar Pelli, designs. At Wake Forest University, she pressed leaves into the wet concrete of a wall under construction around the law and business school building, and in downtown Winston-Salem, she plans a courtyard of native trees to define the entrance to the new Wachovia building.

• Maya Lin took a corner of a park in Washington, D.C., and black granite slabs and changed the landscape to a haunting memorial to those who died in Vietnam.

Visual artists and land/space designers make us see with them. Their vision preserves, records, and reminds. Their response to the landscape helps determine ours.

Our response to their work helps determine our actions.

Our actions illustrate our values.

Our love of plants can often be traced to a single fascination. For Dina Niewenhuis, it was the tulips and hyacinths in the garlands she wore. For me, it was the wild ginger my Brownie leader found for us in the leaf litter of the woods during a field trip. There are women today who draw our attention to the details of plant life.

• Linda Askey, the garden editor of *Southern Living,* issues the invitation to visit small home gardens and helps us focus our attention on the singular plant.

• Nancy Godwin at Montrose Nursery, now closed, introduced many gardeners to her beloved hardy cyclamen.

• Holly Shimizu brought herbs to the forefront of gardening through her work at the National Arboretum.

• Lady Bird Johnson drew our attention to the beauty of wild-flowers.

• Kim Hawkes promotes the responsible growth of native plants for home gardens through her nursery, Niche Gardens in Chapel Hill.

• Jane Dicus' wreaths, garlands, and baskets of herbs and ever-lastings and Karen Harris' culinary and bathing herb treats invite us to create lasting treasures and use all our senses.

• Garden clubs, active and vital in communities across the South in keeping the concept of conservation and beautification of urban spaces before the public, encourage personal education and enrichment through flower and horticulture schools and shows.

• And nearly every day at Reynolda Gardens, I see mothers showing their children the wonders of the garden.

Single interests often radiate and compound, as one passionate and dedicated person inspires another and soon more and more individuals are exposed to needs articulated and solutions proposed.

• Mary Ann Brittain directs the education program for the North Carolina State Museum of Natural Sciences. She encourages teachers to understand their environment by discovery and reflection and to share their understanding with their students.

• When Bibi Moore was working with the North Carolina Botanical Garden at Chapel Hill some years ago, she observed the profound effect horticulture can have on people with mental and physical challenges. Horticulture therapy is now widely used in hospitals, schools, prisons, poverty, and outpatient programs.

• Appearance commissions, community gardens, and urban green committees often begin with a small group of women and grow to include large numbers of women, men, boys, and girls.

Women are in important roles as instruments of change in both volunteer and professional positions throughout the South, as elsewhere. But in my interviews, I heard repeatedly that when it comes to regulation-forming and major decisions, women do not yet hold leadership positions in large numbers. There is much concern over this issue and over the issue of why girls are not excelling in science, a basis for future leadership, particularly in ecological areas.

Fortunately, there are some potential solutions on the institutional level to the problems women and girls face. The National Science Foundation is granting studies that help find out why girls are not staying in science and projects that help girls develop interest, exposure, and expertise in science. Nancy Crouch directs the Western Triad Mathematics and Science Alliance, based at Wake Forest, which received one of these grants.

Enrollment of female students in programs of landscape architecture has increased dramatically over the past twenty years, and there are associations for women in horticulture and landscape architecture.

As women's science networks form, they include women in all areas of research, business, and education, who are developing leadership and offering support. Colleges, including Salem, are sponsoring mentor partnerships. Our head horticulturist at Reynolda Gardens, Preston Stockton, is a Salem College mentor.

In the future, we can expect that there will be more women like Denise Blume, whose education and experience in botanical research led her to found Natural Products, a company that collects plants and extracts and distributes pharmaceutical products from plants. Or like Dale Jaeger, whose firm of landscape architects and historic preservationists, the Jaeger Company, is involved in numerous projects throughout the South, including site preparations for the Olympics, studies for a new road in the Georgia mountains, and the restoration and renovation of Reynolda Gardens.

We know, however, that institutions can't solve all of our problems. Among the women I talked with, there is a common sense that we must not fail in our collective sense of mission, that each of us is part of a greater whole not defined by institutional boundaries, that each of us is making preparation for others to follow us. Even though we live in a true landscape—people who come here from the North to garden can hardly believe it, but it is true—we live also in a landscape of our imagination. We have the experience to remember what has come before—we've witnessed the thoughtless destruction of landscape both worldwide and locally—and in many of us lurks the sinking fear that what has been done cannot be retrieved. Already in our short lives, we know that so much knowledge of the natural world has been lost, even at a time when there is so much to gain.

Somewhere in every conversation or interview, women asked, what will our children learn and how will they learn it? At this time in our development as a society, our children, particularly our girls, are often prisoners inside. Because of security concerns, they are no longer free to explore and discover on their own. Today, there is a movement to enhance the schoolyard, where children spend so much time, so that all children can have the opportunity, within the relatively safe confines of the school grounds, to observe and learn. In Winston-Salem, inspired in part by Flora Ann Bynum's work at Brunson Elementary School in the 1960s and 1970s, teachers like Deanna Moss at Summit School are leading the way.

Maureen Heffernan of the American Horticulture Society has had the responsibility for organizing three national conferences on the education of children in the garden setting. As a result of her work, there is now a network of teachers, 4-H leaders, garden educators, Scout leaders, and others who have a common interest in helping children learn. Teachers and students now exchange gardening information across the globe instantly on the Internet—a modern version of the old garden gate.

Much of our society believes that we will live in a technological future and our children will be ready for it. After all, as babies they know computers as well as we knew roses, tulips, and wild ginger. But as art is showing us now, the picture of the impersonal and often alienated society, where we pretend to be above our natural connections, is far from hopeful. We probably will not be able to create food, clean water, and clear skies with our computers. We will not be able to recreate the intricacy of the world's life systems once they are damaged. Our children must know, for their own survival, about the world in which they live.

There are three stories I want to share with you. One a look ahead, one a look back, one a word of caution, they are all reminders of the circumstances of life today.

The first: Diana Salmons, an oncology nurse, stopped in her neighborhood to visit with a friend, Leigh Ann Kennedy, a pharmacist who works with her at the hospital. Leigh Ann was tending a dooryard garden of brightly colored flowers. Diana, a front-yard gardener herself, asked her what they were. "Oh those are my vinca alkaloids," the pharmacist-gardener said, and laughed. She was referring, of course, to the chemical extracted from this beautiful plant that the two of them use every day to help save the lives of their patients who have leukemia. A familiar activity, two friends talking over the dooryard garden, with a new meaning for thoughtful women in a new society.

The second: On hot summer nights in Salisbury, it was great fun for all of us children to run in the fog spewing behind the bug spray truck on Maupin Avenue. I learned years later that Rachel Carson had seen the danger I didn't see. She watched over me, even in my foolishness, and changed my world, our world. The hawks are back, we hope for good this time, and our children are a lot safer, even if they aren't more sensible than we were, thanks to our early environmentalists.

And the third: Last week, a young teacher brought her class of elementary students for a visit to Reynolda Gardens to make a leaf collection under the guidance of our volunteer educators. She was clearly as interested as the children throughout the walk. At the end, while the group was looking at the hyacinth bean vine in the garden, she asked her leader where the flower came from. She said, not to get an answer from the children, but because she truly did not know, "Does it come from the bud or the seed?" Fortunately, she was able to get an answer to her question. Fortunately, she had someone to ask.

In discussing gardens and the frontier American woman in his book, *The Geography of Childhood,* Stephen Trimble quotes historian Annette Kolodny: "While men sought new Edens . . . altering the landscape to make it comply with their dream . . . women . . . cultivated small gardens in order 'to render Home a Paradise.' "[1]

The South is still a geographical location with its own often puzzling and eccentric climate and conditions, where gardens form a long tradition of making "Home a Paradise." However, we are no longer isolated and defined by our region. Now, with the availability of instant communication, we know that our home and our South are only a part of the worldwide garden we all share. And we know, too, that this same communication offers each of us the opportunity to reach farther, to have greater influence on our world, than women have ever reached before.

We work hard at all we do, wherever we have made our place, despite the difficulties we encounter. We are successful when we remember those who came before us, who helped us, and recognize that others will come after us, whom we will help. The facts and conditions of modern daily life soon become the facts and fictions of history. The technological world and landscape of the future will be just as forbidding and yet as exciting as a new world of exotic plants and animals and landforms must have been for earlier arrivals. Today, our opportunities and responsibilities are great. We are still frontier women in our work, in how we live our lives, and we have a long road ahead. Look around you. This time in our endeavor, we are not isolated and we are not alone.

Camilla Wilcox is curator of education at Reynolda Gardens of Wake Forest University in Winston-Salem, North Carolina.

NOTE

1. Gary Paul Nabham and Stephen Trimble, *The Geography of Childhood: Why Children Need Wild Places* (Boston: Beacon Press, 1994), 72–73.